T0301387

POLITICS, SUBSIDIES AND COMPETITION

Politics, Subsidies and Competition

The New Politics of State Intervention in the European Union

Kostas A. Lavdas and Maria M. Mendrinou

Edward Elgar
Cheltenham, UK • Northampton, MA, USA

Published by
Edward Elgar Publishing Limited
Glensanda House
Montpellier Parade
Cheltenham
Glos GL50 1UA
UK

Edward Elgar Publishing, Inc.
6 Market Street
Northampton
Massachusetts 01060
USA

A catalogue record for this book
is available from the British Library

Library of Congress Cataloguing in Publication Data

Lavdas, Kostas A.
    Politics, subsidies and competition : the new politics of state
intervention in the European Union / Kostas A. Lavdas, Maria M.
Mendrinou.
    Includes bibliographical references and index.
    1. Subsidies—European Union countries. 2. Industrial promotion—
European Union countries. 3. Industrial policy—European Union countries.
    4. Competition, International. I. Mendrinou, Maria M., 1964–   .
II. Title.
    HC240.9.S9L38   1999
    338.94'02—dc21   98–53416
                                                                  CIP

ISBN 1 85898 324 X

Printed and bound in Great Britain by Biddles Ltd, Guildford and King's Lynn

Contents

List of Tables   vii
Preface and Acknowledgements   ix

1. Introduction   1

2. A Story of Restrained Formation and Expansive Enforcement   16
   2.1. Competition and Industrial Policy   16
   2.2. Towards a European Policy on State Aid   26
   2.3. The Evolution of Controlling Capacities   36

3. Institutional Framework and Legal Instruments   49
   3.1. The Definition of State Aid and the Treaties   49
   3.2. Legal Provisions for Reviewing and Monitoring Aid   54
   3.3. Enforcement Mechanisms and Provisions   59

4. Horizontal and Sectoral Aid Regimes: Cases and Policy Trends   77
   4.1. A Case of Horizontal Aid: Promoting Small Business   78
   4.2. Restructuring the Air Transport Sector   89
   4.3. A Sector in Structural Crisis: State Aid and Decline in
        Shipbuilding   98
   4.4. A Critical Sector in Difficulty: Intervention and Overcapacity in
        the Motor Vehicle Industry   108

5. The European Politics of State Intervention   122
   5.1. EU Policy Impact on National Regimes   123
   5.2. The Development of European Policy   130
   5.3. Policy Goals and Policy Means   137

References   157

Index   185

List of Tables

Table 2.1. State aid to industry 1981–94 by member state, breakdown of aid according to sector and function (in percentages)   23

Table 2.2. State aid to industry and *ad hoc* aids in the Community 1990–94 (annual values in constant prices 1993 – million ECU)   43

Table 4.1. State aid to SMEs 1981–94 by member state (in percentages)   83

Table 4.2. State aid to the shipbuilding sector 1981–94 by member state (in percentages)   106

Preface and Acknowledgements

This book developed from a series of joint papers on the evolution of European competition policy. Its main aim is to offer a concise account of the political dimensions of the European policy on competition, concentrating in particular on policy on state aid. Exploring facets of the European Union's policy impact on the management of the European economies, the book traces the interplay of political, economic and institutional–legal parameters in the making and enforcement of EU competition policy.

We are grateful to many colleagues and former teachers who have stimulated our interest in the political economy of European integration. These include George Ross at Brandeis; Richard Samuels at MIT; Michael Moran, Chris Binns and the late Ghita Ionescu at Manchester; Howard Machin at the LSE; and the participants in seminars at the aforementioned institutions for providing an encouraging environment. We are particularly indebted to the scholars who read earlier drafts of the book and provided constructive comments. Many thanks to Stephen George, Chris Binns, Juliet Lodge, Michael Moran, Jeremy Richardson and Geoffrey Roberts. Last but not least, thanks go to the administrators in European Commission DGs IV, XVI, XXII and XXIII for their time and their most useful advice.

This book is a work of joint authorship. Although we each produced first drafts for half the book, our previous discussions and our mutual revisions and rewriting of each other's work have been so extensive that it is now impossible for us to say whose contribution is which. We both deserve half the credit or blame for any analysis contained in the book.

1 Introduction

The years since the 'relaunch' of European integration in the mid-1980s witnessed a remarkable combination of trends. The unmistakable linkage between European integration and *laissez-faire* economic philosophy has persisted and, in certain areas, has clearly been strengthened. At the same time, European-level policies have expanded and have become more significant than ever in their reach and their implications. European policy convergence evolved and eventually became a key parameter in the shaping of the economic programmes of national governments; yet following a period of apparent convergence in domestic political preferences, Europe's political map is again becoming more pluralistic with the advent of new socialist and labour governments. Europe's industrial policy declined, and so did the idea of actively promoting national or European industrial champions; but we have also witnessed growth in active European structural policies, aiming to assist the less developed regions and promote cohesion.

European policy and institutional development since the Single European Act of 1986 have been conditioned by a series of political, economic and institutional parameters that help explain the oscillations and the particular policy mix of the EC/EU. We will see that most relevant parameters are structured around or interact with competition and Europe's policy on competition. Competition policy therefore provides us with a vantage point from which to assess European developments. *Politics, Subsidies and Competition* aims to give a concise account of the political dimensions of the European policy on competition, concentrating in particular on policy on state aid. We explore the interplay of political, economic and institutional–legal parameters in the making of European policy on competition and, in this way, deal with the extent and the limitations of the EU policy impact on the management of the European economies. After examining the evolution of the different aspects of competition policy, this book focuses in particular on the EU control of state aid.[1]

We argue that subsidisation is the only remaining important form of state intervention, because in the integrated European market state aid (ranging from investment and export subsidies to special tax concessions) becomes the only possible national instrument which can be used to favour and protect national industries. The control of state subsidisation is therefore more important than ever, and the European Community's attempts to increase this control since the mid-1970s tell an intriguing story of policy dilemmas, fierce intergovernmental bargaining, business lobbying and increasingly assertive EC/EU institutions (see Lavdas and Mendrinou, 1995). The general argument in the book is illustrated with reference to the evolution of European competition policy and with particular case studies of sectoral aid regimes and their transformation in interaction with EU policy.

Competition policy has evolved in the context of the emergent European regulatory level (see Majone, 1989; 1990; 1994). Indeed, competition policy played a critical role in the formation of the European regulatory level. From the perspective of an influential classification of policy types as regulatory, distributive and redistributive (see Lowi, 1972) and the application of this classification to EC politics (Wallace, 1983; Schumann, 1991; Pollack, 1994), policy on competition is a form of regulatory policy. Aiming to combine this classification with an approach which is based on the positioning of particular policies in the wider context of European policy development, we can distinguish further between 'core' areas (such as competition, established in the Rome Treaty as a principle), 'institutional' areas (which historically have been derivative) and more recent, 'issue-driven' areas (such as the environment). Competition can be specified as a 'core' regulatory policy area (Lavdas, 1997, pp. 45–6).

As this book will make clear, an account of the evolution and current operation of European competition policy touches on several crucial political issues. Politics involves the choices, strategies, configurations and arrangements which influence the contents, the forms and direction of political contestation. We could say, simply, that politics is about the influence over and the management of political contestation. The latter concerns the allocation of political, economic, social and symbolic resources and the arrangements which outline or, in certain cases, aim to fix social norms, obligations and objectives. Politicisation, then, is the emergence of publicly visible political contestation over an issue or an arrangement.

While competition policy has become publicly visible and politically salient as a European policy in the last decade, its role and standing in the treaties have always been central. In agreement with the *laissez-faire* character of the Rome Treaty, the establishment of a regime of undistorted competition was a key principle. The principle of competition was envisaged as the central means towards the fundamental objectives laid down in the Treaty (common market, harmonious development, balanced expansion, economic policy co-operation and raised living standards). With the evolution of integration, competition acquired also a central position in the developing relationships between economic policy, the distribution of economic power, and the EC/EU edifice (see McGowan and Wilks, 1995).

Accordingly, the political salience of competition concerns, first of all, the significance of the policy on competition for the organisation of the European political economy, the forms and degree of concentration of economic power, and the relations between national political economies and European and global developments.[2] Second, competition policy tests the possibilities and the limits of politics: the constraints to political choice developing in complex processes linking national and European policy-making. To what extent do political factors influence the evolution of European competition policy? To what extent does European policy limit national choice? Furthermore, third, the political element in competition policy is linked to different national strategies and manifests itself in the form of intergovernmental bargaining in the Council or, less frequently or at any rate less visibly, in intra-Commission rivalries along national lines. Fourth, the development of European competition policy and, in particular, the control of state subsidisation, and the growth of the enforcing capacities of the relevant European institutions or arrangements, are critical in helping avoid bidding wars among EU states aiming to attract foreign investment (Thomsen and Woolcock, 1993, pp. 76–7).

Last but not least, the politics of competition policy help determine the relations between competition and other European policies, such as industrial, enterprise and structural policies. Such relations can be examined from two different perspectives. We will be looking, first, at the inter-institutional perspective: interactions between different Community institutions as well as within the Commission (between different DGs). At the same time, there is the very interesting question of the impact of competition on other European policies. The issue of the relations between competition and industrial policy has been significant in the past and, as we will see, has occasionally provoked intra-Commission rivalries along policy (or ideological) lines. Competition, however, has a major impact on policies which aim to reduce imbalances and promote 'harmonious development'. For example, the EU monitoring of state subsidies is critical if we want to avoid bidding wars among EU states aiming to attract foreign direct investment. Similarly, the EU control of national subsidisation is necessary if structural policy is to make any difference: indiscriminate use of aid by states which can afford it will undermine the cohesion efforts, as aid in richer states could offset the benefits derived by the poorer states from the funds (see Gilchrist and Deacon, 1990, p. 35; Mitsos, 1992). In other words, if they are to produce results, structural policies are largely dependent on competition rules and how they are applied.

The book's core consists (i) of a political analysis of the factors which influence the formation and implementation of EU policy on state aid to European manufacturing industry, focusing on the process of policy formation and the development of policy enforcement on the part of the European Commission, and (ii) of four case studies on the emergence of particular state aid regimes in different areas, one horizontal (small business) and three sectoral (airlines, shipbuilding industry, motor vehicle industry). Shipbuilding is a sector in long-term structural decline; motor vehicle has been a critical industrial sector but one which has suffered from overcapacity for some time; while airlines, with extensive public involvement in the recent past, are crucial in examining the links between EU impact on national aid regimes and the politics of restructuring and regulatory change. By concentrating on the political and institutional factors which influence the formation of the EU policy on state aid, this book examines in some depth an increasingly important and yet relatively unexplored area of the European political economy. There is still a gap in the political science literature, as competition policy has been examined mainly from economic and legal perspectives. Fifteen years ago, Allen (1983, p. 209) noted the puzzling lack of interest on the part of political scientists in EC competition policy. Although the situation is slowly beginning to change with regard to concentration, mergers and the interaction between industrial and competition policy in the field of large firm regulation, it remains almost unchanged to the present day when one considers the other pillar of competition policy, relatively neglected by political scientists and yet crucial in its implications: the European control of national subsidies.

The Theoretical Prism

We noted that the establishment of a regime of undistorted competition was a central principle of the EC Treaty. Yet competition policy evolved gradually and its development and administration proved challenging for the European institutions. There were several reasons for this. Competition touches on various sensitive areas ranging from the states' economic policies to the market behaviour of leading firms. The sources of change in this area can be located at three increasingly interconnected levels, the domestic, the European and the global. At the same time, EC policy evolution bears the marks of fragmentation in Europe's policy-making mechanisms and inter-institutional rivalries. We will see that competition policy became politicised as soon as it gained momentum. As a result, its development bears the marks of a give-and-take between institutional actors, states, and policy areas. In short, rather than applying a textbook approach, the European institutions had to engage in a process of politically informed clarification and partial redefinition.

Competition and economic life

Although competition has been a central principle in modern capitalist economic systems, the notion of competition has been influenced by the various institutional and cultural contexts in which it operated. Even concepts with a predominantly technical character do not escape the implications of the interpenetration of political life and analytical inquiry (cf. Connolly, 1983, pp. 35–41), and competition combines technical, economic and political elements. The political connotations of different approaches to the concept of economic competition become clearer when we approach the concept in contexts in which it was first received with some reservation. We know that not all successful capitalist economies worshipped competition. This is especially true of late-developer capitalist economies, in which inherited institutions and practices associated with the policies of catching-up remained significant (Gerschenkron, 1962). While extensive state intervention has been a standard companion to late industrialisation, the question is what made such intervention effective in some cases. It has been shown, for example, that the features of economic development in South Korea and Taiwan have been determined by the state's capacity to dispense subsidies to business groups according to an effective set of allocative principles. Dispensing state aid in such a way, and largely avoiding the abuses of gross resource misallocation and corruption associated with subsidies, presupposed considerable state power vis-à-vis big business pressure (see Amsden, 1985; 1989; 1990). In a similar constellation, the agenda of structural adjustment and high growth which became dominant in the economic policy of the postwar Japanese state resulted in industrial targeting, a degree of protectionism and the encouragement of oligopolies in key areas in order to avoid the costs of what was referred to as 'excess competition' (Pempel, 1982, p. 54). Indeed, Chalmers Johnson has shown how a certain 'impatience with the Anglo-American doctrine of economic competition' has influenced the thinking and practice of Japanese economic decision-making bureaucracy (Johnson, 1982, p. 81).

According to the 'Anglo-American doctrine of economic competition', the efficiency of competition is linked to the key role of price as an allocative mechanism. The free-market economy will allocate resources in an optimal way (i.e., so that it is impossible to make an agent better off without making another agent worse off: Pareto efficiency) if certain conditions of perfect competition are met. Firms are in perfect competition if they are unable to influence the market price by themselves, they have free entry to the industry, and they produce under conditions of perfect information (i.e., if the entrepreneurs have perfect information about opportunities and their customers have perfect information about their goods). As is well known, departures from the elegant model of perfect competition may take various forms. Entrepreneurs or customers may have incomplete information about a price disparity which has been generated, for example, by an additional customer; firms may become 'natural monopolies', that is, they may achieve economies of scale up to the entire industry level, and may subsequently raise their prices and reduce their output, earning monopoly rents; there may be rigidities in the labour markets. Furthermore, the free-market system does not take into account public goods or production and consumption externalities. The literature on economic regulation concentrates on market failure rationales for regulation and examines the effects of regulatory policies in terms of efficiency (whether regulatory intervention is efficient or more efficient than doing nothing).

Various approaches, which will concern us directly or indirectly in this book, move beyond the price and the market as such to explore the organisation of economic life and the interaction of competition, institutions and politics in economic change. In *Capitalism, Socialism and Democracy* (originally published in 1942), Schumpeter argued that to assess 'the kind of competition which counts' in economic processes we need to consider competition commanding decisive cost or quality advantages. Such competition comes from new products, new sources of supply, new technologies or new organisational forms (Schumpeter, 1976,

p. 84). With the gradual erosion of competitive market structures, technological and organisational innovation essentially takes the place of competition as was previously understood, that is, as competition among a large number of small firms (the 'invisible hand' acting as a disciplinary mechanism). In Schumpeter's analysis, the emphasis on the technological qualities of products is matched by a certain distrust in large firms, whose impact on economic life is assessed mainly in relation to their interest in perpetuating their economic rents. From a different perspective, concentrating on innovative small-scale production in particular, it has been suggested that small firms engaged in flexible specialisation represent a model of microeconomic regulation in which price has only a limited role as an allocative mechanism (Piore and Sabel, 1984, pp. 265–77). From yet another, but not incompatible, perspective, a long-established school of economic analysis, institutionalism, calls attention to the organisation of economic life and the roles of economic, political and legal institutions in determining economic outcomes. For the institutionalists, the market mechanism is just one among several factors that need to be taken into account in explaining resource allocation, output and prices, and the distribution of income (on institutionalism see Foster, 1991).

The salience of particular regulatory institutions in this area becomes clear when we consider that competition, especially in the broad sense discussed by writers such as Schumpeter, plays a key role and at the same time possesses a systemic quality that makes it challenging for any institutional actor to regulate its mechanisms and implications. The enforcement of a particular normative understanding of competition becomes the domain of particular institutions and policies, which aim to ensure essentially that political intervention does not distort the prevalence of that particular understanding. We suggested above that among the implications of the enforcement of competition at the European level there are some which relate to the symmetrical development of different policies and the structuring of conditions that make it difficult for powerful actors, large firms or leading states, to utilise the European rules to their benefit. This is especially true in the area of state aid. As we will see, this suggests that one of the main functions of a policy on competition is to provide institutional frameworks for the play of market forces in ways that correspond to a normative equilibrium. The latter, as we suggest in this book, is not merely a reflection of particular balances between member states.

We can of course locate various normative viewpoints on economic competition. For example, links between the enforcement of competition and a normative understanding which relates to a notion of fairness have existed in the literature for a very long time and have taken various forms. To concentrate on liberalism, liberal *political* theory approached economic competition often with a certain ambivalence. For John Stuart Mill, whose political liberalism is combined with an anxiety over the social implications of the market economy, the one-sided concern with competition as a means of enforcing efficiency should be supplemented with the search for links between competition and justice. Alan Ryan has shown that Mill's approach to competition was that of a moralist. Mill wants to argue, for example, that while competition among workers can lower wages, competition among employers can drive wages up. The links between competition and justice require that workers understand the role of competition: 'in assessing workmanship, the market must be made to reinforce the desire of the scrupulous workman to demand neither more nor less than the worth of his work' (Ryan, 1984, p. 156). In this light, bracketing the weakness of Mill's particular example, the means of enforcing competition acquire not just a procedural but a substantive dimension as well, since the particular notion of competition and the way of enforcing it interact with the actors' different normative viewpoints and have an impact on their respective positions in the economy.

Interconnectedness and European policy impact

We will see that competition, apart from being a key European policy area, also stands out as an area in which the roles of central European institutions have been crucial in terms of both administration and long-term development.[3] This applies particularly to the European Commission and the European Court of Justice (ECJ). Since these institutions possess generally acknowledged weight in the formation and enforcement of competition policy, it appears promising to apply in this area approaches to European integration which underline the role of European institutions as independent variables which can help explain outcomes or as intervening variables which facilitate certain developments.[4] Policy-making in today's European Union is distinguished by the inter-connectedness of national and European actors and processes, the fusion of boundaries between the national and the European levels, and the increasing Europeanization of national policies and institutions.[5] To capture the complexity of institutionalised interactions between national and European actors and processes, institutionalist approaches seem to be an appropriate starting point for analysis.

The interaction of economic change and institutional parameters has been a major preoccupation for institutional economics, in the classic formulations (Commons, 1934) and in more recent attempts to combine institutional, evolutionary and cultural factors (Hodgson, 1988). The latter attempts, along with the diverse work of theorists such as Williamson (1975) and economic historians such as North (1981), are often referred to as new institutionalist economics. In political analysis, on the other hand, the interaction of political life and institutional factors and the ability of institutions to condition and help define political outcomes have been the research focus of various approaches often referred to, collectively, as new institutionalism.

While the way we approach the interaction of European institutional change and the organisation of economic life is influenced by institutionalist economics and its view of institutions as regulatory structures, the analysis of domestic politics and processes and of the EU institutional edifice draws partly on aspects of recent work within the framework of the new institutionalism in political science and political sociology (March and Olsen, 1984; 1989; Hall, 1986; Steinmo et al., 1992). We endorse new institutionalism's emphasis on the roles of institutional rules and processes in mediating preferences and shaping political outcomes. Furthermore, we note that institutional development is marked by historical inefficiency and unanticipated consequences which make it difficult for political analysis to rely solely on the explication of strategic action.[6] But when we suggest that institutions matter, we need to specify the various levels of analysis at which institutions are to be analysed as intervening variables or, in some cases, as catalysts of development. We need to avoid the potentially misleading significance attached by certain new institutionalists to the perceived resilience of national institutional arrangements.

In the context of the EU, in particular, such an approach appears to be increasingly untenable. We noted that the interconnectedness of national and European processes, actors and institutions makes it difficult to work with a neat distinction between the domestic systems and the EU. One aspect of this concerns the extent to which national policies and, more controversially, national institutions converge into one common model. The conspicuous or subtle shifts in national policies and institutional instruments brought about by policy convergence indicate that we need to focus on the interconnectedness of the national and the European when it comes to policy evolution.[7] We argue that the growth of European policies and the transformation of national policies are the result of interactions between economic shifts, political contestations, institutional capacities and legal instruments at various levels of the EU system. To assess the roles of EU institutions in the complex processes involved we will also need to take into account the unanticipated consequences of decisions and the inefficiency of decision-making (cf. March and Olsen, 1984, pp. 738, 740–41). Institutional politics prompts us to consider particular aspects and cases which contribute to intended or unanticipated shifts in institutional positions, expansion or shrinkage. We will see that such cases are increasingly decided by national courts and the ECJ, judicial politics in the interconnected EU-states system becoming a key arena for the resolution of policy conflicts.[8]

What is the relationship between this politics of interconnectedness and the main analytical frameworks which dominate debate on European integration? The main frameworks are defined today by approaches originating in international relations (IR) or comparative politics. We already noted that neofunctionalism, a prominent IR approach, is generally in agreement with the notion of proactive European institutions. But the same does not apply to intergovernmentalism. The latter approach endorses a view of European institutions which reduces them to epiphenomena of interstate bargaining. The roles of institutions in enacting and enforcing policies cannot be easily accommodated within the confines of this approach. Even in the most refined formulations of intergovernmentalism, the links between interstate bargaining and the operation of institutions aiming to enforce European policies (Garrett and Weingast, 1993) are complicated by the theoretical premises of the approach, which draw on neorealism and on realism. Not only neorealism's depiction of the state as a rational unitary actor but also the view of domestic politics which 'classical' realism presupposes need to be problematised. Realism 'assumes permissive domestic conditions' and ignores domestic non-state processes and transnational linkages (see Jacobsen, 1996, pp. 93–109).[9] In fact, the links between interstate bargaining and the enacting or enforcing impact of institutional action do not conform to a generally applicable theoretical formula in EU politics: different combinations of global and European economic conditions coupled with particular domestic constellations may result in different margins for the autonomy of European institutions.

Exploring the politics of interconnectedness means taking into account approaches from both comparative politics and IR, and working in particular with perspectives which integrate concerns from these bordering fields. Such perspectives have been gaining in significance since the late 1980s, questioning the existence of clear lines of demarcation between domestic and international politics. Perspectives which aim to integrate concerns from comparative political analysis and IR theory do not reduce foreign policy and IR to domestic causes alone, but treat the interaction of domestic and international structures as an historical process, while at the same time recognising that the international is internalised through domestic institutions and/or responses, and that what is being seen as the international (threat, challenge, opportunity, and so on) is the dominant domestic perception of it (cf. Jacobsen, 1996, pp. 93–109).

The analysis of Europeanization in particular requires an analytical framework which utilises insights from both IR and comparative politics approaches to integration (Lavdas, 1997, pp. 36–47). Only in accounts of European international relations and foreign policy it may be possible to retain the primacy of IR approaches, but even in this area, some of the best recent scholarly work endorses the explanatory significance of domestic–international interaction (Carlsnaes and Smith, 1994). In fact, the interaction in question is so intense in the EU framework that national preferences cannot be seen as if they were methodologically 'exogenous' to the EU institutional framework, since EU institutions and arrangements influence the very process of national preference formation (Risse-Kappen, 1994, p. 58).

Hence we concur with Stephen George when he suggests that it is difficult, indeed undesirable, to draw a clear line between approaches to European integration inspired by IR literature and approaches to EU politics inspired by comparative politics (George, 1996, pp. 22–3). There is a meeting of concerns and considerable scope for cross-fertilisation between neofunctionalism, in particular, and comparative politics approaches influenced by both new institutionalism and policy analysis.

Policy analysis plays a crucial role in locating the parameters, the contents and the forms of policy change in the EU system. To account for policy change in the EU we need to follow the politics of 'multilevel governance' (see Marks et al., 1996), which links European, national and regional–local public and private actors. The sources of policy change can be located at various levels. The national level has been significant from this perspective as well during the years of the revitalisation of integration when it came to certain influential policy ideas. For example, debates on deregulation and privatisation in many sectors originated in Britain and, outside the Community, in the US. But for most sectors in most member states for most of the time the source of policy change – indeed, the menu of policy options – has become the multifaceted and multilevel policy process of the EU, rather than any particular national policy solutions.

Accordingly, to explain the occurrence of change in European competition policy we need to encompass the EU as well as the national level and the interactions between them. The latter directs analysis, first, to the emergence of national competition authorities and, second, to the evolution of various forms of co-operation between European and national competition agencies, on the one hand, and between national agencies and other domestic actors on the other. Interactions between the European and the national level define also some of the conditions for the success or failure of European policies and the subtle or not-so-subtle modifications brought about through the processes of implementing European policies and enforcing compliance with European laws (see Mendrinou, 1996; forthcoming; Richardson, 1996a). The gradual and, admittedly, asymmetrical consolidation of a European legal industrial and market culture affects Euro–national as well as domestic relationships. This takes place mainly through the predominance of co-operative solutions in domestic policy games. Again, to account for such processes, an institutionalist prism proves useful. Institutionalism in economic analysis has always had evolutionary aspects. The endorsement of evolution, however, has more recently been evident also in approaches that follow game-theoretical premises in economics and political science (Axelrod, 1984; 1986). It has been argued (Lavdas, 1997) that Europeanization as a process lends itself to the analysis of the evolution of forms of reciprocal co-operation between the main actors in domestic political economy, because it creates the conditions that encourage evolutionary reciprocity. Although some of the most conspicuous effects of Europeanization involve the turn to Eurostrategies on the part of organised interests, such strategies are often combined with more elaborate co-operative solutions at the national level.[10] In other words, there are aspects of European policy impact which encourage new forms of public–private co-operation at various levels, including the national. Participation in European integration and Europeanization help ensure the long-term horizon of relationships, making it meaningful to anticipate future reciprocal returns, and increase interdependency, which necessitates some form of managing the density of interactions.[11]

At any level, economic regulation is linked to issues of power and resource distribution and the prevailing rules of the game (Hancher and Moran, 1989). The rules of the game, which are reflected in institutions and define the cultural environment of interactions, affect the means used by actors seeking solutions to policy problems. The latter are defined with reference to policy ideas. Ideational factors influence the policy options that are considered available, the expression and even the articulation of particular interested positions in generalizable forms, thereby promoting policy coalitions, and the selection of policy instruments.[12] Policy games take place in formal as well as informal relationships between actors who have an interest and a say in policy problems (Richardson, 1982; Richardson and Jordan, 1979) and who seek policy solutions through the mediation of institutional arrangements. Such arrangements concern the state as well as the economic institutions and the structure of the market. As Richard Samuels has shown, the extent to which policy games will be played in a reciprocal fashion will depend on factors such as the concentration of private economic power and the degree of oligopolistic or diversified organisation of interests, the nature of policy coalitions and the prevalent administrative traditions (Samuels, 1987, pp. 14–17). In the EU, as Jeremy Richardson argues, searching for networks of the 'stakeholders' in policy processes helps explain how policy ideas are translated into policy proposals through the involvement of a variety of interested actors and the mediation of the relevant institutions (see Richardson, 1996b). Early attempts to approach the competition implementation network in the EC sought to assess its impact in terms of encouraging compliance informally, that is, without resorting to judicial decisions (Vaughn, 1972). As we noted earlier, however, judicial politics has become a major arena for the resolution of European policy conflicts. Policy analysis should endeavour to encompass legal institutions and assess the impact of competition policy in terms of the politically salient parameters which we identified in this chapter: formal and informal inter-institutional relations, impact on other European policies and implications for the management of Europe's economy. The European competition policy network comprises European and domestic public and private actors and has expanded to include actors as diverse as the national courts in EU member states and the interested third parties in particular cases.

Notes

1. The EU *actual* control of state intervention depends largely on the development of the enforcing capacities of European institutions, the European Commission in particular (see Mendrinou, 1994; 1996; forthcoming).
2. This aspect takes a particularly acute form in member states with highly politicized economies, heavily reliant on state intervention. The Southern European member states of the EU share such characteristics and a highly politicized process of adjustment to European policy development (see Lavdas, 1996; 1997; forthcoming).
3. Competition Commissioner Andriessen suggested in 1983 that competition's centrality in EC development is closely linked to the fact that 'the Commission has its own powers here and is consequently not dependent on the reluctance or inability of the Council of Ministers to reach decisions ... The Commission itself takes a number of decisions in the competition area virtually every week. It considers that Europe cannot afford to run the race with a scratchy team and that the crew has to keep time' (Andriessen, 1983, p. 288).
4. For different analyses pointing to the explanatory weight of EU institutions and inter-institutional relations in accounting for policy outcomes see Kenis and Schneider (1987), Schneider and Werle (1990), Peters (1992), Ross (1992; 1995), Marks (1993), Kirchner (1992), Andersen and Eliassen (1993), and Sandholtz (1993). Such accounts of European institutions are compatible with refined applications of neofunctionalist theory of integration (see George, 1991; 1996). An important discussion of the agenda-setting process in the political system of the EU is Peters (1994). On the role of salient issues in providing stimuli to the politics of institutional development at EU level see Mendrinou (1994).
5. For the analysis of different policy and political aspects of Europeanization see Andersen and Eliassen (1993); Rometsch and Wessels (1996); Machin (1990); Ladrech (1994); Lavdas (1997); Greenwood (1997); Wessels (1997).
6. On the application of new institutionalist analysis to the EU see, *inter alia*, Peters (1992; 1994); Mendrinou (1990; 1994; 1996; forthcoming); Lavdas and Mendrinou (1995); Rometsch and Wessels (1996).
7. For different ways of approaching this interconnectedness see Andersen and Eliassen (1993); Peters (1994); Lavdas and Mendrinou (1995); Marks et al. (1996); Rometsch and Wessels (1996); Kassim and Menon (1996); Lavdas (1997).
8. For extensive theoretical elaboration on these points see Mendrinou (1992; forthcoming); Lavdas (1992; 1997).
9. In his critical discussion of the theoretical issues which confront the study of international politics, Halliday (1994, pp. 84–93) suggests that IR as a field is about the interaction of societies through the mediation of the state and calls

attention to the centrality of the state–society relationship for IR theory. Studying the state–society relationship makes it possible to recognize the broader, socio-economic (capitalist) character of the international system without reducing all relations to transnational linkages.

10. From a different perspective, the significance of domestic co-operative games has been underlined in the analysis of the mechanisms through which regulatory competition (changes in national regulation in response to the actual or anticipated impact of internationally mobile economic factors on national economic activity) works in actual practice. Analyzing the role of government–business interactions in fuelling the process of regulatory competition in the EU context, Sun and Pelkmans (1995) conclude that the process is a complex and unpredictable one, and cannot be considered preferable to Council-driven harmonization.

11. Accounts of reciprocity in policy games have benefited from the analysis of the conditions for biological reciprocity in Trivers (1971, pp. 35–57), even when such accounts do not follow a socio-biological line of argument.

12. On the influence of policy ideas and the ideational factor in policy-making, cf. Hall (1993) and Jacobsen (1995).

2 A Story of Restrained Formation and Expansive Enforcement

An EEC Treaty principle, the establishment of a regime of undistorted competition took considerable time to materialise. In particular, the development of a European competition policy on state aid was gradual and marked by institutional politics and various cleavage lines. It became clear in the process that a strengthened European competition policy contradicted EC-level industrial policy almost as much as it did state intervention. This tendency was reinforced by the neoliberal policy environment of the 1980s and 1990s, which favoured competition policy but not an active industrial policy. The issues, however, which had animated industrial policy debates, did not simply disappear. As a result, competition policy, including, as we will see, policy on state aid, often registers concerns and even negotiates solutions that appear to encompass functions as diverse as the creation of a level playing field, the opening up of a market, the encouragement of small business and the promotion of technological and organisational innovation.

2.1. Competition and Industrial Policy

Beyond direct subsidies, the notion of state aid may encompass special tax concessions and investments from public funds which distort competition. The market criterion in assessing whether an aid measure distorts competition is that it does if no market player would have invested the same amount under the same conditions.[1] In other words, we consider that state aid has been granted when a state makes available to an undertaking funds 'which in the normal course of events would not be provided by a private investor applying normal commercial criteria and disregarding other considerations of a social, political or philanthropic nature'.[2]

This is a recent juridical formulation which we will need to keep in mind. We will see, however, that the market criterion which underlies the notion of competition (and is aptly clarified in the aforementioned formulation) is supplemented and moderated by issues of the social, economic and political environment when it comes to competition policy as such. A somewhat formal way to put it is that, in authorising certain exemptions, the Community institutions make a decision on contributing to one or more of the general objectives of today's Community (for example, cohesion, improved standards of living, or environmental protection). Again, although this formulation is correct, it reduces the range of social and political issues and the variety of factors in response to which competition policy has been evolving.

Shifting policy mix

Although the establishment of a regime of undistorted competition was a central principle of the EEC Treaty, the development and administration of a coherent competition *policy* proved challenging for the Commission. The difficulties had three main sources (cf. Snyder, 1989; 1990; Lavdas and Mendrinou, 1994; 1995). First of all, an ideational framework for the role of competition policy could only take shape in interaction with other policy ideas, concerning mainly the need for an industrial policy at European level. Furthermore, competition policy touches on numerous sensitive areas ranging from the states' economic policies to the market behaviour of leading firms. Last but not least, EC/EU policy evolution bears the marks of fragmentation and inter-institutional rivalries.

In agreement with the *laissez-faire* character of the Rome Treaty, the Commission did not originally favour an active promotion of mergers and scale, despite the endorsement of such prospects by UNICE and several national business and employers associations, notably the *Patronat Française*. The Commission aimed at 'the introduction of greater neutrality in respect of those factors which determined firm size [and at the elimination of] those factors which artificially encouraged or impeded concentration' (Swann, 1988, p. 281). The Treaty did not grant the Commission any powers for an *ex ante* control of mergers, and the Commission has been left lacking some of the instruments it would need for a more active policy. That was because initially the Commission endorsed an approach of minimal involvement, while at later stages (even during periods of Community expansion) there was no consensus for it to become equipped with powers enabling it to pursue a policy of concentration (cf. Tsoukalis, 1993, pp. 109–13).

In the 1960s the *laissez-faire* economic philosophy underpinning the Community's constitutional framework made for an uneasy coexistence with the emerging view of concentration as the principal antidote to the *défi americain*. After the late 1950s French economic policy encouraged concentration particularly in sectors in which the government sought 'to force the creation of national champion firms on a scale suitable for international competition' (Zysman, 1983, p. 148). By 1965 France had the highest rate of mergers in Western Europe. Restructuring and the promotion of mergers entered the Community's menu of policy options once the establishment of a separate DG for Industrial Affairs in 1967 provided the institutional basis for delineating an industrial policy approach (cf. Hodges, 1983, pp. 270–73). As Balassa and others have noted, there have been strains in relations between the Community's industrial and competition policies, resulting in and being reinforced by tensions between DGs III (Internal Market and Industrial Affairs) and IV (Competition) (Balassa, 1973, pp. 311–12).

In its 1962 report on the implementation of the Treaty, the Commission noted that the creation of a common market was conditioned upon the development of a regime of undistorted competition (S/01770/62rev, p. 42).[3] The early adoption of a framework of action with respect to the private sphere, covering mergers, antitrust, dominant position, and so on, led to a workable but often challenged system. The other pillar of competition policy, concerning state aids, proved to be even more controversial. In examining the Community's difficulties in internal market and competition policies, we should distinguish between problems emanating from the Commission's own fragmented approach to these policies and problems associated with general factors inhibiting the development of any Community policy. Difficulties and constraints of the latter kind resulted in a negative interpretation of the Commission's powers, limiting these to the capacity to ban particular types of state aid (cf. Allen, 1983, pp. 216–7). The Communities' political crises of the 1960s along with the economic crises of the early 1970s were causes for self-restraint in policy development.

The former difficulties, focused on the ambivalence surrounding the links between competition and industrial policy and on the organisational reflection of this ambivalence in relations between DGs III and IV, resulted in an asymmetrical pattern of development in the respective policy areas. It was conceivable in the late 1970s that the pattern could be one of alternating influence, whereby an extension of competencies for competition would imply a shrinking of the playground of industrial policy. The Jenkins Commission appeared to be driving in that direction. Industrial Affairs Commissioner Davignon, a Belgian career diplomat who championed a central role for industrial policy, tried hard to co-ordinate the sectoral moves of Europe's leading firms and in the process appeared to weaken the role of competition, led by Commissioner Vouel, a Luxembourger Socialist.[4]

Davignon made an even more memorable comeback as Vice-President in the Thorn Commission, but the zero-sum pattern did not establish itself. In the early 1980s a Commission strategy for the development of a more rigorous and consistent competition policy started taking shape. At first it focused mainly on cartels and anti-dumping and a little later it turned towards the regulation of state aids. Under Commissioner Andriessen, competition strengthened its clout in the context of an emerging accommodation between competition and industrial policy.

Instead of a drastic shift in the power balance between competition and industrial policy, the tightening up of the monitoring regime of competition was achieved as part of a comprehensive package aiming at relaunching integration. In other words, the Single Market project generally promoted a positive-sum evolution of the competition–industrial policy relationship against a neoliberal policy background. Industrial policy on a grand scale became difficult to sustain. On the other hand, it would be erroneous to assume that the zero-sum pattern returned, only this time favouring competition. By the late 1980s competition policy, although considerably strengthened, had become involved in a policy mix which was shifting in response to various economic, political and institutional factors.

The Competition Commissioner conceded that 'the economies of scale afforded by the European market are still not being sufficiently utilised', while a large market 'makes it easier to carry out the necessary industrial restructuring' (Andriessen, 1983, p. 287). At the same time, Davignon's efforts in information technology concentrated on precompetitive collaborative research, which did not offend competition rules (Sharp, 1989, p. 208). The accommodation was and remains fragile, being stretched to its limits when the different policy ideas associated with the different approaches appear in some cases incompatible, or when antagonistic national interests use the industrial policy versus competition tension as a vehicle for promoting different policy solutions.

Differences resurfaced with regard to the European electronics sector on the road to '1992'. In preparing an electronics document, DG XIII (Telecommunications, Information Industries and Innovation) had talked about a strategic industry in crisis, had asked for derogations from the Single Market programme and had put forward proposals for accelerating technological innovation in the field. On the other hand, DG IV rejected the very idea of a strategic industry and insisted that there was no evidence that EC intervention would change anything. DG III stood in the middle, feeling uncomfortable both with the openly Colbertiste approach adopted by DG XIII and with the competition team's equally straightforward rejection of industrial policy. In a meeting with the directors general of the DGs in February 1991, Delors admonished both C.-D. Ehlermann (IV) and R. Perissich (III) for 'making light of industrial policy' (see Ross, 1995, pp. 118–21).

With a new Regulation on merger activity, adopted in December 1989, competition strengthened considerably its position in the area of antitrust. As we will see, this resulted in renewed tensions between competition and industrial policy, different national interests, and different policy ideas and policy programmes.

The basic thrust behind the Single Market project has been the attempt to relaunch integration by stressing a central issue area about which consensus could be achieved. The project aimed to combine the benefits of the internal market, which was in principle acceptable to the neoliberal policy environment, with the anticipated impact on industrial structures, promoting structures better fit to compete internationally. There was potential for considerable cost reductions through economies of scale, with reallocation of resources within each industry and the larger and more efficient firms replacing high-price producers. Mergers and takeovers would permit better exploitation of economies of scale and wider geographical diversification (cf. Emerson et al., 1988, p. 174).

At the same time, and here the ideological distance from the earlier debates on concentration promotion was evident, the benefits of size were not supposed to be the sole solution to the problems of European industry, and in any case, the active promotion of scale was unacceptable in a neoliberal policy environment. The impact of this environment was made clear in part through the readiness to accept more competition as a solution to a number of diverse problems.

Two implications followed, the first of which (that small-scale production should be taken more seriously into account in examining the potential of European industry) will concern us in Chapter 4. The Commission's interest in small business has resulted in SMEs policy being championed as one of the fields of convergence between industrial and competition policies. This convergence, and the Commission's sensitivity towards small business and their problems in securing finance, may become part of a wider functional package of division of labour in the

Community system, incorporating the notion of subsidiarity, familiar from the Community's early years, as signifying the most efficient allocation of functions towards achieving some commonly accepted goals. The desired convergence of industrial and competition policies can leave room for considerable state functions within accepted frameworks, and the assistance to SMEs has been cited as an important example of this (see Ehlermann, 1993b, pp. 701, 703). The convergence in a context confirming subsidiarity is also underlined by the resolve to create a more positive image for EC competition policy.

The second implication was that state intervention in its familiar forms should be checked. To the extent that scale was desirable, rationalisation should be achieved with more competition, and the antitrust wing of EC competition policy should therefore be strong. The advocates of competition within the Commission argued that world industrial leaders could be developed as a result of a process of adjustment in a competitive environment (Brittan, 1989a, p. 20). According to the Commission's White Paper, the completion of the single market ought to be accompanied by a 'strong and coherent' competition policy, involving an 'increased surveillance by the Commission in the field of competition rules to ensure that firms and member states adhere to these rules' (WP, point 19).

The 1992 project was accompanied by a growing emphasis on intra-EC links and a wave of mergers and acquisitions, including increased US and Japanese interest in investing in the EC. The mergers were generally welcomed by the Commission, but they soon raised questions on the relations and the boundaries between efficiency gains from restructuring and collusive behaviour and concentration (see Tsoukalis, 1993).

Accordingly, the strengthening of the Community's general competition policy has been a main aspect of the 1992 process. Greater Community vigilance has been displayed in the implementation of the rules governing mergers, dominant firm position, and so on.[5] Policy on state aid to enterprises has become equally crucial. As Ehlermann put it, in an integrated internal market the control of state aids is more important than ever, because 'state aids remain practically the only possible instrument to favour and to protect national industries', while 'their distortive effect on competition is likely to be so much higher as other distortive measures have been successfully eliminated' (Ehlermann, 1993a, p. 65). Within the framework of an emerging European-level regulatory system (cf. Majone, 1989; 1990), a strengthening of the Community's competition policy is evident also in this area and involves more rigorous enforcement practices in the control of subsidies to industry. In terms of total aid to industry as a percentage of value added, Italy, Greece, Portugal, Belgium and Germany are above EU average (EU average 4 per cent, 1992–4 average; see Commission, 1997b, pp. 7–8). Table 2.1 presents an outline of state aid to industry in the EU up to 1994.[6] Distinguishing between horizontal (for example, SMEs), sectoral (for example, shipbuilding) and regional aid, Table 2.1. shows a breakdown of aid granted by the twelve member states. Germany (especially following reunification in 1990), Ireland and Luxembourg are the main regional aid givers, followed by Italy and the United Kingdom. Spain and Portugal present high sectoral aid concentrations, while in Belgium, the Netherlands, Denmark and Greece horizontal objectives absorb subsidies that range from 82 to 60 per cent of the national total.

We will see that the emergence and evolution of a European policy on national subsidies was a gradual process. At an early stage, it involved subtle shifts in inter-institutional relations within the Community system and a series of difficult administrative tasks for the Commission and, in particular, for DG IV within the Commission. After the mid-1980s competition policy was assisted by the combination of the neoliberal policy environment in Europe and the efforts to relaunch integration. The relative decline in the Community's grand industrial policy projects resulted in greater space for competition policy, but it also made a division of labour between policies and their institutional protagonists less clear. Hence competition policy today needs to incorporate a number of concerns from other areas, not least industrial policy. This, as we will see, often makes for a less than optimal definition of policy goals, policy means and the relationships between them.

National and ideational intra-Commission divisions

The merger Regulation (December 1989) strengthened the Commission's clout in competition policy. DG IV, driven by the 'quest for a good first merger case' (Ross, 1995, p. 135), identified in 1991 the proposed merger between Fiat's Telettra (Italy) and Alcatel (France). DG III opposed the competition team's arguments and approach. In addition, the differences of view between Competition Commissioner Brittan, who sought energetically to expand competition policy competencies, and Delors, who favoured a mix of competition and industrial policy, surfaced in the Alcatel case. Different policy ideas were at stake and this division, as we

Table 2.1. State aid to industry 1981–94 by member state, breakdown of aid according to sector and function (in percentages)

	B	DK	D	GR	E	F	IRL	I	L	NL	P	UK	Total
Horizontal Objectives													
1981–86	67	92	40	64	--	67	26	35	43	59	--	45	47
1986–88	70	92	35	41	19	51	47	34	44	81	71	39	41
1988–90	76	59	29	81	28	66	50	30	39	77	17	45	42
1990–92	82	68	21	64	50	71	31	30	34	72	34	45	38
1992–94	82	72	15	60	40	44	15	27	30	74	29	35	30
Particular Sectors													
1981–86	11	2	5	16	--	25	30	21	0	23	--	15	16
1986–88	9	0	4	20	78	41	14	11	0	4	24	24	20
1988–90	4	38	11	5	67	25	9	15	0	11	78	20	20
1990–92	2	30	8	6	34	18	0	8	0	10	55	25	12
1992–94	3	25	5	19	43	38	11	22	0	11	45	17	17
Regional Objectives													
1981–86	21	7	55	20	--	5	44	44	57	18	--	34	37
1986–88	21	9	60	39	3	9	39	55	56	15	5	37	39
1988–90	21	3	61	15	5	9	42	55	61	12	5	34	38
1990–92	16	2	72	30	16	11	69	62	66	18	11	30	50
1992–94	15	3	80	21	16	18	73	50	70	15	26	48	53
Total	100	100	100	100	100	100	100	100	100	100	100	100	100

Sources: Commission (1989b), (1990b), (1992b) (1995), (1997b)

23

have seen, marked relationships between competition and industrial policies for more than two decades.

There was also another dimension to it. As the reach of competition policy expanded, 'other Commissioners and their staffs, including the Delors team, had try to protect their "national interests" (represent the positions of the member states of their origin) against Brittan's efforts' (Ross, 1995, pp. 57–8). A compromise solution was finally agreed, despite Brittan's clear preference for making the Alcatel–Telettra case the first case of a blocked merger under the new Regulation.

Then later in 1991 the proposed takeover by a Franco-Italian joint venture (ATR) of a Canadian aircraft manufacturer (de Havilland) became the cause of serious controversy within the Commission and in European politics more generally. Both companies manufactured technologically sophisticated turboprop commuter airliners. De Havilland, which was experiencing financial difficulties, had been acquired by Boeing but the latter changed their minds. Brittan and DG IV argued that the merger would result in a dominant position in the EC market. DG III countered that the relevant 'market of reference' was the international not the European, that the method used by DG IV for assessing market share was in any way objectionable, and that the industrial advantages of the merger would be considerable. Europe would possess a world-class champion in commuter aircraft.

DG III was openly backed by DG VII (Transport), led by Karel Van Miert, who later became the Competition Commissioner. Delors initially declared himself undecided, aiming to avoid another conflict with Brittan, but it appears that he was relaxed about the case believing that in the end the deal would not be blocked. When the issue came to the Commission, 'the result was a shock to Delors' (Ross, 1995, p. 178). Brittan's proposal won nine votes (Brittan, Andriessen, Schmidhuber, Cristophersen, Cardoso, Millan, Marin, MacSharry, Dondelinger) and the merger was blocked,[7] despite the fact that it had been supported by the French and Italian Governments and the industrial policy champions within the Commission.

Industrial Affairs Commissioner Bangemann lambasted Commissioner Brittan and DG IV as over-legalistic 'ayatollahs and gurus' oblivious to 'economic realities', while the French Finance Minister talked about a 'technocratic deviation' which, in the name of competition policy, 'denied Europe the weapons to confront economic competition'.[8] The result was damaging for Delors and for the European cause in France, where public reaction was particularly noticeable. George Ross comments that in France the Commission's decision 'fed the anti-European nationalism that would nearly torpedo the Community a year later on the Maastricht referendum' (Ross, 1995, p. 180).

In debates over an industrial policy for Europe, the French and Italian governments usually led the interventionist camp, while the British and the Dutch were prominent among those who believed that the market should decide the fate of firms. Germany was often depicted in the trade press as a waverer. Some German firms openly supported the idea of sectoral aid, although the dominant view in Bonn, expressed mainly through the economics ministry, clearly endorsed free-market principles. When in 1992 the French government launched a campaign in favour of an active European response to the challenges of international and Japanese competition, suggesting the adoption of a more interventionist approach, the Community remained divided over the issue, as was the Commission itself (see *The Economist*, 25 January 1992, pp. 16–17, 79–81).

Intra-Commission divisions along ideational as well as national lines are joined by rivalries which accrue from differences between corporate actors and/or corporate actors and other interests. In a recent merger case, involving major European firms and significant differences of view within the Commission, DG IV moved in spring 1998 to block a digital television alliance between Germany's two biggest media companies, Bertelsmann and Kirch Group. It was a heavily lobbied case and one which brought to the fore intra-Commission divisions. Competition Commissioner Van Miert reportedly went against the wishes of Commission President Santer and other Commissioners in deciding to veto the deal. The digital television alliance would have been marketed under the banner of CLT-UFA, a joint venture between CLT and UFA, the holding for the broadcasting activities of the Bertelsmann group. CLT is the biggest company in Santer's native Luxembourg (see *The Independent on Sunday*, Business Section, 17 May 1998; cf. *Financial Times*, 28 May 1998). In October 1996 the Commission had declared the creation of the joint venture CLT-UFA compatible with the common market. CLT-UFA created a leading European player in the audiovisual sector, but it nonetheless faced considerable competition, in particular from the channels linked to the Kirch group (*Competition Policy Newsletter*, 2/3, 1996, pp. 36–7).

Then, when it came to the Bertelsmann–Kirch alliance in 1998, certain Commissioners reportedly defended a European champion line, arguing that a negative decision would jeopardise European efforts to develop digital television programmes and compete with the US in the international sector. Also according to reports, the Commission took the view that as the two companies would control access to the set-top decoder box viewers will need to receive programmes, rivals would effectively be barred from Germany's digital television market. Interestingly, Canal Plus lobbied the Commission in favour of the deal, fearing that a negative decision would set a precedent in the regulation of the new European television field.

In the British digital TV case, concerning BIB (British Interactive Broadcasting, the joint digital TV venture between British Sky Broadcasting and British Telecom) the Commission's approach was one of conditional approval. The main condition has been that BT's local phone network, which provides the link for the interactive services (home shopping and banking services) should be available to rivals at fair prices.

2.2. Towards a European Policy on State Aid

Gradually, the control of national subsidies to industry became crucial in three respects. First and most conspicuously in an attempt to check state intervention and its distortive impact on competition. Second as a set of institutional–regulatory conditions underpinning the Single Market project. Last but not least, as Chapter 4 will argue, the control of subsidies became significant in the context also of the policy debate about the role and prospects of small business in Europe's economy. The Community was rediscovering in the mid-1980s the contribution of small-scale production. The original discovery was made in the early 1970s, but the second round was instrumental in closing gaps and finding ways out of the dilemmas posed for the relaunch of Europe by the neoliberal policy environment. In all three respects, the emergence of a European policy on state aid was gradual and owed much to the Commission's everyday administrative efforts.

The task entrusted to the Commission from the Community's early days favoured an active role in securing a competitive environment for both private and public enterprises. The task proved challenging. Arts. 85 to 94 EC presented the basic guidelines under which EC competition policy had to be developed. Emphasis was put on the role of competition policy for the Community's development and for the co-ordination of competition and economic policies in the Community.[9]

From restrained pragmatism to flexible expansionism

While the routine processes involved in the application of competition rules, monitored by the Commission, often resemble the interactive implementation processes depending on actors with various actual objectives (cf. Hanf, 1982), our interest in institutional politics prompts us to consider particular aspects and cases which contribute to shifts in institutional positions, expansion or shrinkage. Such cases are increasingly decided by the European Court of Justice, judicial politics becoming one of the key arenas for the resolution of policy conflicts.

The Rome Treaty provided the basic guidelines under which EC competition policy would develop; in 1962 the Council adopted Regulation 17/62 with reference to private enterprises. But developments in the area of state aids and public enterprises did slow. Rules on state intervention encountered difficulties, touching as they were on relations between member states and EC institutions[10] and conferring upon the Commission the strategic task of 'supervising the granting of aids by the Member States, whilst trying to protect the *acquis communautaire* of the Common Market against actions which mainly serve national interests for a short term only' (Pijnacker Hordijk, 1985, p. 67). The predominantly political considerations behind state intervention (Jordan, 1975, p. 237) and the reluctance of member states to undertake clear obligations that would limit their leeway of intervention in national economies (Hornsby, 1987, pp. 89, 92–4) were the factors that left their mark and set the pace of developments in the Community concerning state aids. The significance of subsidies for member states and the rationale behind the unwillingness to restrain themselves are clear for a variety of reasons: 'to ward off the short-term effects of recession; to plant seed capital where financial institutions are reluctant to invest; to facilitate the structuring of industry; to smooth the path to privatisation of industry; and so on' (Green et al., 1991, pp. 286–7).

Against this background, competition policy appeared at an early stage as a challenging task for the new Community. Competition Commissioner Hans von der Groeben noted in 1960 that

> the task of working out a European policy on competition and of seeing that it is applied is one of the four major problems facing the European Economic Community. These four problems are, firstly, the elimination of customs duties and of quotas, as laid down in the Treaty; next, the co-ordination of economic activities; thirdly, the

introduction of the 'four freedoms' covering the right of establishment and free movement of persons, capital and services; and finally, the matter of a regime covering competition inside the Common Market. (von der Groeben, 1960, p. 5)

On its own account, the Commission's role was to 'reintroduce the Community perspective'. The 'Community perspective' implied, first, taking into account the economy of Europe, that is, collective problems which individual states could or would not see, and, accordingly, second, upholding the Community level as the appropriate level for evaluating the overall implications of state policies and assessing overall needs when questions of exemption arise. Exemptions would not be granted to national initiatives which 'could weaken Community cohesion and provoke serious confrontations' (Commission, 1972, pp. 113–15). The pattern of action introduced was based on step-by-step developments and relying on the exercise of self-restraint by the Commission, which had to proceed through individual cases. It was understood that the function of 'reintroducing the Community perspective' would have to operate in a cautious and negotiated way.

Competition Commissioner von der Groeben suggested a 'pragmatic approach' in 1960, implying, first, extensive consultation with member states, and second, taking into account 'a whole series of conditions which strictly speaking do not come into the field of competition policy' (von der Groeben, 1960, p. 9). The 'pragmatic approach' was a cautious strategy of gaining acceptance and achieving a degree of consolidation for the Commission's role in competition policy.

The Commission followed this approach throughout the 1960s and on the occasion of the *First Report on Competition Policy* (published in 1972) it renewed its commitment to adhere to the basics of such an approach (point 139), although, as we will see, there was also change. The *First Report* presented in a more explicit manner the main principles which guided the approach to state intervention taken by DG IV. The Commission emphasised the risks that anarchical state intervention would entail for Europe's economy as member states did not evaluate the effects of intervention from a Community, i.e., a collective perspective. The Commission declared that it did not approach state aids negatively, because it .recognised that subsidies might constitute an appropriate instrument for structural adjustment and development of the national economies, while also playing various social functions (Commission, 1972, p. 17, point 133). However, unlimited national intervention would result in reciprocal neutralisation of national policies, transfer of difficulties from one member state to another and costly rivalries (Commission, 1972, pp. 17–18).

While it indicated that it considered necessary a system according to which all aids would be evaluated before their implementation, the Commission did not raise issues directly pertaining to its monitoring powers. It stressed that it intended to adhere to its realistic attitude, and that the social concerns behind particular schemes of national intervention would be given serious consideration.[11] The Commission insisted that Community action with regard to aid must not be treated as 'a confrontation between unrealistic principles of competition and the need to promote orderly structural changes', since 'it tends to make an essential contribution to the latter by being a factor of effectiveness and better control rather than a disturbing element in national initiatives' (Commission, 1972, point 134).

In the *First Report on Competition Policy*, the Commission argued that a state aid generally implies 'a conflict of interests' between the recipients and their unsubsidised competitors in other member states, the latter being placed in a less favourable position on the European market compared to that which they would have held in the absence of the aid (Commission, 1972, p. 113). Why did it take so long for DG IV to apply vigorously the provisions on state aids?

The economic growth of the 1950s prevented the issue from becoming politically salient. At the same time, most member states were reluctant to commit themselves to an agreement governing subsidisation of industry, even more so after the monetary crisis of 1963 and in view of the coming of the end of the transitional period specified in the Treaty. The effects of the monetary crisis of 1963 and the industrial decline experienced in certain central areas of the Community in the late 1960s had among their effects the strengthening of economic nationalism. As a result, there was an increase of the volume of state aids with a regional focus and the intensification of antagonisms among member states (cf. Mathijsen, 1972, pp. 381–3).

Learning to work without a Regulation

Against this background, in 1966 the Council refused to adopt the draft Regulation proposed by the Commission (in April) on the basis of Art. 94 EC[12] for the application of Arts. 92 and 93 EC. Apart from the general factors noted above, the Council's position can be explained against the background of the 'empty chair' crisis in 1965 and the subsequent Luxembourg Compromise which weakened the Commission's role (cf. Lambert, 1966, pp. 212–28), deterring any further attempts towards the refinement of the rules on state aids (Sassen, 1970, p. 7).

In the absence of a Regulation, the Commission started developing state aid policy through cases, notices, communications and, generally, the application of state aid rules in an individualised and flexible manner based on a consideration of the characteristics of each case. Thus the pragmatic approach advocated early on by von der Groeben was subtly transformed to embrace a flexible strategy of enforcement aiming at utilising the absence of a Council Regulation in the direction of gradually forming a practice founded on the Commission's political sense of possible impact.

According to the Commission, what was lacking was the willingness of member states to place their intervention policies under Community control by agreeing to create the necessary framework of action, a state aids Regulation. A second proposal to the Council for making recourse to Article 94 was equally unsuccessful in 1972. It confirmed the Commission's determination to adapt and proceed without a Regulation. As a result, the Commission was nonetheless 'deprived of a reference system which would facilitate its assessment of the legality of the aims and methods of Member States' intervention' (Commission, 1972, point 138). What was needed was a way of moving forward in spite of the absence of a Regulation. The solution was 'pragmatic action', signifying a combination of cautious pragmatism (von der Groeben's 'pragmatic approach' of the early 1960s) and flexible expansion of the controlling capacities. In the words of the Commission,

> this pragmatic action constitutes, at present, the main instrument for bringing to light common views on structural intervention and for reducing, by means of arbitration, partitioning and rivalry which may exist between the various national policies. The time-limits and transitional periods ... should not be a reason for slowing down action as required by the Treaty and failing which, the necessary convergence would become more remote. (Commission, 1972, point 139)

The legal instruments which the Commission had at its disposal were rather vague (see Chapter 3). The EEC Treaty addressed potential state interventions that are or may be excluded from the prohibition of Art. 92(1) (Arts. 92(2) and (3) EEC) on an individual basis according to the set criteria.[13] In contrast to the ECSC, the EEC Treaty did not abolish all state aids as illegal. It encouraged the development of a system for the evaluation of the compatibility of each individual scheme, seeking to secure undistorted competition while leaving room for aids in specific areas.

State aids were defined in a negative fashion as any state measure which, independent of form, distorts or may distort competition by favouring certain undertaking or the production of certain goods affecting interstate trade (Art. 92(1) EEC). Procedural practice has attached a broader meaning to state aids, reinforced by both the Court's case–law (Cases 290/83; 10/85) and the Commission (see, *inter alia*, Surveys on State Aids). Emphasis is put 'on ends rather than means, on effect rather than form' (Flynn, 1987, p. 124) in the evaluation of state aids.

This was the result of the variety of forms that state aids could take (Cases 57/86; 67, 68 and 70/85). State aids may be difficult to distinguish from other government measures, while the interplay of politics and legal constraint often results in complicated forms of subsidisation (cf. Fromont, 1988, pp. 153–4). The strains for national economies which resulted from the oil shock in 1973 and the recession led to protectionist measures with governments increasingly resorting to state aids (cf. Caspari, 1988, p. 48). The Commission's cautious attempts to control distortions of competition were met with more intractable modes of intervention and evasion of Community rules (cf. Cownie, 1986, pp. 248–9; Wulff, 1988, p. 16; and Steenbergen, 1987, pp. 194–5).

In the mid-1970s the Commission, evaluating the actual parameters of the crisis, which had also increased state intervention in the EFTA group, and considering the social character often attached to state aids, followed a more relaxed approach expecting that to an extent the increase in state intervention was of a temporary nature. It did not represent the beginnings of a re-nationalisation of economic policy. It soon became evident, however, that the tendency of 1975–6 towards the increase in state aids was not 'short-term' and of a conjunctural nature but reflected instead a 'more deep-seated structural' tendency (see COM(78) 221, points 5.1-2).

The recognition of the structural basis of the problem led the Commission to abandon its more lax attitude and aim to develop a systematic policy. After the mid-1970s the Commission, benefiting from the gains of the previous years of 'pragmatic' enforcement, tried a gradual shift in the direction of developing criteria that would allow the application of the rules in ways that would be acceptable to member states, emphasising recovery purposes (COM(78) 221, 3-9). The Commission suggested that 'the Treaty rules are not a static instrument but give the Commission a flexibility to accept the realities of the situation at both Community and Member States level' (COM(78) 221, point 6). The case-by-case examination of state intervention continued and, while the procedural instruments were gradually refined, the number of negative decisions remained low and there was limited recourse to the Art. 93(2) EEC procedure. As de Jong argued, the Commission's aim was to proceed but to proceed with caution, 'assembling information and trying to device schemes which avoid both the Scylla of directly contravening the national states and the Charybdis of unlimited financial support' (de Jong, 1982, p. 80).

The aim was to consolidate the Community involvement in the control of national subsidies by working closely with governments on mutually acceptable criteria. The perceived lead of the US and the Pacific economies further stressed the need for adjustment and restructuring, offering a systemic Community perspective to the debate. The Commission declared that its aim was to influence a channelling of aid in order to help restructuring of industry, boost investment, and curb inflationary tendencies while avoiding adverse effects on other member states (Vouel, 1977, points 1.5.1.–14.). The purpose of overcoming the structural problems inflicted upon the member states by the recession (COM(78) 221 final) was underlined. Even as Vouel's softer approach gave way to the more determined shaping of competition policy during Andriessen's tenure, we should note that during Vouel's term the Commission realised that national state aids could be regarded, in a realistic manner, as part of the Community system's direct or indirect policy instruments, which could be assessed in positive or negative ways at EC level and with reference to given objectives.

Through Communications and Notices to the member states, supported by test-cases to the Court, the Commission strove to create a framework for the application of state aid rules by introducing further criteria and by refining its legal instruments for evaluating aid compatibility with competition rules. Despite a relatively late start, the Commission's interest in state aids resulted in a steady increase in the 1980s of the use of procedures based on Art 93(2), decisions, and so on.[14] The Commission was often rigorous in trying to curb member states' opposition, particularly related to the tendency of avoiding to notify 'new' state aids (Commission, Letters SG (77) D/122; SG (80) D/9538; SG (81) 12740;

SG (83) D/13342). The Competition Commissioner argued at the time that the emphasis was not on abolishing all aids but on achieving co-ordination with the aim of ensuring that these would not endanger interstate trade or export economic difficulties from one member state to another (Andriessen, 1983, pp. 292–5).

A 'fine balance of views' between the supporters and the opponents of state intervention was therefore necessary (Andriessen, EP Debates, 15.10.1981, pp. 190–91). This policy explains the increase in the 1980s of cases related to state aids that reached the Court's docket, enriching the Court's case law. As Andriessen explained, 'the Commission too cannot but make the best of the means at its disposal or as the Dutch say, it can only row with the oars it has, but it is resolved to use them as effectively as possible' (1983, p. 295). In the 1980s DG IV initiated a bold approach towards strengthening its controlling function with respect to state aids,[15] responding to the tendencies developed in the member states with an increase in the volume of aids, cumulation of aids among different schemes (OJ C 3 1985), indirect aids, and an increase in cases of non-notification of aid schemes (OJ C 252/2 1980; OJ C 318/3 1983). The move to a more rigorous policy was supported by the European Parliament,[16] and can be discerned in the increase in the negative decisions and in the restrictions and alterations that could be found in its positive decisions (Andriessen, 1983, p. 394).

The Single Market initiative

The adoption of the White Paper and the SEA was a green light for the Community also in the area of controlling state aids. The establishment of the internal market gave a new boost to the attainment of conditions of undistorted competition (Brittan, 1989a, p. 20; 1989b, pp. 12–14; COM(87) 100 final). The Delors Report on economic and monetary union (1989) targeted the issue of government subsidies as one that should be tackled, while the Padoa-Scioppa Report (Commission, 1987) and the Cecchini Report (Commission, 1988) confirmed the role of competition as the major precondition for the internal market.

Against this background, the Commission initiated a more rigorous policy on aid control insisting on transparency for state intervention and on the development of co-operation with the states in this area, through multilateral meetings (Commission, 1990a, point 126). Apart from refining its legal instruments, the Commission embarked on the examination of the weight of state aids in the national economies, providing for the first time an overview (*Surveys on State Aid*). The early 1990s saw further attempts at tightening the control of both 'new' (SG(91) D/4577) and 'existing' aids,[17] stressing strict adherence to the rules (Delors, 1990, p. 20; cf. also SG (89) D/5521).

According to the White Paper, 'a strong and coherent competition policy must ensure that the partitioning of the internal market is not permitted to occur as a result of protectionist state aids or restrictive practices by firms' (WP, point 19; cf. 6 and 157). It was plain that if the states were serious in their commitment to the internal market, the control of state aids should be encouraged. The White Paper stressed that

> it will be particularly important that the Commission discipline on state aids be rigorously enforced. There are tendencies to spend large amounts of public funds on state aids to uncompetitive industries and enterprises. Often, they not only distort competition but also in the long run undermine efforts to increase European competitiveness. They represent a drain of scarce public resources and they threaten to defeat efforts to build the internal market. As the physical and technical barriers inside the Community are removed, the Commission will see to it that a rigorous policy is pursued in regard to state aids so that public resources are not used to confer artificial advantage to some firms over others. An effective Community discipline will make it possible to ensure that available resources are directed away from non-viable activities towards competitive and job creating industries of the future. (WP, point 158)

The Single European Act (SEA) was a crucial opportunity for the Commission to start applying tighter criteria (Commission, 1989b, point 5; 1988b, points 170–1). Although it brought no changes to the articles concerning EC competition policy the addition of new policies, as are the environment, research and development and the economic and social cohesion, the SEA indirectly affected the salience of competition policy and particularly of state aids (cf. Ehlermann, 1992, p. 257).

The adoption of the single market programme raised further concerns with respect to its impact on the European industrial structures, setting competition's policy choices as the mid-ground arena. The co-ordinates of the Commission's competition policy are to be found in the interactions between the realisation of the internal market and the attributes of industrial policy (cf. Ehlermann, 1993b, p. 699). Two opposing poles developed with respect to the desirable goals and the means to be used. The basic thrust behind the first was the attempt to overcome the problems associated with the fragmentation of European industry and to promote a rationalised industry better fit to compete in international markets. There was potential for considerable cost reductions through economies of scale, with re-allocation of resources within each industry and the larger and more efficient firms replacing high-price producers. Internal restructuring was also held to be significant, with some firms being compelled to rationalise and possibly concentrate on particular products, but the crux of the story was external restructuring.

Mergers and take–overs would permit better exploitation of economies of scale and wider geographical diversification, it was hoped, creating 'truly European companies which have no special links to a particular country and are thus able to escape from the national champion mentality' (Emerson et al., 1988, p. 174). The other approach, however, argued that the benefits of size were not the sole solution to the concerns of restructuring European industries and their position in world markets. The promotion of mergers leading to industries of a monopolistic scale even at the national market level would have various adverse effects. The advancement of European industry could only succeed adjustment and functioning in a competitive environment (Brittan, 1989a, p. 20).

The latter approach, combined with the impact of the Single Market project, gave considerable impetus to the Commission's role in state aid control (cf. Brittan, 1989a, p. 20; 1989b, pp. 12–14; COM(87) 100). As Ehlermann put it,

> in a truly integrated internal market ... the control of state aids is more important than ever before. The reason is simple: state aids remain practically the only possible instrument to favour and to protect national industries. Their distortive effect on competition is likely to be so much bigger as other distortive measures have been successfully eliminated through the process of establishing the internal market without internal frontiers. The Commission has therefore to become even more vigilant. (Ehlermann, 1993a, p. 65)

Furthermore, the internal market initiative extended the application of state aid rules to further areas, such as banking, insurance, transport, energy, telecommunications, and other service sectors such as entertainment and leisure industries (Ehlermann, 1992b, p. 260;

Commission 1992a, point 158). The Commission's tasks had expanded not only through the development of a system of monitoring and control but also by providing the intermediate means (with individual decisions and guidelines) for the application of the legal provisions and of the various prohibitions and the exceptions under the state aid rules (see Ehlermann, 1992b, p. 263).[18]

More generally, examined from the perspective of inter-institutional relations in the Community system, the main implication of the White Paper and the SEA was the strengthening of the Commission's role. As Ehlermann explained, the Commission's 'more decisive approach to the exercise of its powers of implementation and control reflects its increased influence in relation to the Council and the national governments'. Ehlermann used two examples to illustrate the point: first, 'the bold application of a previously little-used provision to apply the rules of competition in the member states'; second, 'the new practice of demanding the repayment of illegally granted aids, which was unthinkable a few years ago' (Ehlermann, 1990, p. 70). The gradual development of the Commission's capacities in controlling state aids was therefore given a major thrust with the Single Market project.

2.3. The Evolution of Controlling Capacities

The control of state aid has become a central field in the Commission's use of its monitoring powers, especially since the Commission and to some extent the Court[19] managed gradually to make a virtue of the Council's refusal in 1966 and 1972 to adopt a Regulation on state aid. The Council's stance, which was meant to delay for as long as possible putting subsidisation under the Community regulatory framework, led to the gradual development of a flexible policy by the Commission, building on the earlier notion of a pragmatic approach. This development, which was unanticipated from the Council's viewpoint, has far-reaching implications for the system of enforcing EC rules in the area of state subsidisation of industry. The experience of applying the Treaty provisions along with the Court's extensive case-law have led to the gradual refinement of the legal instruments[20] and the criteria for evaluation[21] at the Commission's disposal.

Council–Commission relations: the reversal of positions

As it became clear that the lack of an implementing regulation for the control of state aids failed to keep the Commission's enforcing capacities at bay, and as DG IV gradually adapted to the gap and even used it to expand its monitoring, the views about the instrumental significance of a state aids Regulation were changed and even reversed. The lack of a 'reference system', as the Commission had put it in 1971, had encouraged instead of a binding framework the development (by the Commission and the Court) of a pragmatic and flexible one which in effect expanded the discretionary powers granted to the Commission under Art. 93 EC. With a view to preserving its gradually acquired powers, the Commission preferred to refrain from submitting further proposals to the Council on envisaged Regulations (cf. Caspari, 1988, p. 43).

On the other hand, against a background of increased relevance of the EC control of state aids in the context of the Single Market, the member states discovered that the use made by the Commission and the Court of the lack of a Council Regulation was unanticipated by the Council. The Council moved to reverse the process, spearheaded by states whose intimate involvement in their industrial structures made them worry most about the effects of a tightening of the competition regime and its enforcement.

The Italian President of the Industry Council suggested in 1990, in a letter to Competition Commissioner Brittan, that the time had come for the Commission to submit and for the Council to adopt a Regulation on the implementation of the Treaty Articles on aids.[22] The Commission responded that a more elaborate framework would be unnecessary.[23] The practice developed during years of efficient operation enabled the Commission to argue that proposals for a Regulation under Art. 94 would be inappropriate, since 'the objectives of juridical certainty and transparency can be best attained by continuing the well-established practice, *inter alia* of bilateral and multilateral dialogue and consultation in the decision-making process' (Brittan, quoted in Slot, 1990, p. 743). In the context of the compromise reached, the Commission came off with its basic position unmodified, but undertook the obligation to strengthen member states' participation in the policy-making process by holding a multilateral meeting of national experts on state aids twice a year.

Assuming that the Commission (along with the other EC institutions) is an organisation seeking to enhance its position in the Community system, we can attribute the change in its preference from a binding framework to a flexible approach to the fact that developments advanced rather than constrained, as was anticipated by the Council, the discretionary powers granted to the Commission under Art. 93 EC. Submitting proposals to the Council for an implementing Regulation 'would no doubt have led to responsibility for the control of state aids being transferred to the Council, which would have been unacceptable to the Commission' (Ehlermann, 1992, p. 275). The threat of retrogression and of the curtailing of the Commission's powers has been a constant point of reference for the Commission. According to then Competition Commissioner Andriessen, because the Commission has its own powers in competition policy, it is not dependent on the divisions, reluctance or inability of the Council of Ministers to reach decisions on proposals which the Commission has put forward. The Commission 'considers that Europe cannot afford to run the race with a scratchy team and that the crew has to keep time' (Andriessen, 1983, p. 288).

The strong connection between competition policy and the 1992 programme was evident in the Delors Report on economic and monetary union (1989). Government subsidisation was defined as a crucial area. Subsidies were in any event a threat to the programme: they could take the place of the eliminated tariff barriers and risk transferring problems from one member state to another (Brittan, 1989b, p. 12). Furthermore, the changes in the national economies associated with the 1992 programme raised concerns that 'losers' in the national economic structures might respond by exercising increased pressure on domestic institutions for state aids (Brittan, 1989b, pp. 19–20). The question was whether member states would be willing to accept the new 'rules of the game', or whether they would prefer to go through protracted political and legal battles over subsidy regimes (cf. Emerson et al., 1988, pp. 7–8).

The strategy of the Commission for the initiation of a more rigorous enforcement policy on state aids was supplemented by its insistence on securing transparency in state intervention[24] and by favouring the development of co-operation with the member states through multilateral meetings (Commission, 1990a, point 126). Concerning monitoring and enforcement, in 1985 the Commission focused on three main areas: 'improvement in the effectiveness and transparency of the procedure, increasing information on the current situation regarding state aid and the aid rules', and 'priority handling of cases that are important for competition policy' (Commission 1986, point 170).

In addition, along with boosting the legal instruments for its controlling function through procedural practice and the European Court's case–law, the Commission during this period embarked on the examination of the state aids' weight in member state economies providing for the first time an empirical overview of the situation (*Surveys on State Aid*). The Surveys aimed to overcome the legacy of the protectionism of the 1970s, which was based on multiple and intractable modes of state intervention.

The Commission seemed also determined to adopt a harder line against infringements, declaring that

> it has instructed its services automatically to open the Article 93(2) procedure in case where the Member State does not reply to a request for notification within a limited time period. Furthermore, it is examining whether non-notified aids which have been paid out, or aids paid before the Commission has taken its final decision on them and which are therefore illegal on procedural grounds irrespective of whether or not in an examination they are found to be compatible with the common market, should automatically be subject to a demand for reimbursement. (Commission 1986, point 173)

DG IV sought to enhance its instruments with the adoption of the White Paper. The newly introduced measure of repayment had to be utilised fully supporting the Commission's action. The application of this tougher line of action against non-notified state aids was resisted by the member states. In a case brought to it by France, the European Court rejected both positions demarcating the limits within which responses against non-notified state aids should be placed (Case C–301/87; see Chapter 3). Guided by the Court's case–law, the Commission formulated a system of conduct for cases of non-notified state aids (Commission SG(91) D/4577). In its attempt to free resources in carrying out its 'realistic' approach, concentrating on cases that both attract the interest of member states and constitute potential threats of competition (Brittan, 1989b, p. 13), the Commission introduced a faster and more effective way of evaluating aids of minor importance granted to small enterprises[25] or, more recently, in 1996, of minor aids granted to all enterprises.

A further dimension that should be added to the Commission's control of state aids in the 1990s is that the tightening of the discipline in state aids, by strict adherence to the rules and favouring reductions of the amounts involved (Delors, 1990, 20; see also Commission SG (89) D/5521), was perceived as inadequate to the extent that it only referred to 'new' aids. 'Existing' aids should also be scrutinised with equal vigour if consistency and effectiveness of policy was to be reached.[26] The result was a change of emphasis in the Commission's policy on state aids 'from merely reacting to new schemes, to a more positive one of the Commission actively selecting the important areas it should critically examine' (Brittan, 1989b, p. 14). The rigour demonstrated by DG IV in this area led not only to reactions by member states but also to certain intra-Commission conflicts (between DG IV and DG XVI, which is responsible for regional policy).[27]

Co–operative institutional relations and enforcement

The enforcement strategy of the Commission in this area, a strategy which was described by Brittan as realistic, laid great stress on finding creative ways to combine the legal powers assigned to the Commission and its discretion in monitoring and enforcement. The Commission adopted an active approach, realising that by strengthening its controlling function in 'existing' aids it would be possible for it to select particular areas and cases of interest, with the aim of supporting and developing further its policy priorities. The review of existing aid schemes provided an opportunity for the Commission to focus on cases and types of aid that corresponded to its priorities. Brittan noted that aid schemes that would receive attention first included export aids, general investment aids, nationalised industries, state holding companies, and capital injections (Brittan, 1989b, p. 14).

A related dimension has been suggested by F. Snyder with respect to the enforcement strategy of the Commission, which concerns 'not only the classic aims of competition policy, but also other policy objectives' (Snyder, 1989, p. 151). It is worth quoting at some length former Director General of Competition C.-D. Ehlermann, who explained that

> the Commission's more decisive approach to the exercise of its powers of implementation and control reflects its increased influence in relation to the Council and the national governments. Two examples will suffice as an illustration: first, there is the bold application of a previously little-used provision to apply the rules of competition in the member states; second, there is the new practice of demanding the repayment of illegally granted aids, which was unthinkable a few years ago. (Ehlermann, 1990, p. 70)

The *modus operandi* which DG IV had cultivated in the absence of a regulation involved both the European Parliament and, in a different capacity, the European Court of Justice in critical institutional roles. In the area of state aid policy, the initial reluctance of the Council to regulate had been the catalyst behind the development of the Commission's relationships with the other institutional pillars of the Community with respect to monitoring and enforcement. We noted above that the EP supported a more rigorous approach to state aid policy in the 1980s. The EP was a consistent supporter of the Commission's extended competencies and increased vigour in controlling state aids (Caspari, 1988, p. 40). It raised the crucial issue of the political authority of the Commission with respect to its tasks on state aid policy, and on various occasions it exercised pressure in favour of a more determined attitude in state aid control (EP Debates, 14.10.81, 112–13, 120). The discussions of the annual reports on competition in the EP often lead to considerable political support being offered by the EP to the Commission for its functioning in competition policy.

More importantly, as we have seen, the Commission turned towards the European Court. The Commission's view has been captured in Flynn's argument that

> little or no help can be expected from the Council in the field of State aids. A combination of caution and jealousy paralyses it. ... Thus, the burden is on the Commission. The letter to the Member States (OJ C252/2 1980) ... is a sign that the Commission's line is going to toughen up. Having thrown down the gauntlet, the Commission should now enter the lists. It is common knowledge that many aid schemes have been implemented in breach of Article 93 since the date of the letter, and are causing serious damage to the economies of the more law-abiding Member States. In taking firm action, the Commission will be strongly supported by the Court, as previous rulings show. (Flynn, 1983, p. 312)

The remedy was to be found in the ability of the ECJ to exercise guidance and, as Judge Mancini argued, state aid constitutes one of the prime arenas for doing so. The Court exercises guidance by providing through its case-law the necessary legal instruments for effective surveillance of the corresponding rules (Mancini, 1991, p. 190). The role of the Court is critical in supporting the fulfilment of the Commission's function by delivering authoritative (legal) solutions to pressing problems. For the

Commission, recourse to the Court for clarification, legal solutions or endorsement usually led to increased potential for enhanced institutional position and the ability to influence policy developments. In any event, the peculiarity of the legal framework of state aid control, which promotes the institutionalisation of all actors involved with respect to the litigation potential, strengthens the Court's role considerably, especially in view of the fact that, as Caspari observed, the increase in negative Commission decisions led to more appeals to the ECJ (Caspari, 1988, p. 40). The Court of First Instance had jurisdiction over many state aid cases since 1993 and has been able to concentrate in a thorough manner on the underlying facts and their economic and policy appreciation by the Commission (Ehlermann, 1995, p. 3).

On the part of member states, a tendency towards withdrawal or modification of proposals has been discerned since 1985 (Commission 1986, point 169). This was followed by the attempt of member states to notify schemes in line with the ones introduced by the Commission (Caspari, 1988, p. 49). Although this may be due to changes in the governments' approach to state intervention, the effects of the initiation of a more rigorous policy by the Commission should not be underestimated as an interconnected factor. Intensification in the Commission's monitoring function in one issue area may be effective in changing national tendencies on subsidies in that area while at the same time driving private firms (under the risk of repayment) to reformulate their demands (e.g., turn to R&D projects) and/or diversify their lobbying strategies. Since the mid-1980s there has also been a tendency by member states to withdraw proposals because they anticipated a negative decision by the Commission (cf. Vogelaar, 1985, pp. 31–2).

In the long run, the success of the Commission in improving and developing the very conditions of its functioning has been mainly due to the tendency to set priorities and work on them (cf. Ehlermann, 1992, p. 265) exercising a margin of essentially political discretion (Ehlermann, 1995, p. 3). This has become a powerful means for a relatively small bureaucracy, assisting the latter to clarify and develop its tasks at the same time as it expands its capacities (cf. Mendrinou, 1994; 1996; forthcoming). Council–Commission relations remain at the centre of developments in the late 1990s as state aid control reaches a turning point. The number of negative decisions on state aid has increased considerably. At the same time, available data indicate that strict monitoring will be essential if a level playing field is to be taken seriously as an objective. As Table 2.2 shows, there is a considerable increase in *ad hoc* aid (from 7 per cent of cases in 1990 to 36 per cent in 1994), indicating the crucial yet transitional nature of subsidy regimes in Europe. Armstrong, Glyn and Harrison suggested in 1991 that while government subsidies to industry in the private or public sector have been 'a favourite target of free market rhetoric', actual reductions have been small (Armstrong, Glyn and Harrison, 1991, p. 318). Yet the gradual refinement and extended reach of European state aid control is evident in the fall in levels of industrial aid excluding *ad hoc* cases. On the other hand, the increase in *ad hoc* aid signifies the persistent nature of the issues associated with subsidies as we approach monetary union.

Table 2.2. State aid to industry and *ad hoc* aids in the Community 1990–94 (annual values in constant prices 1993 – million ECU)

	1990	1991	1992	1993	1994
Amounts *including* ad hoc cases	43777	39827	41196	43890	42830
Amounts of *ad hoc* cases	3163	5237	6914	12069	15486
Amounts *excluding* ad hoc cases	40614	34590	34282	31821	27344
Ad hoc *cases as percentage of overall industry aid*	7	13	17	27	36

Source: Commission (1997b).

The effort to tackle state aid on the road to monetary union assigns important functions to decentralised enforcement. In particular, the role of the national courts has become instrumental in the development of a decentralised enforcement system for European competition policy.[28] In 1995 the Commission published a notice with the aim of encouraging the national courts to use their powers in state aid cases. The Commission invited the national courts to co-operate with it in the field (OJ C 312, 23.11.1995). Proceedings before national courts may require that the courts interpret and apply the concept of aid in Art. 92 in order to determine whether aid introduced without observance of the preliminary examination procedure specified in Art. 93(3) ought to have been subject to the procedure. The ECJ had clarified that the involvement of the national courts is the result of the direct effect of the last sentence of Art. 93(3) on the enforceability of the prohibition on implementation until the Commission has reached a decision (Case C–354/90).

The role of the national courts is twofold in this respect. First, when dealing with a case in which the Commission has not decided, the national court must ensure that no effect is given to a proposed aid measure until the Commission has reached a final decision on the measure's compatibility with the common market. Second, if the Commission has taken a decision on an aid measure, the national courts must ensure the application and enforcement of that decision (Faull, 1994, pp. 57–8).

Towards state aid Regulations

We noted that state aid policy has arrived at a turning point. In the second half of 1996 the Commission launched a joint initiative with the Irish presidency with the aim of clarifying and, to an extent, re-orienting state aid control in the European Union. The Commission was given the green light to prepare proposals for a procedural Regulation and for a Regulation on block exemptions (to exempt aid categories from the notification obligation).

A key factor behind this development was the combination of the completion of the Single Market and the increasingly assertive drive towards monetary union. The Treaty on European Union confirms undistorted competition as a necessary precondition for further integration, emphasising 'the principle of an open market economy with free competition' (Art. 3(g) and 3a(1,2) EU). The need for controlling state aid is increasing further under the convergence objectives of the monetary union, which is affected by the governments' volume of spending for industrial purposes. EMU and the apparently irreversible drive towards a single currency, with the accompanying commitment to the Maastricht convergence criteria, cleared the way for a general acceptance of the need for debating a possible Regulation.

Apart from the coming of monetary union, by 1996 there were other factors that made possible this changed approach to state aid Regulations (cf. Mederer, 1996, pp. 12–14; Van Miert, 1997, pp. 7–9; Commission, 1997a, pp. 69–75). First, the completion of the single market and greater exposure of Europe's economies to competition strengthened the tendencies to liberalise previously protected sectors (such as transport, telecommunications, energy, postal services). Accordingly, there was need for monitoring and control of state aid in these important sectors. Such control should be extensive and at the same time predictable and based on agreed criteria.

Second, the increasing involvement of third parties in state aid procedures and the growing realisation of the role of national courts by third parties (such as businesses) reflected the growing propensity to engage in litigation under conditions which were less than ideal in terms of legal certainty. Furthermore, third, the continuous increase in the workload of DG IV (594 cases in 1994, 802 in 1995) exercised considerable pressure for modernising the rules of procedure in order to enable the DG to cope with the increasing volume of cases with speed, efficiency and transparency.

Last but not least, by 1996 there was a significant change in political climate. The politics of Council–Commission relations, which led even to a reversal of these institutions' positions with regard to the need for a state aid Regulation between 1972 and 1990, had been associated with the years of difficult negotiated development of European policy. The aforementioned factors indicate that, despite oscillations, state aid control is becoming an increasingly acceptable process. It does not follow that the envisaged Regulations would necessarily consolidate the power which the Commission acquired through years of pragmatic, flexible and politically sensitive application of the rules. But it appears certain that, since the actual and extensive control of state aid became a major and legitimate issue in EU politics, the eventual transformation of national practices will be confirmed.

In February 1998 the Commission submitted a proposal for a Council Regulation laying down the rules for the application of Art. 93 of the EC Treaty (COM(98) 73 final). The proposal covers all areas in which the Commission, in accordance with the jurisprudence of the European Court, has developed a practice for the application of Art. 93 (procedures regarding notification, unlawful aid, misuse of aid, existing aid schemes, monitoring, and certain common provisions regarding interested parties, professional secrecy and the role of an advisory committee on state aid). It is now considered 'appropriate', in order to ensure 'effective and efficient procedures' and 'increase transparency and legal certainty' to 'codify and reinforce this practice by means of a regulation'.

Regarding horizontal aid in particular, the proposal for a Council Regulation on the application of Articles 92 and 93 to categories of horizontal state aid (COM(97) 396) aims to simplify the processing of cases and focuses on block exemption decisions in the case of aids coming under regional policy and granted to SMEs, R&D, environmental protection, employment and training and export credits and credit insurance. When it comes to aid granted under the various exemption decisions, the member states will have to publish and to pass on relevant information to the Commission so that the latter will be able to exercise *a posteriori* control (in other words, there will be no prior notification requirement for such aid). The Commission will also be able to grant a general authorisation for state aids below a certain amount.

Notes

1. On the criteria of a market economy investor as used by the ECJ in order to clarify state aid which distorts competition see, for example, Case 234/84 ('whether in similar circumstances a private shareholder, having regard to the foreseeability of obtaining a return and leaving aside all social, regional policy and sectoral considerations, would have subscribed the capital').
2. Advocate General Jacobs's Opinion, Joined Cases C–278/92 to C–280/92 (Spain v Commission), ECR 1994, par. 28.
3. See an analysis against the background of the 1966 Zijlstra Report by P. Verloren van Themaat (1969, pp. 311–22); cf. Deringer (1963, pp. 30–40).
4. See Jenkins (1989, p. 278), diary entry for 20 June 1978: '10.30 meeting with Raymond Vouel, who complained, with some justification, about Davignon running around and organizing all sorts of cartels which were offending the competition rules of the Commission'.
5. While the influence of US federal competition law has been significant in the formation of the provisions of European competition policy, there are limits to the influence exercised by more recent developments in American antitrust law, particularly developments moving in the direction of a minimalist policy on enforcement (cf. Fejo, 1989). We will argue that the Commission's role in competition policy and its administration has instead been on the increase, often diverging from the economic efficiency criteria of the Chicago approach (cf. Frazer, 1990), and has been characterized by a combination of elements of greater decentralization and more rigorous strategic involvement in the emergent enforcement system (see also Chapter 5).
6. The most recent Survey on State Aid, the Fifth, does not include data on the period after 1994 (see Commission, 1997b).
7. The vote in the Commission College was nine to four with four abstentions. Delors abstained.
8. See *The Economist*, 12 October 1991, pp. 17–18; *Financial Times*, 12 February 1992 and 25 October 1993; cf. Tsoukalis (1993, pp. 111–12); Ross (1995, p. 179).
9. See an analysis of this on the basis of the Zijlstra Report of 1966 by Verloren van Themaat (1969, pp. 311–22); see also Deringer (1963, pp. 30–40).

10. It has been suggested that the difference in the development of the two areas of EC competition policy is owing to the fact that cases involving state intervention necessitate a political rather than economic approach (Jordan 1975, p. 237). The reluctance of the member states in limiting their leeway of intervention in the national economies has greatly influenced developments in the Community. See Hornsby (1987, pp. 92–4, 89); Joliet (1981, p. 442).

11. See Commission 1972, pp. 18–19 and points 132, 135; cf. Commission 1985 on the use of Art. 93(2) EC when the scheme in a first examination appears to be incompatible with the common market (point 197).

12. This provision has only been used with respect to procedures in specific sectoral aids in transport. Regs. (EEC) 1191/69, OJ L 156/1 1969; 1192/69, OJ L 156/8 1969; 1107/70, OJ L 130/1 1970.

13. The categories of aid listed in Art. 92(3) EC cover the middle ground between compatibility and prohibition, and the Commission is entitled to scrutinize them.

14. Interview with senior official, DG IV (Competition), Commission of the EC, Brussels, November 1992. Name and interview notes with the authors.

15. On the Commission's supervisory function more generally see Audretsch (1986); Steiner (1995). For a political analysis of the Commission's strategic considerations in monitoring see Mendrinou (1996; forthcoming).

16. See Debates of the EP 14/15.10.81; EP Resolution 1–608/81, OJ C 287/61–62 1981; EP Resolution 1–610/81, OJ C 287/63 1981.

17. The result was a change of emphasis in aid policy 'from merely reacting to new schemes, to a more positive one of the Commission actively selecting the important areas it should critically examine' (Brittan, 1989b, p. 14; cf. Commission, 1991, point 171).

18. Indicative is the introduction of guidelines for the granting of state aids to SMEs (OJ C 213 1992). See discussion in Chapter 4.

19. As Slot (1990, p. 759) notes, the Court has repeatedly pointed to the gap resulting from the absence of a Regulation on the basis of Art. 94. Furthermore, in a number of cases (e.g., Case 301/87) the Court has restrained the Commission. However the Court's judgements offer clarifications and fill gaps, generally contributing to the development of a system of enforcement in the area. This is an area in which the Court feels it needs to exercise guidance. If clear rules on notification of aids do not exist, 'sooner or later ... such rules will have to be written by the Court'. See Judge Mancini (1991, p. 190).

20. Two indicative developments are the recovery of the illegally granted amounts (Case 70/72; Commission OJ C 318/3 1983) and the new procedures for illegally notified aids (Case C–301/87; Commission SG(91) D/4577).

21. Of considerable use to the Commission in its evaluation of aids has been the compensatory justification criterion. See Case 730/79, cf. Commission (1981, point 213).

22. Minister Battaglia maintained that the Council's failure to act a long time ago would be no excuse for the Commission to continue avoiding to submit a proposal, for 'the parallel maturing of the European institutional process and economic and social requirements make this issue ripe for examination'. Quoted in Slot (1990, p. 742).

23. See the response of Sir Leon Brittan on behalf of the Commission to the letter of Mr Battaglia from the Council in October 1990: *Agency Europe*, no. 1656, Oct. 1990, quoted in Slot (1990, pp. 742–3).

24. See, *inter alia*, Commission, 1988b, point 173; Commission, 1990a, point 170. Furthermore, the Commission seems to have been particularly preoccupied in succeeding to secure transparency in member states interventions in national economies, a concern related also to the provisions of Art. 90 EEC. Of particular significance is the Commission's stance towards public undertakings, both with respect to state participation (see Commission, Guidelines Bull. EC 9–1984; also see EP Debates 14.10.1981, pp. 111–12, 121; for the more general issue of the financial relations with public enterprises see Commission, Dirs. 80/723/EEC; 85/413/EEC). The Commission viewed the implementation of the Directives as a valuable means for improving supervisory powers by promoting information. For objections by member states against the First Directive see Cases 188–190/80. For extensive analysis of developments in the area of public undertakings in the 1980s see Hellingman (1986, pp. 111–33).

25. This policy of the Commission had been initiated in 1985 with a letter to the member states (Letter SG(85) D/2611), that was later expanded to include a more detailed formulation of the legal framework (Commission OJ C 40 1990). The Commission in 1992 introduced a detailed code of action with respect to aids of minor importance and the schemes for SMEs (Commission OJ C 213 1992). See Chapter 4.

26. The Commission turned towards the examination of 'existing' state aids by the summer of 1990. See Ehlermann (1992, p. 276); Commission, 1990a, point 120; and Commission, 1991, point 171 on the desire for a more regular review of existing schemes.

27. For a detailed exposition of the crisis see Wishlade (1993, p. 148).

28. On the combined roles of the ECJ and the national courts cf. Weiler (1993; 1994); Volcansek (1992); Shapiro and Stone (1994); Faull (1994).

3 Institutional Framework and Legal Instruments

As part of its role as guardian of the Treaties, the Commission aims to ensure that state aid is allowed only where it complies with Community rules. Generally speaking, state aid complies with Community rules when it is compatible with the common market. It is the job of the Commission to detect and pursue cases which it considers to be incompatible with the common market. This chapter is concerned with exploring the institutional framework in place and the legal instruments available for the Commission in its role of monitoring and enforcing Community rules on state aid. Certain specialised legal regimes covering particular sectoral or horizontal categories are examined in greater detail in the analysis of the cases in the next chapter.

3.1. The Definition of State Aid and the Treaties

A combination of legal rules and procedural practice indicates that state aid is considered incompatible with the common market if four cumulative conditions apply to it. First, the measure in question must provide the recipient firm with an advantage. Second, it must be granted by a state or through state resources. Third, it must have a particularistic character, that is, it must favour only certain firms or the production of certain goods. Finally, fourth, it must affect trade between member states (see Commission, 1997a, p. 71).

The rules governing the control of state aid in EU competition policy can be found in Articles 92–4 of the Treaty. These Articles constitute the general framework for the review and monitoring of national subsidies to industry, with the aim of avoiding distortions of competition in the Community. The very idea of a common market presupposes the attainment of conditions of undistorted competition (Art. 3 EC). Since the early years of the Community the realisation of the objectives of the common market has been considered conditional upon the development of an EC competition policy (Commission, 1962, p. 42). The White Paper and the Single Market project reaffirmed the significance of competition policy for integration. The Maastricht Treaty and the convergence criteria underlined further the significance of competition policy on state aid.

In contrast to the European Coal and Steel Community (Art. 4(c)), the EC Treaty does not abolish all state aids as illegal. It provides instead for the development of a system for the evaluation of the compatibility of each individual aid scheme. Thus it seeks to secure conditions of undistorted competition while at the same time allowing state aids in areas or sectors in which state intervention is considered acceptable or necessary. Little documentation is necessary, particularly after the creation of the internal market with the removal of all trade barriers and the establishment of the 'four freedoms', to back the imperative to control general state intervention in the EU in order to avert potential distortions of competition in the member states.[1]

The EC Treaty advances no particular definition of what state aid is in the EC context. It embarks instead on a discussion of forms of state intervention that may be excluded from the prohibition of Article 92(1) EC on an individual basis, according to the fulfilment of the specific criteria which are delineated in Article 92(2–3) EC or as may be provided for by actions of the Commission or the Council (Art. 94 EC). State aids are defined in a negative fashion, as any state measure which, independently of its form, distorts or may distort competition by favouring certain undertakings or the production of certain goods and affecting in this fashion interstate trade in the Community (Art. 92(1) EC).

Through procedural practice, reinforced by the practice of the Commission and the Court's case–law, a broader meaning has been attached to the concept of state aid.[2] In the examination and evaluation of state aid cases the emphasis is 'on ends rather than means, on effect rather than form' (Flynn, 1987, p. 124). As Caspari noted, 'it is not a question of form taken by the aid, nor whether it is a direct or an indirect aid and by which public body it is granted; what matters is the effect' (Caspari, 1988, p. 43). This appears justified in view of the multiplicity of forms in which state aid may be granted, often beyond any clear transfer of public funds and with the use of various channels through which aid may be given by public authorities.[3] Even state participation, although in principle not incompatible with competition rules, has under particular circumstances been considered an aid measure.[4]

The Court with its case law has made a key contribution in the Commission's efforts to clarify and define state aids.[5] As we saw in the previous chapter, the early failure of the Council to adopt a Regulation that would provide guidelines for the application of state aid rules under Art. 94 EC[6] led to the adoption by the Commission of strategic procedural practice as the main alternative.[7] State aids present an inherent difficulty in that it is sometimes difficult to distinguish them from other measures employed by governments, based as they are on the interplay of political choice and legal constraints (Fromont, 1988, pp. 153–4). These difficulties, along with the renewed interest in state aid control due to the relaunch of integration since the mid-1980s, contributed to the Commission's decision, exemplified in the *Surveys on State Aid*, to try to acquire more accurate information on the national aids granted in the 1980s in order to be able to devise appropriate strategies of enforcement.[8]

Aid categories that may be exempted

Article 92(2–3) EC provides the general guidelines for exemptions from the prohibition of Article 92(1) EC. The Commission is bound to authorise the categories contained in Article 92(2) EC, although it is true that different views have been expressed regarding the notification procedure.[9] This derogation refers to aids of a social character to consumers and should not discriminate against the origins of the goods concerned; to aids granted in order to neutralise the effects of national disasters; and, finally, to aids for the former eastern German regions following reunification.[10]

The categories of state aids listed in Article 92(3) EC are positioned in the middle ground between compatibility and prohibition. Although in principle these categories distort competition, exceptions may be granted by the Commission or the Council on particular grounds.[11] Five categories are listed under this heading (the fourth is a relatively recent addition introduced with the Maastricht Treaty). First we have aids to under-developed regions, with low living standards and high percentages of under-employment compared to the European average.[12] Second, there are aids for projects of a common European interest[13] or counterbalancing aid measures against cases of serious disturbance in a member state's economy.[14] Third, there are state aids for the development of specific economic activities or regions. Then, fourth, there are aids promoting culture and heritage conservation which do not distort competition or trade to a degree contrary to the Community interests (a Maastricht Treaty addition). Finally, as a fifth category we have aids provided from derogations decided by the Council on the basis of the Commission's proposals.

In addition to the aforementioned categories of state aids that may be admitted compatible, general measures granted by the member states are in principle accepted.[15] Although of course general measures affect competition, their dispersion across the whole economy minimises any distortive effects. Their compatibility depends on the condition that they do not support particular sectors or regions (Commission, Letter SG(79) D10478). If they do, the relevant plans should be notified separately to the Commission for evaluation under the relevant legal provisions.[16] But still a 'grey area' appeared to exist and the Commission has been aiming to achieve further elucidation and development of criteria. General aid schemes may indirectly favour specific sectors, for example certain fiscal or social security measures may offer advantages to specific sectors depending on how they are used (see Commission, 1990b, points 8–10 and Technical Annex, point 10.5).

Of a similar character but falling under the meaning of aid of Article 92(1) EC are aids of a horizontal nature. Horizontal objectives in manufacturing cover state aids for SMEs, R&D,[17] environmental purposes,[18] and energy conservation, that do not fall within the scope of other regional or sectoral objectives. In current debates, the tendency towards curbing general aid schemes has affected the attitudes regarding the importance of the distortive effects that horizontal schemes may cause, leading to the development of specific guidelines for partial objectives. Of considerable interest in this area has been the relatively recent general prohibition of investment aids with the exception of firms defined as SMEs for state aid purposes (OJ C 213 1992, point 4.1).

Evolving criteria

The experience of applying the Treaty provisions along with the creation of extensive case–law by the ECJ have advanced the implementation of the state aid rules, leading to the gradual refinement of the legal instruments at the Commission's disposal. Certain principles have developed through practice, testifying to the crucial role of the Commission and the Court in this area. Particularly from the early 1980s the Commission embarked on the development of 'general principles' and criteria for the evaluation of state aids, which compensated for the lack of a detailed framework of action in the early years of the Community (Ehlermann, 1992, pp. 274–5). The effects on intra-Community trade (cf. Case 47/69), that is, on trade and competition among member states, have been the key criterion for evaluation. The locality and intensity of the aid have also been considered (see Cases 40/75; 173/73; 730/79), an issue that is of particular relevance to regional aids (cf. Andriessen, 1983, p. 293), also in view of the very real danger of transferring difficulties and strains from one member state to another.

As regards principles developed through practice, an example of great significance is the well-known 'compensatory justification criterion'. In order to fulfil the compensatory justification requirement an aid scheme should, along with satisfying one of the set objectives, be of such kind and have such effects that could not have taken place under normal market conditions and/or as a result of the beneficiaries alone, while its justification should extend beyond the interests of the member state granting the aid or of the beneficiary firms and/or regions. Its justification would depend on the measure being beneficial from the perspective of the general interest of the Community.[19]

More elaborate criteria have evolved according to the type of state aid examined.[20] For sectoral aids the following are included (cf. COM(78) 221). First, rescue aids for specific companies or sectors are generally not compatible with the common market, and only under special circumstances, for example, certain social problems, may derogations be granted (Andriessen, 1983, pp. 292, 294). Second, the aid should promote restructuring and/or reduction of the sector's capacity, and should not function as operating aid. This approach follows the rationale of combined action that encourages discipline by avoiding competition distortions along with promotion of industrial restructuring (Andriessen, 1983, p. 293). Third, the aid should progressively diminish, or be of short duration, a criterion compatible with the early recognition of the expediency that medium/short–term state aids have for the Community (cf. Verloren van Themaat, 1969, pp. 311–22). Fourth, the aid should not result in distortions of interstate trade or export problems to other member states. In addition, special regimes have developed for specific sectors that attract member governments' concerns. The special regimes set frameworks of regulation for schemes in these sectors and ensure predictability and control of the related schemes.[21]

For regional aids also, detailed frameworks have evolved covering the necessary principles under which the granting of regional aids is compatible with the Treaty.[22] The significance of regional policy for integration is reflected in the emphasis on the co-operation and co-ordination principles covering cases of existing as well as new regional aids. Furthermore, the attempt to achieve complementarity between national and Community regional schemes has led to the development of a number of principles for setting a working framework of co-ordination in the Community.[23] The significance of regional aids and their co-ordination has acquired particular weight in the framework of the internal market project.

3.2. Legal Provisions for Reviewing and Monitoring Aid

The EC Treaty has a separate set of legal provisions for the review and monitoring of state aids. Political and legal considerations alike attach particular significance to this legal procedure. Compared to the general monitoring procedure (Art. 169 EC), the emphasis here is on speeding up the procedure, even though a conciliatory phase is also available under Art. 93(2) EC. Distortions of competition are often considered to be more urgent, because their prolongation may cause considerable damage to other member states and to market conditions. State intervention may undermine intra-Community trade and/or export difficulties from one member state to another; it may also complicate the Commission's efforts at re-regulation in an area or it may weaken EC policy impact.[24] Finally, the existence of an illegal state aid is regarded as inimical to the very spirit of the Treaty's principles (Arts. 3, 6 and to an extent 5 EC).

The likelihood of deliberate elements being present has required strict procedures in order to ensure compliance. Compliance seems to be more likely with the provisions of Art. 93(2) EC than with those of Art. 169 EC.[25] The practices associated with ensuring compliance in this area combine an inclusionary character (various actors may be involved) and an unusually swift pace with extensive and flexible powers for the Commission. The result appears to be a rigorous system of enforcement in a sensitive area of relations between member states and Community institutions.

According to EC competition law, all cases of state aids that do not fall under the scope of the provisions of Article 92(2) EC or have not been exempted under the provisions of Article 92(3) EC, or do not belong to any of the exception categories and/or have been granted unlawfully, are considered illegal. Article 93 EC sets the framework for the control of state aid. It distinguishes between two categories of state aids: 'existing' (Art. 93(1) EC) and 'new' aids (Art. 93(3) EC). The examination of all 'existing' and 'new' state aids is performed by the Commission, which assesses their compatibility with the common market and decides on their adoption, revision or abolition.

Art. 93(1) EC entitles the Commission to constantly review 'existing' schemes and authorises it to suggest any necessary changes or improvements or even the abolition of a scheme altogether. The review of 'existing' schemes was a much more relaxed process until relatively recently. The result of the previous process was that member states were encouraged to present new state aids as existing, avoiding the obligation of prior notification. Since 1990 the Commission has adopted a firm attitude towards the review of existing schemes.[26] This change has caused lively debates concerning the tenacity with which the Commission had initiated its review policy on existing regional schemes.

Publicly visible controversies surrounding the new approach acquired significant dimensions not only between the Commission and member state authorities but also within the Commission, particularly between DGs IV and XVI. An agreement was reached by combining the time-spans of regional aids with that of their review by the Commission for competition purposes (see Wishlade, 1993, pp. 143–50). This development may potentially serve as a pattern for the review of long-term existing schemes. Bearing in mind the Commission's views behind the policy of a more active review of 'existing' schemes, this development may be viewed as a relative setback for the Commission. First, by undermining the idea of an active role in selecting the cases to be pursued (Brittan, 1989b, p. 14), and, even more so, second, by retaining the prominent role of controlling new aid schemes if their prospective review is set according to their time stages.

According to Article 93(3) EC, member states are under the obligation before implementing any 'new' state aid (referring both to totally new schemes and to alterations introduced in 'existing' ones) to notify the Commission and to wait until it reaches a final decision on the compatibility of the scheme. Procedural practice and the Court's case-law have set the time for the Commission's response to two months (Cases 84/82; 120/73). The time-limit may be suspended if within two weeks from the receipt of the notification the Commission requests further information on the aid plan,[27] and may be reactivated with the receipt of the relevant information.[28] The Commission during this period should either reach a decision or initiate the procedure of Article 93(2) EC (see Case 120/70).

A 'new' state aid is legally implemented, and its legal status becomes that of an 'existing' one, either after the Commission's final positive decision under Articles 93(3) or 93(2) EC (save for the carrying out of modifications if such are required) or in the case of the Commission's failure to respond before the elapse of the time-period.[29] The failure of the Commission to respond within a reasonable time period entitles the member state concerned to challenge the Commission, bringing an action before the Court under Articles 175 or 173(1) EC; or the state may implement the aid measure after an additional notification to the Commission. A limit has been set by the Court on this discretion of member states by asking them to notify promptly the Commission of their intention to implement the aid, giving the Commission reasonable time to respond (Case 84/82).

The importance of the notification obligation imposed upon member states can be seen in the breadth of its originally intended application. New aids should be notified even if they belong to categories that are generally permitted, the only exceptions being the *de minimis* category for small business[30] and the newly introduced *de minimis* category. In 1996, in a new notice on *de minimis* aid, the Commission separated the relevant rules from policy on SMEs, extending it to all enterprises. Under the new rule, all aid of less than ECU 100,000 per firm over a period of three years, with the exception of export aid, will be regarded as not subject to Community control and need not be notified to the Commission. However, certain sectors (including shipbuilding, transport, agriculture and fisheries) are excluded from eligibility under the *de minimis* rule (Commission, 1997a, pp. 69–70, 75). As we noted in Chapter 2, the recent proposal for a Council Regulation on the application of Articles 92 and 93 to certain categories of horizontal aid (COM(97) 0396) specifies that when it comes to aid granted under the various exemption decisions, the member states will have to publish and to pass on relevant information to the Commission so that the latter will be able to exercise *a posteriori* control. According to the proposal, there will be no prior notification requirement for such aid.

The exemption of more cases from the prior notification obligation (for example, through the extension of the *de minimis* category to all enterprises) is the result of the efforts to modernise state aid control by focusing on the significant aspects and cases while rationalising the use of the Commission's limited resources. The prior notification obligation, which continues to be a very significant instrument, draws upon a broader concept of aid than the one expressed in Article 92(1) EC, calling upon the Commission to examine not only the compatibility of an aid measure with the Treaty but also the extent to which the scheme notified constitutes state aid proper (OJ C 318/3 1983).

Cases of non-notification of new aid schemes by the member states have been relatively common, a fact which speaks in favour of a combination of a more rigorous control by the Commission (Slot, 1990, pp. 751–3) and certain rationalisation measures, such as the ones we mentioned above. In a number of communications to the member states, the Commission has emphasised their obligation to promptly notify new schemes (OJ C 252/2 1980; OJ C318/3 1983; SG(91) D/4577). The Commission was even inclined in its communications to provide clarification on the question of the time elapsing between notification and implementation, recommending a period of at least two months or in some cases 30 days (OJ C 252/2 1980; OJ C 318/3 1983; SG(91) D/4577).

Special legal provisions on particular aid regimes

State aids in the production and trade of agricultural outputs are governed by the provisions of Arts. 40–43 EC, particularly by Art. 42 EC as refined by the corresponding Council regulations (see Reg. 26/62). Special guidelines apply to fisheries. In transport, state aids are governed by Arts. 74–84 EC, particularly Arts. 77 and 80 EC. Further exceptions are provided by Arts. 108(1) and 109(1) EC, referring to difficulties in the balance of payments of member states, and Art. 223(1) EC for matters pertaining to national security (affecting only sectors related to military products and national military purposes). Certain industrial sectors, owing to their particular circumstances, are governed by special regimes (e.g., textiles, synthetic fibres, shipbuilding, motor vehicle industry). In the analysis of the case studies in Chapter 4 the particular aid regimes for each case will be discussed in some detail.

We have seen that it was the significance of ensuring conditions of undistorted competition that made the Rome Treaty include special provisions on the general legal framework for the control of state aids. Although this framework has remained basically unchanged,[31] its content has gradually been refined and adjusted to the demands of competition in the EC/EU. It was the peculiarities and complexities of this task undertaken by Community institutions that led during the process of applying the rules on state aid control to the emergence also of particular legal frameworks. Although they are compatible with the general rules on state aid control, these frameworks have been adjusted to the special conditions pertaining to a specific sector or a particular category of state aid. In this way, specialised partial legal regimes were formed with the aim of regulating subsidies in particular sectors.

It was the ECSC experience that had demonstrated the importance of sectoral arrangements. Although in the ECSC Treaty state aids were generally prohibited, special regimes had formed on some occasions in order to address the particular market conditions in a sector. This policy of specialised arrangements appears to function in a manner that is both efficient and pragmatic, having to address the dual and often contrasting tasks of promoting competitive conditions in a sector with particular problems while at the same time limiting state intervention. But conditions under the ECSC Treaty for the granting of state aid were much more straightforward compared to those under the EC, in which member states may grant aids so long as these are compatible with competition rules.

The variety of sectors, along with the intermingling of European policy objectives and the dependence on the economic conditions in a given time period and a particular member state, contributed to a complex set of parameters affecting state aid rules. Although to an extent reflecting the different economic and institutional circumstances of a sector or an area, the development of specialised legal frameworks, which are able to take into account the particular parameters applicable in each case, has performed three main functions. First, it has averted the confusing effect for a particular policy area resulting from the cumulation of often divergent general policy objectives. Second, it has balanced the opposing effects exercised by different policies in a specific area in a manner which is compatible with the general objectives of the EU. And finally, third, it has allowed the development of rules compatible with the needs and the peculiarities of specific areas of policy.

The links between EU policy areas are significant when it comes to explicating the parameters which can account for the realisation of objectives in state aid policy. By its nature the control of state aids expands beyond any specific policy area and cuts through or supplements developments in other EU policies. State aid control makes the interconnectedness of EU and national policies clearly felt. Along with policy links, important in its consequences is the impact on policies of the distinction between horizontal and sectoral types of state aids. Hence we witness the emergence of further distinct legal frameworks to govern the granting of state aids in corresponding categories of aids, along with those concerning particular sectors.

As the previous chapter demonstrated, the Commission approached the realisation of the Treaty objectives in a flexible and dynamic manner. It aimed constantly to adapt Treaty rules, facilitating the evolution of a correspondence between policy needs and the actual use of the available policy instruments. The pertinence of this approach has been clear in state aid control, since policy responses in this area are essentially contingent upon changing economic conditions. A 1978 Commission Communication to the Council (COM(78) 221 final) provided one of the most explicit expositions of the rationale behind that approach. Independently of the basis of the aid (be it sectoral or objective-specific), this approach touched upon the imperative of focusing policy responses with respect to state aids control. The advancement of specialised partial legal frameworks for examining and reviewing aid was considered to be among the means available to the Commission in fulfilling its tasks.

3.3. Enforcement Mechanisms and Provisions

The review and monitoring of state aids, an important sphere of action for the Commission, are governed by specific rules, delineated in the Treaty, and have been particularly significant for the Community's economic and institutional development. The realisation and the functioning of a common market was from the beginning conditional, *inter alia*, upon the establishment in the Community of conditions of undistorted competition (Art. 3(f) EC). In addition, the role of the Commission in particular has been upgraded in this area. In a nutshell, the control of state aid presents qualities of particular interest because it connects three critical parameters, which allow us to discern the roles and development of European institutions. The control of state aid combines the characteristics of (i) being of great significance for the Community's functioning and development, (ii) arming the Commission with extensive powers and (iii) being particularly sensitive to the member states.

The dependency of a key aspect of state intervention on the Commission for evaluation and approval of state aid schemes constitutes a limitation in the ability of member states to pursue nationalist economic policies. As we have seen, awareness of the importance of this development was heightened with the Single Market project.

The various practical and tactical issues involved in the enforcement of the Commission's decisions under Articles 93(1) and (3) EC and the acute problem of the breaches of the member states' obligation to notify new schemes have encouraged the Commission to use, refine and try to expand the legal instruments at its disposal. In what follows we discuss briefly the legal means available to the Commission for securing compliance with state aid rules.

Enforcement provisions and interested parties

The Treaty has separate provisions for the review and monitoring of state aids, derogating from the general infringement procedures. In Treaty provisions as well as in developing practice it is easy to detect an interest in swift processing, as distortions of competition are often considered to be of an urgent nature. The evaluation of the compatibility of an aid measure with the common market is performed by the Commission which decides on its adoption, revision or abolition.[32] The Treaty makes the distinction, which we discussed above, between 'existing' and 'new' aids.[33] It introduces a complicated but potentially robust monitoring process, which took some time for the Commission to apply to its full potential.

The Commission in its review of state aids is supported by the provisions of Article 93(2) EC.[34] When the Commission forms the opinion that a state aid is either incompatible with Article 92(2–3) EC, or has been introduced improperly or even abusively,[35] it is entitled, after having invited the member state concerned to submit its observations, to decide on the abolition or the amendment of the aid.[36] The Commission's decision under Article 93 EC is legally binding for the member state concerned. This is derived from the provisions of Article 90 EC in conjunction with that of Article 189 EC (see Case 227/87; Commission, 1989a, point 324). The ECJ has established in judgements that the Commission's decision should be based on detailed evaluations of the economic circumstances providing a clear analysis of the effects of the planned aid and the extent to which it affects intra-Community trade. The Commission is bound to demonstrate its reasons for arguing that an aid distorts competition by presenting in its decision a lucid and verifiable justification of the potential or existing distortion of competition.[37] Nevertheless, the Commission in this function enjoys considerable discretion in taking into account various economic and social considerations before reaching a final decision, particularly if it is going to be a negative decision.[38]

Art. 93(2) EC asserts that if the member state in default does not comply, the Commission and any interested member state are entitled to bring a direct action to the Court, derogating from the time-consuming provisions of Arts. 169 and 170 EC (see Cases 31/77R and 53/77R; 52/83; 52/84). The latter derogation, that grants a member state direct access to the European Court, indicates the significance attached to distortions of competition by state aids and safeguards injured member states both against the injuring party and the possible reluctance of the Commission to act. Furthermore, it acts as a deterrent mechanism for defiant member states. Last but not least, it prompts the Commission to take the lead and pursue the case further in order to avoid the tensions that might result from direct litigation between member states.

The procedure of Art. 93(2) EC applies also to cases that raise difficulties during their evaluation. The Court has prompted the Commission to resort more often to Art. 93(2) EC procedure in order to characterise a scheme as an aid measure (Cases 290/83; 84/82), or when difficulties arise during evaluation. The procedure is particularly convenient in that it provides for all interested parties to participate in the proceedings by submitting their observations, and, by so doing, assist the Commission to reach a final decision. The Court has even declared that the Commission's reluctance to resort to the procedure may be viewed as a violation in case an action under Art. 173 EC is brought against the Commission (Cases 84/82; 166 and 220/86 at 6501).

The Court has given a broad definition of 'interested third parties'. Under Art. 93(2) EC the Commission should notify all interested parties by both direct notifications to the member states and by notices in the *Official Journal* for all interested third parties to submit their views on the case; lack of proper notification may lead to claims of procedural defects in the Commission's decision (Case 323/82). Participation in the procedure by a third interested party may be evoked in cases where the latter intends to appeal for annulment under Art. 173(2) EC, since the Court has accepted that it constitutes sufficient proof for admissibility purposes of the action, by substantiating the direct interest of the appellant (Case 169/84).

As has already been shown above, the procedure of Art. 93(2) EC provides a robust legal instrument for the Commission's control of state aids. Violations, however, of the obligation of notification of new aids are not a new phenomenon. In the course of refining and expanding the legal instruments at its disposal for securing compliance, and supported by the Court's case–law, the Commission introduced a number of vigorous mechanisms. The recovery of aid granted illegally has been one of the most interesting measures introduced by the Commission in the context of this process.

The idea of repayment of illegally granted amounts from the recipients had been first put forward by the Court in Case 70/72. It took almost a decade for the Commission to follow that line and introduce as a rule of conduct in the area of state aids the recovery from the recipients of the illegally granted amounts.[39] The power of the Commission to order the repayment of the aid became a mechanism of deterrence by making potential beneficiaries of aid sensitive to the legality of the relevant schemes. The acceptance by recipients of an aid measure that has not been previously notified and authorised by the Commission exposes them to the risk of repaying the amounts in question at a later point. The Commission provides special notices in the *Official Journal* for potential recipients who may be at risk from state aids of questionable legality. In view of such notices, recipients are liable for repayment. Recovery is made through the relevant national legal provisions and although no harmonisation has taken place, the Court has made it clear that the national provisions used should be such that they do not render recovery tenuous, a possibility which then renders member states liable against Community law.[40]

The measure of recovery of illegally granted amounts puts pressure on member states to observe the prior notification requirement for new state aids for which the requirement exists. For example, the Commission has suggested that the increase in the number of notifications in 1991 was partly the result of the enforcement by the Commission of the repayment measure (Commission, 1992a, point 159). This was due mainly to two factors. First, the intention to grant aid may be frustrated by the potential adverse effects on the beneficiaries of the aid measure. Second, recipients risk coming under considerable strain if the aid received is subsequently found to be illegal. They tend to require clarification of the terms under which an aid measure is granted to them. Furthermore, non-compliance with the Commission's decision and/or the Court's judgement cannot be maintained for long after the introduction of the repayment measure, because the execution of the order of recovery is made in accordance with the relevant national provisions and is under the rule of the national courts, which the member states would not defy. The introduction of the repayment measure and its enforcement by the Commission and the Court appears to be highly effective, both in substance and in procedural terms, in compelling state compliance.

The enforcement mechanism for state aids under Art. 93(2) EEC allowed the Commission to petition the Court for interim measures. The Commission has in this way a powerful instrument in cases of blatant violation of the aid rules for terminating the implementation of the aid.[41] Recourse by the Commission to the procedure of Art. 189 EEC for non-notified schemes constitutes also a particularly effective instrument (Case 70/72). In recent years, this power of the Commission has been further enhanced by the addition of further means of enforcement against member states which defy the obligation of prior notification under Art. 93(3) EEC. Even though the new instrument possesses less clout than the one preferred by the Commission, it still has enough power to compel member state compliance.

The Commission had argued in the past that any non-notified state aid should be characterised as illegal, in terms of procedural defects resulting from the violation of the non-notification obligation, and without resorting to the evaluation of its compatibility with the Treaty.[42] The Commission's preference for a strict approach on this particular matter had been expressed at various earlier points. The Commission intended to make the most of the introduction of the recovery measure and suggested also the declaration of the illegality on procedural terms of notified aids that had been implemented before its decision, thus putting pressure upon the member states for breaches of procedure (Commission, 1986, point 173). The European Court, however, rejected the view that breach of the prior notification obligation is irreparable. According to the Court, this view is incompatible with the spirit of the Treaty, which bestows upon the Commission the obligation to examine the substance of the aid along with its procedural legality. But in the relevant case the Court equally rejected the French Government's argument that a violation of the notification requirement does not affect in any way the rights of the member state in default.

The Court ruled that the declaration of illegality of an aid measure on procedural terms and independently of its substance can only be ruled by national courts through the direct effect of Art. 93(3) EC (cf. Winter, 1993). The Court, by also rejecting the view that procedural defects do not affect the rights of the member state in default, established that the Commission may resort to conservatory measures against the scheme concerned, at the same time as it embarks upon its evaluation. It ruled that member states are under the clear obligation not to implement new aids before the Commission reaches a final decision under Art. 93(3) EC, and if this is abused the Commission is eligible to go to the Court for an injunction against the member state in default.

By providing the Commission with the power to take conservatory measures, the Court advanced further the case law developed in Case 70/72, in which it had ruled on the possibility of ordering specific steps for the member state concerned, dismissing the German Government's claim on the declaratory character of the action (Pescatore, 1974, pp. 113–14). Failure of the member state to concede during the procedure of evaluation under Art. 93(2) and (3) EC grants the Commission the right to proceed with the evaluation of the aid and, if necessary, to order the recovery of the illegally granted amounts. In short, although the Court did not sanction the more drastic approach proposed by the Commission, it provided the latter with a rigorous procedure in order to compel member states' compliance.

Following the above Court judgement, the Commission proceeded to formulate a rule of procedure for cases of infringements of the prior notification requirement and to set a strict framework for the evaluation of such schemes (Commission SG(91) D/4544). According to this, the member state in default should submit to the Commission all relevant information within 30 days (in urgent cases the period could be shorter). Failure of the member state to respond empowers the Commission to order, by a provisional decision, the suspension of the aid measure. If the member state within 15 days complies with the provisional decision then the Commission initiates the procedure of Art. 93 (2) EEC, notifying the member state concerned to submit within a month all necessary information for the Commission to proceed with the evaluation of the aid measure. If the member state does not respond within the set time-limit, the Commission may reach its final decision on the basis of the information available and may order the recovery of the unlawfully granted amounts plus interest from the date of the award of the aid in accordance with the national provisions for late payment of amounts owed to the government. Finally, non-compliance of the member state with either its provisional or final decision entitles the Commission to refer the case to the Court under Art. 93(2) EEC or to apply for interim measures.

The Commission has acquired under this framework a robust procedure that is swift, while also diminishing the benefits of the member state in default and, correspondingly, those of the recipients by nullifying any advantage they might gain from the early implementation of an aid measure. Member states are compelled to participate in the procedures, since failing to do so destroys their chances of reversing the Commission's initial view (more often than not initial information to the Commission on illegally implemented aids comes from competitors), and, consequently, its decision on the compatibility of the aid scheme. Furthermore, the Commission has gained the power to resort to the Court both under Arts. 93(2) and 189 EC and retains the power to do so even if the member state fails to comply with its provisional decision. The Commission retains a wide margin of discretion in terms of both the promptness of recourse to the Court against the infringement in question and the legal instrument to be employed.

The potential violations in the area of state aid, which cuts across other policy areas of the Community, present a further peculiarity with respect to enforcement. Recourse by the Commission to the general infringement procedure is not ruled out in this case and has often been employed.[43] The use of the infringement procedure under Art. 169 EC is not uncommon. This is especially true when it comes to borderline cases in which the legal aspects of the infringements relate to other areas of policy, while the direct effect of these provisions allows for referral to the national courts.[44] Cases that combine violations of state aid provisions with those of other provisions (such as those of Arts. 30, 37, 90, 95 EC), or cases in which, although a state aid is compatible, its use may violate other provisions, are not rare.[45] Depending on the particular violation, the Commission resorts to the relevant infringement procedures having often a wide margin of discretion.[46] In the early years of the Community, resorting to the general infringement procedure for cases involving state aids was a relatively frequent phenomenon, owing to the fact that these procedures possess features that are less rigorous and less threatening (for the states) compared with the procedures of Art. 93 EC.

Discretionary powers of the Commission

We turn to the legal grounds of the Commission's discretion in monitoring. The Commission in monitoring exercises its power of selecting the means best suited for its response to particular breaches of member state obligations.[47] The legal provisions in the Treaty do not restrict the Commission's responses to violations, allowing enough leeway for it to act in accordance with the particular circumstances, in terms of both policy considerations and the specific conditions concerning the alleged violation.

In the infringement procedures proper under Art. 169 EC, the Commission is furnished with extensive powers of discretion. These can be examined in a number of different instances with respect to the legal process. Even the very initiation of the procedure rests upon the Commission's consideration of a member state's default. But the control of subsidies is a critical area in examining both the powers and the limitations associated with the Commission's discretion in monitoring (see, *inter alia,* Mortelmans, 1984, pp. 419–21, 431). As in the case of Art. 170 EC, the Commission's discretionary powers are in some ways limited compared to those under the general infringement procedures. Still, in this area the Commission enjoys exclusive powers for effective and swift responses along with considerable discretion during the evaluation process of state aids, exercising considerable power to choose the appropriate enforcement strategy. This is linked to the fact that the Commission's discretion in state aid control, the result also of developments brought about through case–law, relates more to the substance of the aid measure than to its legal form.

In terms of legal form, the Commission's discretion in the control of state aids is curtailed to an extent by the availability of remedies for both member states and interested third parties. These remedies may be employed not only against negative or positive Commission decisions but also against failure to act. This is not immediately apparent from the relevant Treaty provisions, which endow the Commission with significant discretionary powers. But the latter appear weaker when we consider the provision of Art. 93(2) EC. Under this provision, any interested third member state is entitled to bring a case before the Court against another member state for non-compliance with the final decision of the Commission, issued under Art. 93(2). This is a means that member states may use if they want to encourage the Commission to expedite the processing of a case against a member state in default. Thus the Commission is sometimes keen to initiate proceedings in order to avoid direct actions between the member states. The logic of this situation is similar to the one we discussed above concerning Art. 170 EC, which encourages the Commission to act so as to avoid potential tensions between member states.

A further limitation on the Commission's discretion is derived from the Court's case–law, which elaborated further on the conditions under which the Commission may be challenged in the control of state aids. Case–law expanded and affirmed the options for potential litigation open to third interested parties. This development acquires particular relevance in view of the increasing tendency of DG IV to develop a more rigorous approach to the control of state intervention in the EC/EU.

Nonetheless, the limitations on the Commission's discretion should not be overestimated for two main reasons. The first is derived from legal considerations linked to the Commission's general discretion in monitoring, while the second concerns discretionary powers in a more specific and context-related sense. The first factor is linked to the recourse to the general infringement procedure for cases involving state aids, a possibility that remains open. In a relatively recent decision (see Case 227/87; Commission, 1989a, point 324), the ECJ ruled that a Commission's decision under Art. 93 EC is of a legally binding character, as derived from Art. 90 EC in conjunction with Art. 189 EC and, therefore, in a case of non-compliance by a member state with the Commission's final decision under Art. 93(2) EC, it is in the Commission's discretion to initiate the infringement procedure of Art. 169 EC against a member state for failing to fulfil its obligation under the Treaty. As a result, the use of the general infringement procedure provides the Commission with considerable discretion, while at the same time it offers a renewed possibility for an extensive conciliatory phase that may lead to an amicable settlement.[48]

The second factor is linked to the specific powers of the Commission when it comes to the review of the compatibility of aid schemes with the principle of undistorted competition. The discretion involved here concerns also the ability to take into consideration wider social, regional or economic parameters. The peculiarities of both the content and the context of different aid schemes have resulted in provisions that have furnished the Commission with the powers necessary to enable it to review state aids in the EC while actually taking into account the particular parameters mentioned above. It is in this context that the Commission was granted additional discretionary powers, in order for its review to be constructive in terms of the economic and social development of member states. Consider, for example, the provisions of Art. 92(3) EC, which confer on the Commission enough leeway to proceed with the review of aid schemes by making an exception to the principle of undistorted competition, in circumstances where the common interest dictates the granting of aid, even if the latter affects competitive conditions. The Commission has under this provision the power to accept as compatible with the Treaty aid schemes that may distort competition.[49] Finally, a further potential discretionary power is bestowed upon the Commission: the latter has the right to review its own decisions on the compatibility or incompatibility of an aid scheme (see Gilmour, 1981, p. 72).

Remedies and safeguards

That the monitoring procedure has acquired considerable bite can be inferred from the increase in the relevant cases as well as in the number of litigations against the Commission's decisions, while the annulment procedure has also been invoked by various interested actors.[50] The result has been the transformation of all relevant actors into institutional ones. The increasingly rigorous character of the monitoring procedure and the significance of state aids made necessary a number of safeguards and remedies against the powers of the Commission. This particular aspect also distinguishes the monitoring system which concerns state aids from the system which follows the general infringement procedures. The remedies for both member states and interested third parties and against both negative and positive Commission's decisions have acquired particular significance in the Court's case-law in the area, while an important body of literature has been emerging (see, e.g., Schina, 1987, pp. 152–66; Ross, 1986, pp. 867–94; Ross, 1989).

Third interested parties, such as large or small firms, which remain unsatisfied by the Commission's decisions, may also resort to the provision of Art. 173(2) EC (Cases 166 and 220/86; also Commission, 1989a, point 323). Direct action against the Commission for negligence has also been invoked by member states and third interested parties. As we noted in Chapter 2, a further remedy of increasing salience is available for competitors' interests through the direct effect doctrine, which provides for an action to be brought to the national courts against the legality of a state aid granted by a member state.[51] Reference has already been made to the right of injured member states to refer directly to the Court, derogating from the provisions of Art. 170 EC against member states that fail to observe the Commission's decision with respect to an aid measure. In the following discussion we focus in greater detail on other important safeguards and remedies available for both member states (whether granting aid or alleging injury by an aid measure) and third interested parties.

The conciliatory phase under Art. 93(2) EC is considerably shorter than that of the general infringement procedure under Arts. 169 and 170 EC, even though consultations between the Commission and the interested parties do take place. The rigorous character of the procedure and its effects on states' economic policies underlined the need for a special safeguard clause. In this context we have the only occasion upon which the Council may intervene in the monitoring function. The Treaty establishes that the member state concerned may petition the Council to decide by unanimous vote on the admissibility of the aid scheme, by amplifying the provisions of Art. 92 EC or by referring to the provisions under Art. 94 EC, if special circumstances can be said to exist. Recourse to the Council has been rare, especially since the end of the transitional period that allowed for resort to the provisions of Art. 226 EC.[52] If this safeguard is invoked after the initiation by the Commission of the procedure under Art. 93(2) EC, the procedure is suspended till the decision of the Council. With a view to encouraging the swift processing of cases, the Treaty sets a limit of three months for the Council to respond. After three months the Commission may decide.

While the aforementioned procedures provide safeguards in favour of both the member state(s) which granted the aid measure and the allegedly injured state(s), further remedies against the powers of the Commission are available. Given the economic and political sensitivity of the matter and the increasingly active approach of the Commission, the number of litigations against the Commission's decisions has risen considerably. Remedies in this area for both member states and interested third parties and against both negative and positive decisions by the Commission, as well as against the failure of the latter to act, have grown in significance in the Court's case-law.[53] The availability of remedies against the Commission emphasises the difference between its monitoring function under the state aid rules and its function under the general infringement procedure, limiting the wide discretion enjoyed by the Commission in the latter.

The annulment procedure of Art. 173 EC has in recent years often been invoked, particularly by member states, in order to challenge Commission decisions; procedural defects referring to delays in the Commission's response are often the cause.[54] Third interested parties not satisfied by the Commission's decisions may also resort to the provision of Art. 173(2) EC (Cases 166 and 220/86; also Commission, 1989a, point 323); the strict admissibility criteria employed by the Court do not affect beneficiaries (Cases 26/76; 191/82), but often give rise to difficulties for competitors. In this respect there was a landmark Court decision that accepted for admissibility purposes, as substantial proof of interest, the participation of third parties during the procedure under Art. 93(2) EC.[55]

Direct action against the Commission under Art. 175 EC for failure to act may also be invoked by member states and third interested parties. The European Court has further accepted that any third interested party may invite the Commission to act with respect to a state aid invoking Art.

175(2) EC against the Commission for failure to act under 175(1) EC.[56] Recourse to both the provisions of Arts. 173 and 175 EC recognised by the Court for third interested parties with respect to the Commission's monitoring function in state aids had been introduced for the first time in this context, and provides in that fashion remedies that do not exist for cases falling under the procedure of Art. 169 EC (cf. Ross, 1986, pp. 873–87; Pijnacker Hordijk, 1985, pp. 91–2).

A further remedy is available through the direct effect doctrine applicable to Art. 93(2) and (3) EC. This opens the possibility for an action to be brought before the national courts against the validity of the Commission's decision[57] or against the legality of a state aid measure granted by a member state with respect either to the compliance of the implemented aid with the Commission's decision or the obligation of prior notification (cf. Schrans, 1973, pp. 185–6; also Cases 78/76; 120/73). The direct effect of Art. 93(3) EC provides national courts with the means to enforce the relevant prohibition.

As we explained in Chapter 2, the role of the national courts is twofold. First, when dealing with a case in which the Commission has not decided, the national court must ensure that no effect is given to a proposed aid measure until the Commission has reached a final decision on the measure's compatibility with the common market. Second, if the Commission has taken a decision on an aid measure, the national courts must ensure the application and enforcement of that decision (cf. Faull, 1994, pp. 57–8). In competition policy referring to private enterprises, particularly important have been the new guidelines suggested by the Commission with respect to Arts. 85–86 EC, which establish the national courts as a second tier of control and enforcement in the area of competition. But, as the ECJ made clear, it should be noted that the roles of the national courts and that of the Commission with respect to state aids should be clearly distinguished, as the Commission is the only body responsible for referring to the substance of a case.[58]

Last but not least, actions for damages against the wrongful exercise of power by Community institutions may be brought by third parties against the Commission's decisions before the national courts under Art. 215 EC. Although they involve the difficulty of proving the link between the unlawfulness of the Commission's act and the damages incurred upon the claimant, such actions have often been characterised as a disguised action of annulment (cf. Pijnacker Hordijk, 1985, pp. 93–6; Lasok, 1986, pp. 79–80).

Notes

1. Various analyses have focused on the role of state aids and their adverse effects when it comes to the creation and maintenance of a competitive environment in the EC/EU. For a good review of the relevant theories of state intervention in the European economy before the 1990s see Lehner and Meiklejohn (1991, pp. 17–29).
2. See, *inter alia*, Cases 730/79; 290/83; 310/85; 173/73; Commission (1989b; 1990b; 1992b; 1995; 1997b). See also the analysis in Lehner and Meiklejohn (1991, pp. 49–54).
3. Public and sometimes private authorities and agencies may be involved, while regional and local entities are often given the power to grant state aid (see, *inter alia*, Cases 57/86; 67, 68 and 70/85; 248/84). Indicative is the view expressed by the Commission on the matter: see Commission (1989b; 1990b, points 28–33).
4. See Cases 6 and 11/69; 47/69; 290/83; 78/76; 61/79; 213–215/81; 173/73; 323/82; 296 and 318/82; see also Bull. EC 9–1984. For extensive discussion see Hellingman (1986, pp. 111–33).
5. On the definition of state aids see Mathijsen (1972, pp. 378–81); Green et al. (1991, pp. 287–90); on prohibited state aids cf. Lasok (1986, pp. 54–63); and on the different types cf. Cownie (1986, pp. 260–66); Slotboom (1995). For a list of examples on the difficulties faced by the Commission in monitoring state aids see Vogelaar (1985, pp. 35–6). See also Commission (1989b; 1990b; 1992b, Technical Annex, points 3–9).
6. This provision has been employed in the case of inland transport; see Council Regs. 1191/69; 1192/69 and 1107/70.
7. On the significance of the avoidance by the Council of a state aids Regulation see Lavdas and Mendrinou (1994; 1995).
8. See the introductory remarks of the Commission to the *Surveys on State Aid*. On the rationale behind the Surveys see Brittan (1989b, pp. 12–14).
9. Schrans (1973, pp. 178–9) suggests that the provision requires no notification, while Schina (1987, p. 38) maintains the view that notification is required, even if the Commission cannot refuse the aid.
10. The German Government notified the Commission that from the end of 1991 it did not intend to use the derogation further (see Commission, 1991, point 178).
11. It should be noted that in the 1990s the Commission has made wide use of the provision that allows distortions of competition in the name of the common interest. In its guidelines for aids to SMEs the Commission provided a clear statement of its rationale: see OJ C 213 1992, points 3.3., 3.4.; cf. Lavdas and Mendrinou (1995). On the current position of SMEs in European competition policy see Chapter 4 in the present book.
12. Particular emphasis had been given to regional aids; co-ordination principles were developed at a relatively early stage, in 1971 (OJ C 111/1 1971). The

Commission in 1978 in a Communication set detailed co-ordination principles for this category of aids (OJ C 31/9 1979), while in all cases the contribution of the promoted investment and the number of jobs created are evaluated by the Commission. In 1988 the Commission published a Communication with a systematic approach to the evaluation of aid in less developed regions (see OJ C 212 1988). For legal analyses of regional aid systems see, for example, Schina (1987, pp. 63–75); Schrans (1973, pp. 174–94).

13. See, *inter alia*, cases related to developments in telecommunications, transport, new industries, as well as energy policies (particularly during 1970s see Council Resolutions OJ C 153/1 1975 and COM(77) 183) or concerning environmental purposes.

14. Their particular importance may be discerned in the energy crises of the early 1970s that underlined issues linked to the restructuring of national economies.

15. The Commission is of course particularly sensitive to the distinction between the definition of state aids falling within the scope of Art. 92(1) EEC and general measures; see Commission (1989b, points 13–18; 1990b, points 8–10).

16. On general aid schemes see the analysis in Schina (1987, pp. 32–3).

17. COM(85) 350; OJ C 83 1986. Of particular interest are the potentially distortive effects that R&D schemes may have by reproducing and widening the differences between poor and wealthy member states. See Caspari (1988, p. 50); and Gilchrist and Deacon (1990, pp. 42–50).

18. SEC(74) 4262; Letter S/74/30.807; Letter SG (80) D/8287. The adoption of the SEA that provided for an environmental policy as such has led to an increase in its significance.

19. Commission (1981, point 213); the principle had been generated in Case 730/79, that had functioned as a test–case for the Commission. For an analysis of the principle see Mortelmans (1984, pp. 405–34) and Andriessen (1983, p. 289).

20. On types of state aids see Commission (1989b; 1990b, Technical Annex points 3–9).

21. On the significance of such developments cf. EP Debates 15.10.1981: 191; 14.10.1981: 110–142. Sectors such as textiles (cf. SEC(71) 363; SG(77) D/1190; SEC(77) 317), synthetic fibres (cf. OJ C 183 1987; OJ C 173 1989), shipbuilding (see Dir. 81/363/EEC; Dir. 85/2/EEC; Dir. 87/167/EEC), motor vehicle industry (OJ C 123 1989), or the case of the steel (see, *inter alia*, Decisions 73/287/ECSC; 3544/73/ECSC; 145/85/ECSC; 3612/85/ECSC; 2064/86/ECSC) and coal mining industries under the ECSC Treaty (see, *inter alia*, Decisions 2320/81/ECSC; 1018/85/ECSC; 3484/85/ECSC; 322/89/ECSC), are all under regulatory frameworks that tend to be evaluated, renewed and adopted according to particular developments that take place in the particular sectors.

22. See Council Resolution, OJ C 111 1971; cf. Communications, OJ C 111 1971; OJ C 31 1979; OJ C 212 1988; of 12.8.1988 and 4.7.1990 annexed in Lehner and Meiklejohn (1991, pp. 92–9).

23. For an analysis of the co-ordination principles with respect to national regional aid schemes see Schina (1987, pp. 63–75).

24. As we have seen, the Community's regional policy, for example, often encounters difficulties which weaken its impact on less developed regions, since co-ordination and cohesion prospects may be easily undermined by counterbalancing schemes in other member states.

25. To illustrate briefly the enforcement power behind this procedure, it should be noted that the final decision of the Commission under Art. 93(2) EEC has a binding effect on the member state concerned and it may be reinforced by a Council's unanimous decision and/or a Court's judgement, while the provision for interested member states to bring direct actions to the Court may be a further strength of the procedure.

26. See Commission (1991, point 171); also Brittan (1989b, p 14; 1989a, pp. 19–21); and Ehlermann (1992b, p. 276). On the investigating practices of the Commission in the area of competition see especially Kuypers and Rijn (1982). For legal analyses of enforcement in general cf. Audretsch (1986); Steiner (1995).

27. SG(81) 12740. The Court has ruled on the possibility of the Commission resorting to petitioning for an injunction to the Court; see Cases C–301/87; C–142/87.

28. The Court does not usually favour extensions of the set time-limit (Case 84/82). It has once more repeated the obligation that member states have to notify anew the Commission of their intention to implement the aid measure in cases where the Commission delays its decision. Furthermore, the annulment procedure of Art. 173(1) EC may be employed by the member state concerned against the Commission's failure to act, pleading abuse of procedural requirements (see Case C–312/90). On the other hand, the Commission in practice follows its view expressed in Case 84/82; see also Notice N340/89.

29. See Case 120/73. It should be noted that the latter development has been a cause of some controversy.

30. On the *de minimis* rule before 1996 see OJ C 213 1992, point 3.2. It concerned aid of not more than ECU 50,000 for a three-year period granted to small enterprises (defined as the enterprises which employ less than 50 employees and have an annual turnover of less than ECU 5m or a balance sheet total of less than ECU 2m and with no more than 25% owned by companies not falling under this category). On the regime for SMEs more generally see Chapter 4.

31. Exception is the addition by the Treaty of European Union of a further subcategory of potentially compatible state aids in Art. 92(3)d EU which concern aids aiming to promote culture and heritage conservation.

32. For the details of the review procedure see Schina (1987); Commission (1991).
33. 'New' aid schemes account for most of the Commission's review and monitoring function. The Commission has only recently started employing its powers in reviewing 'existing' schemes. Cf. Commission (1990b); Brittan (1989a); Ehlermann (1992). The attempt to employ the powers fully caused a minor intra-Commission crisis (mainly concerning regional schemes) and tensions with member states (see Wishlade, 1993, pp. 143–50).
34. The robust features of the procedure have been among the main considerations behind the Commission's early reluctance to use the procedure in full.
35. Cases of non-notified state aids fall under this category (see Case 173/73).
36. In the case of non-notified state aids the Commission is not bound by the time-limit of the Art. 93(2) procedure. Despite the Commission's expressed reservations in examining illegally granted aids (see Case C–301/87), the Court, based on the procedural functioning of the provisions, ruled that the Commission is bound to examine the compatibility of an aid before declaring it illegal, and that only the rulings by national courts on the legality of an aid brought before them under Art. 93(3) are rulings on its legality *per se* (see Case C–142/87; cf. discussion in Winter, 1993). A critical development in the area of illegally implemented state aids has been the recovery of the amounts involved (Case 70/72 at 829, and particularly Commission Communication OJ C 318/3 1983).
37. See Cases 248/84; 52/84 at 103; 323/82; 730/79. The Court tends to criticise and reject the Commission's explanations when a cogent analysis is absent: see Cases 70/72; 296 and 318/82. On the legal reasoning of the Commission in state aid cases cf. Ross (1986, pp. 877–85).
38. See von der Groeben (1960, pp. 5–9). In Case 730/79 the Court stressed that Art. 92(3), unlike 92(2), 'gives the Commission a discretion by providing that the aid which it specifies "may" be considered to be compatible with the Common Market'. The exercise of the Commission's discretion, noted the Court at another point, 'involves economic and social assessments which must be made in a Community context' (Case 730/79).
39. OJ C 318/3 1983. For cases of illegal aids in the agricultural sector, the Commission stated that it would refuse the EAGGF advance payments or charge expenditure relating to national measures that directly affect Community measures to the EAGGF budget as a means of recovering the unlawfully granted amounts. The latter policy had been also accepted by the Court in earlier cases (see Cases 15 and 16/76).
40. Cases C–147/87R. If recovery fails to take place an action before the Court under Art. 171 EC may be initiated against the member state in default: see Case 5/86. An exception is found in cases of aids implemented after the expiration of the time-limit set for the Commission's response (Case 223/83).
41. The first time that the Commission petitioned for summary procedures was in Cases 31/77R and 53/77R.

42. Cases C–301/87; C–142/87. See also the account of the Commission on the matter (Commission, 1991, point 172; 1992a, point 343). For discussions of the new developments resulting from the Court's case–law and their impact see Lasok (1990, pp. 125–7) and Winter (1993, pp. 313–4). On the legal analysis of enforcement more generally cf. Steiner (1995).

43. In terms of legal certainty the Court tends to favour recourse to the procedure under Art. 93(2) EC instead, as it allows the participation of all interested parties to participate and it provides significant remedies for third parties not available under the general infringement procedure. See the use of this reasoning on the inadmissibility of a case under Art. 169 EC (Case 290/83); and analysis of its impact in Pijnacker Hordijk (1985, p. 73).

44. Arts 30 EC (quantitative restrictions on imports and measures having equivalent effect), 37 EC (measures taken by state monopolies of a commercial character in favour of the production and marketing of domestic products), 90 EC (state intervention with respect to public enterprises) and 95 EC (fiscal discrimination against imported products) refer to actions of the member states that may have effects similar to that of state aids due to their highly interventionist character.

45. See, *inter alia*, on Art. 30 EC: Cases 249/81; 73/79; on Art. 37: Case 91/78; on Art. 90 EC: Cases 188–190/80 – against Commission First Directive 80/723/EC on the transparency of the financial relations between member states and public undertakings. On Art. 95 EC see Cases 47/69; 73/79; 142 and 143/80.

46. On the relationship between Arts. 169 and 93(2) see Gilmour (1981, p. 63); for an extensive analysis of the rules on state aid in conjunction with those on the free movement of goods under Arts 30–36 EC and the procedures against member states' violations see Flynn (1987, pp. 131–7). For an analytical exposition of the connection between state aids and Art. 95 EC and the legal remedies against violations see Flynn (1983, pp. 301–11), who praises the use of the general infringement procedure in cases where the violation lies deeper in the financing of the scheme, since its use avoids the evaluation of the compatibility of an aid that violates Art. 95 EC.

47. On the legal basis of the Commission's discretion in monitoring and enforcement see, *inter alia*, Case 324/82; cf. Evans (1979); Dashwood and White (1989, p. 399).

48. For an analysis of the possibilities for amicable settlement inherent in different steps of the infringement procedure see Mendrinou (1996; forthcoming).

49. Indicative in this respect is the use by the Commission of this provision for the introduction of exemptions of aids to SMEs from the normal review procedure (see OJ C 40 1990; OJ C 213 1992; Commission, 1993a; for a political–administrative analysis see Lavdas and Mendrinou, 1995).

50. The Court in Case 323/82 provided a broad definition of the third interested parties that extends well beyond the direct beneficiaries.

51. As we noted in Chapter 2, the crucial role of the national courts in the enforcement of Community law is present in competition policy. The Commission's guidelines to the national courts on the application of Arts. 85–86 EC encourage the emergence of the national courts as a tier of enforcement in the Community.
52. The first case was in 1960 and concerned France (Council Decision OJ 1972 1960). On questions raised with respect to the role of the Council in the procedure see especially Colliard (1969, p. 867).
53. Also, as we noted above, an important body of literature has been developing. In addition to the works mentioned above to illustrate the point, on citizens' complaints in competition see also Vesterdorf (1994, pp. 77–104).
54. See analyses of the remedies available to both member states and third interested parties in Ross (1986, pp. 868–73); Pijnacker Hordijk (1985, pp. 77–91).
55. Case 169/84. See analysis of the impact of COFAZ in Ross (1986, pp. 868–73).
56. See the Court's judgements in Cases 166 and 220/86; also OJ C 17/15 1985. See also Commission (1989a, point 323).
57. See Case 62/70. Analysis in Lasok (1986, p. 69); and Pijnacker Hordijk (1985, pp. 92–3).
58. Case C–354/90. For an extensive discussion see especially Winter (1993, pp. 315–16).

4 Horizontal and Sectoral Aid Regimes: Cases and Policy Trends

This chapter illustrates some of the main issues raised in the book by concentrating on four case studies on the emergence and operation of particular state aid regimes. As we noted in the previous chapter, there are special legal provisions covering certain aid regimes: the result of particular economic features as well as political–administrative developments. Aid regimes examined in the pages which follow include a case of horizontal aid (small business) and three important sectoral aid cases (airlines, shipbuilding, motor vehicles). The selection of cases reflects their contribution to and interaction with the EU management of crisis and change in crucial areas of economic activity and the development of European policy on state aid. Accordingly, the links between the cases have little to do with the features or patterns of development of particular sectors. They concern the suitability of the cases in terms of providing important examples of competition policy development. Focusing on the manufacturing of cars (motor vehicle industry) and of ships (shipbuilding), on the operation of airlines (air transport) and on a key category of horizontal aid (small business), this chapter illustrates different ways in which EU institutions, national governments and industry interests interact in the development of aid control policy. Because we are dealing with only one case of horizontal aid, the case of small and medium-sized enterprises (SMEs), and because of the significance of that particular case both for the politics of EU policy-making and for the Union's economy, we examine SMEs at some length. As we saw in previous chapters, a recent Commission proposal for a Council Regulation on the application of Articles 92 and 93 to categories of horizontal state aid aims to simplify the processing of cases and focuses on block exemption decisions in the case of aids coming under regional policy and granted to SMEs, R&D, environmental protection, employment and training and export credits and credit insurance. The Commission will also be able to grant a general authorisation for state aids below a certain amount.

4.1. A Case of Horizontal Aid: Promoting Small Business

The single market coupled with a tighter competition regime was bound to have considerable impact on Europe's small businesses. The particular characteristics of that impact, however, were influenced by the way in which the role of SMEs was incorporated as a parameter in European policy development. Because the problem of finance is a crucial one for SMEs, examining how this problem has been tackled in the Community system allows an analysis of the ways in which domestic political concerns and EU institutional prerogatives are interlinked in the process of policy development.

We have seen in previous chapters that the policy on general state aids to industry has presented considerable challenges for the Commission. With regard to the case of small business in particular, Commission control has been minimal. Since the argument that the apparent laxity in dealing with the states' subsidisation of small enterprises is due to their negligible impact in terms of competition policy can be dismissed as untenable (see, for example, Schina, 1987, p. 94), the Community's policy vis-à-vis small-scale production in Europe requires examination. Why is there no rigorous EU control in the case of state aids to small business? Does the lack of such control suggest limitations in the capacity of Community institutions to play key and proactive roles in policy development? Policies contributing to the persistence of small-scale production in Europe were the result of interactions between political considerations, institutional capacities and legal instruments at various levels of the EC/EU system. In order to assess the roles of EC/EU institutions in the complex processes involved we need to take into account the unanticipated consequences of decisions and the inefficiency of decision-making (see Lavdas and Mendrinou, 1994; 1995).

Small firms make for the vast majority of enterprises in the EC. Firms with less than 100 employees claim shares of total employment ranging from approximately 40 to more than 70 per cent in the member states, while the Community average for firms with less than 200 employees is 62.7 per cent of total employment (Commission, 1993a, p. 399). More impressive still is the percentage of such firms in the total number of the Community's enterprises. Firms employing less than 100 represent 99.3 per cent of the total, while 'micro-enterprises' with less than 10 employees represent 91.3 of the total.[1]

The difficulties in defining small business are compounded by the recognition of the implications of the adoption of a particular definition, especially in the area of exemptions from Community rules. Optimal firm size may of course vary from sector to sector; and national definitions of small business do vary considerably. Recognising that the concept varies between sectors and between countries, and that the definition accepted will depend on the aims pursued, the Commission chose to work with a general definition of 'small and medium-sized enterprises'[2] which was different from the concepts used when considering exemptions from the rules on state aids. The latter concepts, which concern us in this book and which are closer to the notion of small firms in the political economy literature, have undergone transformations. In a letter to member states in 1985 the Commission defined aids of minor importance with reference to recipient firms having less than 100 employees and less than 10m ECU in annual turnover (SG(85) D/2611). In 1990 the limit was expanded with respect to employment (less than 150 employees) and annual turnover (less than 15m ECU) (OJ C40 1990). The definition was expanded further in 1992 to include enterprises with up to 250 employees and up to 20m ECU in annual turnover.[3] But this last change created a new tier of 'small' enterprises with up to 50 employees, which are now to be normally exempt from the prior notification requirement.[4] As the level of analysis in this book is the Community rather than the states, we will work with the definition of SMEs used by the Community in the context of controlling state aids.

European policies and small businesses

Given the developing system of controlling state aids which we followed in previous chapters, what was the Community's approach to small business subsidisation? Since 1970 small businesses have been on the EC agenda. The Community's role in encouraging the persistence and development of small businesses can be examined at two levels, concerning first direct action and measures (industrial policy – enterprise policy) and second the elaboration of a framework conducive to small business development (through competition policy). Four main points can be distinguished in the development of the Community's role in small business promotion: the first in the early 1970s, the second in the mid-1980s, the third in the early 1990s and the most recent in 1996.

The targeting of small business as an area in need of special EC policy had begun in the late 1960s to early 1970s. In March 1970 the Commission's *Memorandum on Industrial Policy* (Colonna Report), despite its overall thrust which was favouring restructuring and concentration, identified the need for a policy on SMEs acknowledging the problems these firms face, especially with regard to medium and long-term finance (Commission, 1977, p. 132). A year later the Economic and Social Committee commissioned a study on the position and the problems of SMEs in the Community and advised the Commission to consider measures which would assist such enterprises. The Commission proved especially receptive, and soon afterwards a Division for 'small, medium-sized and craft enterprises' was established (cf. Dyson, 1990, p. 23). In 1978 the European Investment Bank was first used to administer finance raised in the money markets by the Community (the New Community Instrument or Ortoli Facility). The New Community Instrument acquired a component which was meant to function as loans to SMEs on the basis of the experience of the EIB's original 'global loan' programmes. These were aimed at financing SMEs in underdeveloped regions and have operated independently since 1968 (Pinder, 1986, pp. 172–5).

In this way policy was directed at what we term the first level of Community involvement with small business. We have seen in previous chapters that the Single Market project was a push factor in the direction of more consistent state aid control in the context of a reinvigorated competition policy, affecting the development of relations between industrial and competition policies. A European Year of SMEs and Craft Industry was championed by the EP in 1983. That was followed by a number of Community initiatives surrounding and following the White Paper and the SEA. An action programme for SMEs was adopted in November 1986 (OJ C 287 1986), designed to offer guidelines for future development in Community action towards SMEs. Also in 1986 the Commission established an SME Task Force aiming to co-ordinate the relevant aspects of the different Community policies and to liaise with SMEs providing information and assistance.

The active way of assisting small business would fall into the domain of European industrial policy. However, the efforts to assist and promote small business led to the creation of a separate DG (XXIII) in 1989, with the twofold implication of a potentially more thorough investigation of the problems associated with small firm size (e.g., through the SMEs impact assessment of EC policies) and further fragmentation within the Commission.

Although industrial policy was in certain respects more visible, competition policy had from an early stage contributed towards the survival of small enterprises. The contribution has three aspects. The Community supports small business first by applying the rules of competition on mergers, dominant position, and so on, to large firms and second by exempting small business from its scrutiny of agreements, and so on. Two implications follow from the first two aspects. First, small business was exempted from a substantial part of the cost of regulatory compliance inflicted on large firms. Second, some co-operative measures and agreements between small firms being accepted, the Community moved on to advance a number of active pro-small business measures and instruments of its own, aiming at a direct (EC level) policy of small business promotion.[5] Yet these measures, usually as part of the Community's industrial or enterprise policies, could only provide a minor compensation for the major problem of small business, the difficulties associated with self-financing and the search for credit and assistance. Therefore the most salient aspect of the Community's policy for small business was the third, that is, its ability to influence the regime of state aids.

In its first comprehensive policy statement on state aids to promote SMEs, included in the *Sixth Report on Competition Policy* (1976), the Commission reviewed the problems faced by SMEs and suggested that small business played crucial roles for the future of the Community's economy (Commission, 1977, p. 132). The Commission stated that it would take a positive view of specific forms of state aids to SMEs, such as loans at preferential rates or guarantees helping provide finance for investment, grants for R&D, and technical assistance with commercial and management policies. SMEs being a rather vague concept, it was suggested that in terms of staff employed a small firm would be one with up to 100 employees, and a medium firm would employ up to 500. The precise criteria were left open to further specification and it was noted that the Commission would assess each individual case 'in a pragmatic fashion', although the examples offered (from Danish and Irish cases) concerned assistance to firms with less than 75 employees (Commission, 1977, pp. 133–5).

In view of their function in the European economy (cf. Commission, 1992a, point 165; OJ C 213 1992, point 1.1.), SMEs deserve a simplification of the regulatory requirements, provisions for incentives for the *smaller* aiming mainly at solving the capital shortage experienced by the SMEs, and even taking care of the regulatory burdens imposed on them by governments, because the compliance costs of small business with respect to a number of government regulations may be higher.[6] The *Surveys on State Aid* confirmed that subsidies granted to small businesses cover a significant part of overall state aid. As we saw in Chapter 2, Italy, Greece, Portugal, Belgium and Germany give total industrial aid above the EU average. It appears that the group of leading overall aid givers and the group of main aid givers to SMEs (as a proportion of total industrial aid) do not coincide. There is an overlap (Italy, Greece, Belgium) as well as divergence (Luxembourg, Spain). Table 4.1 presents state aid to SMEs as a percentage of horizontal aid and as a percentage of total aid to industry, based on the *Fifth Survey on State Aid* (Commission, 1997b). Aid to SMEs relative to total aid has been on the increase in Belgium, Greece, Spain and marginally in Luxembourg, while France and the Netherlands clearly reduced the proportion of total aid devoted to SMEs. Greece, Spain and Ireland display a tendency to increase the percentage of aid to SMEs as a percentage of aid to horizontal objectives.

The Commission has sought gradually to clarify criteria and provide guidelines. Aids to small business in industry – excluding industrial sectors under specific regimes of aid (Case 259/85) as well as export and operating aids – were characterised as being of 'minor importance', were governed by simplified procedures of notification and would in principle be regarded as compatible with competition policy. In 1985 the Commission delineated the criteria for the characterisation of aid as one of minor importance, the approach to such cases being that there is no objection in principle but notification is obligatory (SG(85) D/2611).

The threshold for defining small business in the context of approving state aids was increased in the Commission's second notification to the member states for state aids of minor importance (OJ C 40 1990). For new aid schemes the main precondition for consideration under this clause is enterprise size with respect to both employment and annual turnover, both of which have been expanded from less than 100 employees to less than 150 employees and from less than 10m ECU to less than 15m ECU. The Commission further set four criteria for governing existing aid schemes.[7] Work towards a codification of small business policy involved numerous consultations with national officials in the context of the multilateral meetings during 1990 and 1991 (Commission, 1992a, points 162–3). DG IV was concerned about a tendency of non–notification despite the introduction of simplified procedures in 1990 (Commission, 1990a, point 125).

Table 4.1. State aid to SMEs 1981–94 by member state (in percentages)

	B	DK	D	GR	E	F	IRL	I	L	NL	P	UK	Total
State aid to SME as percentage of state aid to horizontal objectives													
1981–86	21	1	20	6	--	1	12	20	33	51	--	9	13
1986–88	36	1	23	10	11	12	13	29	48	44	4	26	22
1988–90	33	2	24	12	18	22	16	33	54	40	0	27	24
1990–92	32	1	19	19	20	15	23	30	47	28	3	33	24
1992–94	18	4	33	20	30	7	33	30	57	8	0	20	20
State aid to SME as percentage of state aid to the total of state aid to industry													
1981–86	14	1	8	4	--	1	3	7	14	30	--	4	6
1986–88	25	1	8	4	2	6	6	10	21	36	3	10	9
1988–90	25	1	7	10	5	11	8	10	21	31	0	12	10
1990–92	26	1	4	12	10	11	7	9	16	20	1	15	9
1992–94	15	3	5	12	12	3	5	8	17	6	0	7	6

Sources: Commission (1989b), (1990b), (1992b), (1995), (1997b).

In 1992 DG IV introduced the new Guidelines, establishing the first-ever detailed Community policy framework on aids to SMEs (OJ C 213 1992). The Guidelines underlined the various beneficial effects of SMEs for the economy, and focused on two sets of problems: capital shortage and governmental regulatory burdens. SMEs for state aid purposes are independent enterprises with less than 250 employees and with either an annual turnover of less than 20m ECU or a balance-sheet total of less than 10m ECU, and with less than 25 per cent owned by companies not falling under this category. This wide definition covers more than 90 per cent of businesses in the EC. A new concept of 'small' enterprises is introduced, which reduces the thresholds to 50 employees, 5m and 2m ECU respectively and with less than 25 per cent owned by companies not falling under this category (OJ C 213 1992, point 2.2).

The new system is in a sense undermining Art. 92(1) EEC in a dual mode, by on the one hand expanding further the thresholds in defining SMEs, while on the other exempting the new category of 'small' business from the notification procedure. The innovation concerned this new category of 'small' business and the fact that it is exempted from the requirement of prior notification: with the 1992 framework the Commission decided to wave notification obligations for granted amounts of a figure *de minimis*, set at ECU 50,000 with no cumulation for a period of three years (OJ C 213 1992, point 3.1). Such aid was regarded as falling outside 92(1) EEC (points 3.2.–3.4.). The crucial implication was that the new category, even as the Community regulated its ability to receive aid (more than ECU 50,000 would be under Commission scrutiny), was in this particular respect put 'outside' the Community control system.

The new development complemented the renewed emphasis on small business found in the Maastricht Treaty. Aiming to reduce the costs for small business from regulatory compliance in social policy, the Social Agreement attached to the Treaty stresses that implementing directives 'shall avoid imposing administrative, financial and legal constraints' which would 'hold back the creation and development' of SMEs (Agreement on Social Policy, Art. 2(2)). As regards subsidisation, the Commission's pragmatic approach reaches a crucial turning point, as a politically significant field of government – small business relations is left to the states to manage as they see fit. But the objective of assisting small business was, as we saw, an objective that the Commission from an early stage shared with voices in the member states. Having established a common objective, and having recognised that 'national governments, too' can contribute towards the objective mainly by 'some direct financial assistance' (OJ C 213 1992, point 1.5), the sharing out of the function of aid could be seen as a division of tasks in the Community system.

In 1996 the Commission adopted a new version of the Guidelines on state aid for SMEs (OJ C 213 1996). In accordance with the White Paper on *Growth, Competitiveness and Employment*, intangible investment in the form of technology transfer (licences, acquisition of patent rights, know-how or unpatented technical knowledge) can qualify as expenditure eligible for state aid. Also, aid to help the takeover of SMEs can be granted if the buyer, too, is an SME. Furthermore, the *de minimis* rule was separated from the Guidelines and now forms a separate text which concerns all businesses.[8] But SMEs continue to be the main beneficiaries of the rule. The new version reiterates the Commission's belief that small business is a factor of both economic dynamism and social stability, and the recognition of the series of handicaps which SMEs face due to their size, particularly as regards access to capital and loans. The Commission's view was also confirmed in its reply to the relevant points raised by the European Parliament in its Resolution on the Commission's *Twenty-Fifth Report on Competition Policy* (see Commission, 1996a, pp. 86, 369–73).

Explaining small business promotion

European policy aiming at exempting small business from the tightening of the competition regime as well as from other regulatory costs, the active measures aiming at providing small business with services and assistance, and the member states' contribution in addressing the problem of capital haunting SMEs can all be analysed as aspects of the Community policy of small business promotion (Lavdas and Mendrinou, 1994; 1995).

The enabling approach adopted by EU competition policy vis-à-vis small business can be explained by one direct and three background factors. This explanation suggests that Community institutions and especially the Commission have played key and proactive roles even in developments apparently involving an abdication of competencies on their part.[9] The direct factor was the development of a more rigorous enforcement system in the area of state aids, resulting in part as an unanticipated consequence of the Council's decision to reject an implementing regulation, a decision which created the opportunity for the Commission to develop gradually a sophisticated enforcement practice. There was an inverse relationship between the refinement of the enforcement system and the Community's reach in the field of small business: the more developed the system, the less the Commission applied it to national subsidisation of small-scale production. The enforcement system was becoming so elaborate and potentially so rigorous that any attempt to apply it to small businesses would be counterproductive in a dual sense: it would be politically too risky while at the same time it would cause a Commission overload. The Commission could not increase the costs of enforcement by committing resources as well as risking the whole development.

The first background factor was the development of policy ideas in the Community about the position of small-scale production in the European economy. As we have noted, Community institutions took the initiative in suggesting various schemes and approaches. The advocacy of the EP has been the main stimulus from within the EC institutional system. The EP has represented the interests of small businesses by pointing to the alleged disadvantages in the single market and the need for special policies. The Commission has often relied on the EP's support to get political backing for its policy on competition and aids (cf. Caspari, 1988, p. 40). Thus the concerns expressed in the EP debates over the fate of small business in the single market have been taken seriously by the Commission, especially since they often also tackled the question of state subsidies benefiting large firms.[10] EP debates appear to reflect a genuine concern of small business owners in Europe.[11] From the viewpoint of small firms, the difficulties encountered in the Single Market could be aggravated first by industrial policy schemes which would benefit mainly large firms and second by a more rigorous control of state aids which might sharpen their problems with finding capital, while the relatively time-consuming process of evaluation might affect them considerably by delaying the absorption of granted aid.

The second background factor was the neoliberal environment of the 1980s which encouraged competition and promoted the image of small business at the same time. The result was more room for competition policy and, stemming from a relative convergence of national policies in the 1980s, an ambivalent view of an industrial policy approach to small business. Thus small business assistance was at once promoted as an issue and kept within bounds by the ideological policy environment. The latter encouraged the Community's competition policy almost by default, as it generally supported greater competition and deregulation but not the emergent regulatory properties at EC level, brought about in part through EC competition policy.[12]

The third background factor is linked to the domestic political conditions influencing the chances for the success or failure of the implementation of Community policies (cf. Puchala, 1975, pp. 506–20). Domestic patterns of links between small business and politics are too diverse in organisational forms and the links themselves usually too strong for the Commission to be able to enforce effectively competition rules on subsidisation. Domestic conditions include a number of political linkages, which the Community did not want to disturb.

The future of the Community's sensitivities vis-à-vis small-scale production will depend on the changing policy environment, the evolution of policy ideas, related policy interactions (particularly relations among EU institutions and between these and the member states) and the use being made of the EU enforcement system. But it appears certain that the politics of small business promotion remains rooted in the domestic contexts, even if Community policy is a factor which reinforces this. For example, as regards the impact of competition policy on industrial culture, the effects appear much less pronounced in the case of small business. Competition's implementation network is often able to deter general infringements and encourage compliance without decisions having to be made (Vaughn, 1972, pp. 54–5). As a senior administrator at DG XXIII put it, the impact on 'industrial morality' has been significant and can be evinced from the great number of firms which choose to change their course (following closely the Community framework or correcting their practices when the Commission investigates similar cases) without any formal measures being taken.[13] The impact is more qualified when it comes to small firms, because direct Community–firms interactions are less significant and less continuous, and much is left to the states.

Regulation and the division of tasks in the EU system

The EU impact on small business is likely to remain primarily in terms of a regulatory framework, mainly through competition policy, rather than resulting from a more active enterprise policy. In organisational terms, the fragmentation of the Commission is compounded by the fragmentation of small business associations at EU level; put against a background of organisational asymmetries at the national levels, these factors suggest that there are difficulties in the Community's enterprise policy (cf. Grote, 1992, pp. 151–66). The embeddedness of small business in national and regional industrial cultures makes EU-level associations both fragmented and relatively inconsequential. There appears to be no move in the direction of a more homogeneous pattern of interest representation at EU level, and it is conceivable that the small business sector will remain fragmented. This is not to suggest that the societal corporatist model is definitely irrelevant at EU level; some sectors achieve greater organisational coherence and may acquire some corporatist characteristics.[14] But a sectorized and segmented approach is likely to be the general norm at EC level interactions between Community institutions and associations (Mazey and Richardson, 1993b, pp. 256–7).

The Community interest in small business promotion is amplified by the fact that the latter is championed as one of the fields of convergence between industrial and competition policies. This convergence may be seen as part of a wider functional package of division of labour in the Community system, incorporating the notion of subsidiarity, familiar from the Community's early years, as signifying the most efficient allocation of functions towards achieving some commonly accepted goals. The desired convergence of industrial and competition policies can leave room for considerable state functions within agreed frameworks, and the assistance to small business has been cited as an important example of such an area.[15] The convergence in a context confirming subsidiarity is also underlined by the resolve to create a more positive image for EU competition policy, an issue to which we will return in the next chapter. With regard to small business assistance, this division of tasks may appear, *ex post*, as a functional solution, but it emerged as a result of the politics of inter-institutional bargaining.

From a normative policy viewpoint, the pattern that emerged is not necessarily the best possible in terms of policy content. The Community's involvement in the business of small firm promotion registers several of the familiar political considerations behind this business at national level, and seeks to accommodate these considerations with EU institutional objectives. There may be problems of effectiveness in the emerging solution, as it has grown out of the need to register and accommodate different institutional views, often at the expense of advancing a coherent Community policy on the potential, the prospects and the limitations of small-scale production in Europe.

Nonetheless, the policy which emerged, in interaction with the changing environment, made it possible to avoid a situation where the promotion of national or European champions leaves no room for a consideration of the needs and potential of small firms. Another promising aspect of Community policy vis-à-vis small firms to date has been provided through links to structural policy, an area which has managed to activate and mobilise subnational governments and in which the Commission's role has been instrumental (Marks, 1993, pp. 406–7). Given the fragmentation within the Commission, the crucial question in this area may be the relative roles of structural and enterprise policies in administering the relevant instruments. An emphasis on the former would imply greater roles for subnational governments and the Commission (and possibly the Committee of the Regions), while opting for the latter might lead to more direct links between the Commission and small business, with intermediary non-public agencies being used for the administration of Community funds.[16]

The emergent Community system of small business promotion, in which regulatory (competition) policy plays a key role, resembles certain features of the US federal support for small firms. In the American regulatory order, small business manages to gain considerable exemptions from federal regulations, thus reducing the costs associated with regulatory compliance while continuing to receive substantial public (mainly state) funding (see Brown et al., 1990, pp. 82–91).

4.2. Restructuring the Air Transport Sector

While the Treaty of Rome established the legal basis for a common transport policy, its application was restricted to road, rail and waterway transport. The Treaty gave the Council of Ministers powers to add marine and aviation transport at a later stage if they unanimously agreed. This was agreed in 1974 and the regulation of maritime and air transport has followed diverse paths since then. The international context of deregulation and regulatory change in the air transport sector entered a phase of transformation in the late 1970s. As in other areas, US deregulation processes (Airline Deregulation Act, 1978) provided the stimulus for global change. In the EC, a tighter European enforcement regime on competition emerged at a time when national airlines in Europe began entering a new phase of development, which was introduced with the privatisation of British Airways in 1987. The Council proceeded slowly and for the most part remained in the area of various technical issues (e.g., noise limitation certificates for aircraft). The European Commission, on the other hand, aimed from the early 1980s to get to the crucial question of market operation (Moussis, 1992, pp. 390–91; cf. Doganis, 1991). The Commission presented its first document on airline liberalisation in 1979, followed by a 1984 memorandum on the liberalisation of the prices and route licensing regimes (Cullen and Yannopoulos, 1989). In 1986, in view of difficulties in Council decision-making, the Commission sought to initiate action against restrictive practices such as tariff fixing and capacity sharing (*International Herald Tribune*, 10 July 1986, p. 9).

While the British Government pursued a policy of full privatisation, in the 1990s flag carriers in several EU member states had to face at least the possibility of partial privatisation.[17] One major cause behind such considerations has been the need for restructuring accruing from the various constraints imposed on both governments and airlines by international competitive pressures and the application of European competition policy. In the process of restructuring, the need for state aid to bail out national airlines has been felt by a number of EU member states, and this has resulted in protracted negotiations with the Commission.

Three packages of measures

The liberalisation of the air transport sector in the EC/EU has been implemented through three packages of directives and regulations (1988, 1990, 1993). The Community has pursued a more systematic policy of liberalisation of civil aviation since the late 1980s, through the clarification of the applicability of European competition rules to the air transport sector (Council Regulations 3975/1987, 3976/1987, 2342/1990, 2343/1990, 2407/1992, 2408/1992 and 2409/1992). The European Court of Justice supported the Commission's objectives in the area of air transport, by accepting in an important 1985 judgement (in the *Nouvelles Frontières* case) that the EC Treaty competition rules could be applied in the area (Mathijsen, 1990, p. 190; cf. Balfour, 1994, pp. 1026–7). While this application initially concerned merger control, collusionary practices and the abuse of dominant market position (Button and Swann, 1989), after 1987 the Commission increasingly looked at the subsidies received by flag carriers. That transport policy (DG VII) should observe and apply competition policy (DG IV) is a relatively recent development. Hancher, Ottervanger and Slot (1993, p. 137) have noted that state aids in transport were supervised by DG VII not DG IV. Although, as we will see, the situation has shifted since 1993, observers still appear to be confused about the important issue of the administration of competition policy in the air transport sector.[18] Because the differences between DGs in terms of administrative cultures, 'turf' protection or expansion and policy and lobbying styles are important (Mazey and Richardson, 1993a; 1993b; Wishlade, 1993; McGowan and Wilks, 1995; Lavdas and Mendrinou, 1995), we need to take into account the issue of the administration of competition policy in air transport.

By 1994, more than half the EU states had applied for Commission approval for packages to rescue ailing national airlines. As we will see, the cases of Sabena (1991), Iberia (1992), Air Lingus (1993), Air France, Olympic Airways and TAP (1994) gave the Commission the opportunity to clarify the rules and expand their combined application in liberalisation-promoting rescue deals. In most cases, governments turned to a combination of forms of state aid prohibited by the developing competition regime which we have discussed in this book. The usual recipe involved the state taking over the carrier's debt while injecting a one-off capital increase to cover losses. The Commission approached such aid as rescue aid; in terms of general competition policy, rescue aid 'aims to provide the firm with the liquidity it needs to maintain its position while a restructuring plan is worked out' and must satisfy a number of criteria concerning adverse effects on competitors and the implementation of the restructuring plan (Bull. EU 7/8–1994, point 1.2.42).

Against the background of processes of liberalisation of air transport since the late 1980s, the strengthening of the Commission's control of state aid in this context has a number of functions (cf. Lavdas, 1997).[19] First, it is meant to reinforce and extend processes of liberalisation and competition, mainly by breaking up relations or pockets of relative closure (e.g., access to airports, ground handling liberalisation). In other words, state aid control and liberalisation policies are closely interlinked in their implementation. This is a function which promotes marketization in the context of a European space with fewer and fewer barriers to carriers competing for business. Second, the strengthening of the Commission's control is meant to mediate and moderate liberalisation processes, by ensuring that any 'chaotic effects' of liberalisation are avoided (Van Miert, 1998, p. 2) and that states and players with different levels of development and/or states of finances are given a chance: the rescue and restructuring packages are seen as one-off attempts to rescue state enterprises which would appear to be in a disadvantaged position even if privatisation options were immediately followed. The Commission gives the go-ahead for rescue and restructuring deals which have a number of aspects: agreed predominance of market criteria in the future management of such enterprises; opening of several of their functions to competition;

avoidance of political confrontation with the states; last but not least, the states' agreement on the impossibility of future state aid. Restructuring aid is a one-off measure. New aid cannot be allowed, except for truly exceptional and unforeseeable circumstances (hence the principle of 'one time last time').[20] We will call this an accommodative function. Third, the Commission as an institutional mediator is supposed to take into account social parameters (for example, socially unacceptable levels of unemployment for a national or regional economy resulting from the closure of a major employer): a social function. In sum, the Commission's role in enforcing a tighter regime of competition control acts both as an amplifier and as a buffer of wider liberalisation processes. In so doing, it co-ordinates European responses to such processes while expanding the EC institutional involvement in the policy areas concerned.

We noted that the Commission gives the go-ahead for rescue packages on the basis of certain conditions, including the states' agreement on the future impossibility of public intervention. It follows that future problems will have to be addressed through other means, possibly privatisation. The TAP restructuring package (1994) included an understanding on partial privatisation by 1998. Of course, the Treaty (Art. 222) explicitly recognises public ownership systems and, therefore, the right for member states to invest or disinvest in company capital. State aid control and the principle of 'one time last time' apply only in so far as a financial transaction can be seen as an aid measure. As we saw in Chapter 2, Community institutions apply the market investor criterion to ascertain whether a transaction constitutes state aid.

At the same time, the fact that by 1996 Iberia was successful in its lobbying for a new aid package underlines the political nature of states–Commission bargaining over the future of flag carriers. But the new package was agreed after Iberia accepted even stricter conditions (which included substantial restructuring and the sale of loss-making subsidiaries). State aid would be in instalments, and release of further instalments of aid will be contingent upon the successful implementation of the agreement. Predictably, the Commission was attacked by private carriers like BA for authorising the new aid package.

In 1998, as a result of judicial action by private sector litigants, FFr 20bn of state aid to Air France was called into question by the European Court of Justice. The ECJ ruled that the Commission had failed to provide sufficient justification for its decision to authorise the aid package to Air France. In particular, according to the ruling, the Commission had failed to take into consideration the purchase by the airline of new aircraft and the airline's position on the transatlantic routes which nonetheless affected intra-EU competition. The Court stopped short of demanding repayment (*Financial Times*, 26 June 1998).

In view of the often repeated argument that the Commission has been rather feeble vis-à-vis flag carriers, it is worth noting that the position reflects both political balances and pressures and the transitional nature of the airline subsidy regimes. First, it is important that agreements on restructuring are meant to be transitional arrangements on the road to liberalisation. Second, the implementation of such agreements in effect transforms the operating patterns of the carriers involved. As a rule, they subsequently turn to restructuring and strategic alliances in order to increase their competitive position and market viability (cf. *Financial Times*, 20 December 1995; *The European*, 21–27 December 1995). Finally, third, the case of Air France shows that private sector firms acting as litigants are able to bring judicial pressure to bear in order to counterbalance the political pressure exercised on the Commission by governments on behalf of state groups. In other words, the sector's response to regulation indicates the increasing divergences among industry interests, reflecting the different and changing patterns of relationship between governments and airlines (see, e.g., Holmes and McGowan, 1997, p. 180).

Liberalisation-promoting deals

The control of state aid has been 'the most important and most contentious policy area' in the sector (Niejahr and Abbamonte, 1996). While until 1993 the Commission had taken a pragmatic or even lenient view when it came to a number of aid schemes to airlines such as Air France and Sabena, a stricter line was followed after the end of 1993 (see, for example, Kassim, 1995, pp. 200–1). But this, far from being solely the result of developments in DG VII policy, was the combined outcome of (a) the Transport Commissioner's taking over in Competition and attempting to expand his new area of competence while retaining some of his previous tasks,[21] (b) the experience of the lobbying campaign to which the Commission was subjected in 1993 by the competitors of Aer Lingus on the occasion of the attempts of the Irish government to inject an IR£ 175 million aid into the carrier (cf. Soames and Ryan, 1995, pp. 291, 304–5), and (c) the crisis in air transport and airlines' losses which intensified domestic pressures for states to increase financial injections to flag carriers while at the same time underlining the extent to which air transport was indeed suffering from overcapacity, an issue affecting the Commission's approach. Capacity limitations were first imposed on restructuring packages linked to state aid in the case of Aer Lingus in 1993.

On 1 January 1993 the third and final package of measures for the liberalisation of the sector entered into force. The package consists of three complementary sets of regulations which establish common rules on the licensing of air carriers, provide that a carrier holding such a licence enjoys free access to all intra-Community routes, and allow a carrier to set its fares and rates for the services operated within the internal market. There are various safeguard clauses for the member states. For example, member states may intervene in the pricing freedom under clauses which allow them to withdraw excessively high passenger fares or to stop sustained downward spirals of air fares (see Niejahr and Abbamonte, 1996).

The fact that member governments devised plans for additional aid to carriers contravened the agreements reached with the Commission in the first round (before 1993), in which it was understood that governments would 'abstain from granting any further aid or other new measures favouring directly or indirectly' the national carriers (see OJ L 300, 31.10.1991, p. 48, on Sabena). In the first round, the Commission had argued (relying on reports from the Association of European Airlines) that the sector was experiencing growth. After 1993, its decisions are based on the assumption that the sector suffers from overcapacity (in which case authorisation of aid is more difficult and involves an agreement on capacity reductions). The latter view had been suggested in 1993 by the *Comité des Sages* on air transport, although the Commission did not immediately endorse that view, granting the next aid package (to Air France) on the assumption that aviation did not require capacity cutbacks (see Soames and Ryan, 1995, pp. 290–309).

Since EC Treaty Articles 92–4 apply to air transport (cf. Hancher, Ottervanger and Slot, 1993, p. 146), the Commission produced, in late 1994, the first-ever competition guidelines for state aids in civil aviation (Bull. EU 11–1994, point 1.2.109; cf. OJ C 350, 10.12.1994). The guidelines made clear that state aid injections were considered to be one-off rescue efforts, exceptions being authorised in 'exceptional and unforeseeable circumstances', and laid down the conditions for aid (a comprehensive restructuring programme, capacity reduction, non-interference by public authorities in management). In addition, DG IV became actively involved in supervising the application of these guidelines.

To take a very interesting case post-1993, the Greek government approached formally the Commission in July 1993 requesting the go-ahead for a rescue package for Olympic Airways, focusing on a debt write-off. Following months of largely informal negotiations, a new proposal was submitted by a new Greek government in May 1994, by which time the carrier's debt had reached Dr 545bn (see Lavdas, 1997).[22] The proposal envisaged a restructuring of the company and subsequent liberalisation according to EU regulations, which had already been suspended for Greece, Ireland, Spain and Portugal, granting a transitional period of up to 1998. Once a formal rescue proposal has been submitted, the Commission (DGs IV, VII) follows a procedure which allows other member states and interested parties (such as other airlines) to submit their observations on the proposed package.

The Commission rejected the view of the Greek Government that the state aid could be granted as a derogation from the competition rules because of 'serious disturbances' in the Greek economy (Art. 92. 3b of the Treaty). The aid in question was aimed at the carrier and 'could not possibly have as either its object or effect the remedying of a serious disturbance in the Greek economy' (OJ C 94/4 1994, p. 10). The Commission then turned to the restructuring package *per se*, suggesting a liberalisation plan with four main aspects.[23] In addition, the Commission requested that the carrier should not take advantage of its special position during the restructuring period in order to further expand its services in the European market: the number of seats available for its busiest European routes for 1994–5 should not exceed the number for 1993, while the carrier would not be permitted to act as 'price leader' for the London and Stockholm routes for the duration of the restructuring programme. Since most of the Commission's conditions concerned areas in which there were either exemptions for Olympic until 1998 or no general EU regime in place, the negotiation with regard to the rescue package was bound to involve difficulties for the company (see Lavdas, 1997).

Negotiations between member states and the Commission in the cases of TAP (Portugal) and Iberia (Spain) presented similar characteristics. Both companies accepted a degree of domestic routes liberalisation and greater personnel cuts than Olympic. The Commission's general tendency has been to try to apply often more stringent criteria than those already in place, not only with regard to the restructuring aspects of the deal (in order to ensure that subsidisation does not amount to EC-sanctioned, lame-duck rescue), but as concerns also the competition regime (e.g., when it comes to the opening up of ground-handling). From the viewpoint of the Commission, restructuring/rescue packages operate also as liberalisation-promoting deals, extending further the competition regime and the Commission's capacities in its monitoring. From the viewpoint of other carriers, the negotiation procedure for rescue packages provides an excellent opportunity for the opening of new routes or surface activities.

In the case of Olympic Airways, an agreement with the Commission was reached in July 1994. It then became the responsibility of the Greek Government to ensure that the airline would adhere to the terms reached. The government sought to pass a law on the carrier's restructuring as soon as possible after the agreement, but was only able to do so in November 1994. When it did, the agreement had already been tampered with as a result of government concessions to various union demands. Nonetheless, the available evidence indicates that the restructuring package has been moderately successful in its first year, despite changes and a softening of many of its provisions. The government was able to write off Olympic state debts of Dr 427bn in early 1995 as a result of the aid and restructuring package agreed with the Commission, and another Dr 64bn of debt was converted to equity with an agreed state injection of Dr 54bn into the carrier as equity in three instalments. Olympic was able to post profits of Dr 6bn for 1995, the first bottom-line profit since 1977. But several issues remained open.

A first issue concerned the continuing argument between the Commission and the Greek Government over ground handling (even after the agreement and the formal approval of the package with the Commission decision on 27 July 1994). As a result of new complaints by BA, KLM and SAS on Olympic's continuing monopoly over ground-handling, DG IV made further enquiries in November, just before the government's first effort to pass the bill through the parliament. DG IV was now moving in the direction of closing the gap on ground-handling and producing legislation (as it did on airport slots in 1993). The DG has been keen to achieve an opening up of ground-handling and its approach to the negotiation of rescue packages for national airlines has been to see them as instrumental in that direction also. Interestingly, the Commission's consultative paper on opening up the ground-handling services to competition was met with a cautious response by the Economic and Social Committee in 1994 (see Bull. EU 9–1994, point 1.2.124). The Commission's determination to proceed was ultimately successful in achieving an endorsement by the ESC for a proposed Council Directive in

September 1995, although the Committee reiterated its preference for a 'gradual, progressive approach' to a 'reasonable degree' of opening up (Bull. EU 9–1995, point 1.3.79). The proposed Directive was endorsed by the EP in November 1995 subject to various amendments (Bull. EU 11–1995, point 1.3.122).

It has been reported in the Greek trade press that DG VII was taken by surprise by the renewed efforts of DG IV on the Olympic case in November 1994 (see Lavdas, 1997, pp. 199–201). It has also been reported that both the Greek Government and Olympic Airways were taken by surprise by DG IV, as they both understood that the argument had been settled following agreement with DG VII on the rescue package. The case of Olympic Airways was among the first to be implicated, and the Greek side indicated that it intended to stick to the July approval and, if necessary, pursue the matter against the Commission at the ECJ. DG IV softened its approach later in 1995, in view of the general EU agreement reached on the liberalisation of ground-handling by January 1999. While obviously increasing future competitive pressures on the carrier, the general agreement has different implications for the short and medium-term: putting the particular case of the Olympic under the new regime has the consequence of alleviating immediate pressures associated with Commission–state negotiations, while at the same time taking advantage of transitional clauses. Ground-handling will be liberalised in January 1999 for Greece's larger airports (over 3 million passengers a year). But other issues remained open, concerning especially industrial relations in the carrier and various union demands which the Greek Government sought to neutralise through protracted negotiations. In 1996 the Commission requested that Greece abstain from paying the second instalment of aid to Olympic pending the Art. 93(2) procedure, which was reopened. The Commission noted that, while the carrier 'is largely meeting the objectives of the restructuring programme', the Greek Government seems 'to have granted further aid' to Olympic and 'to have interfered in the management of the airline to an extent which goes beyond its role of shareholder' (Commission, 1997a, p. 80). In any event, the 1994 restructuring plan was seriously diverted in subsequent years, resulting in a more drastic package being negotiated in 1998.

Several important cases have demonstrated that the EU possesses a developed competition system. These cases indicate also that the difficulties involved in the operation of this system may lead to rivalries at various levels, including intra-Commission tensions (consider, for example, the public controversies over Iberia between Transport

Commissioner Oreja and Competition Commissioner Van Miert). The function of European competition policy in the air transport sector has been to try to promote liberalisation in a symmetrical way across Europe, although the pressures exercised by national governments have sometimes been too heavy for the Commission to resist. On balance, the Commission's crucial mediating role (increasingly assertive control of state aids and authorisations based on competition-promoting deals) helps ensure that a change in the response pattern to international transformations will have to take place, albeit in a negotiated manner.

4.3.   A Sector in Structural Crisis: State Aid and Decline in Shipbuilding

Unlike air transport, the market for sea transport has not been directly subject to state authority. This has been a major background variable in explaining some of the key developments in the sector since the Second World War. During the 1950s conditions in the shipping industry were gradually transformed due to a combination of international economic factors and technological change. Developments in the international economy, involving the substantial growth of maritime commerce and sea transport of goods, contributed to substantial changes in the structure of the shipbuilding sector. At the same time, changes in the methods of ship construction allowed the establishment of large modern shipyards close to steel mills in the Far East, Brazil, Yugoslavia and the Soviet Union.

Old-established shipyards in countries such as Britain and the US faced considerable competition. As Susan Strange notes, because it was hard for governments to stop shipping operators from placing orders for new ships wherever they were produced most cheaply, shipbuilding capacity expanded very rapidly. But the other side of internationalisation was that once in production, all shipbuilders were all the more vulnerable to a change in market conditions (Strange, 1988, p. 143). In the 1950s and 1960s the shipbuilding industry experienced conditions of expansion in the Far East, notably Japan, leading in the late 1960s to an overcapacity crisis in the sector. The situation was seriously aggravated by the energy crisis of the early 1970s. In the European economies the impact of the rapid growth of shipbuilding industry in the Far East and elsewhere and the subsequent international crisis of overcapacity in the sector put tremendous pressure on governments.

The global recession that followed the quadrupling of oil prices in 1973–4 transformed the economic scene in many ways. As a result of the quadrupling of oil prices, approximately 2 per cent of gross world product was transferred from the OECD to the OPEC countries. The latter could not spend that money so quickly and real demand was cut internationally even as inflation rose. 1974 saw the beginning of large public sector deficits as government revenues fell with the reduction in taxation yields while expenditure rose as unemployment benefit and other payments rocketed.[24]

In Japan, shipbuilding, which 'had grown to make good war-time losses and established itself as the largest in the world on the construction of super tankers and bulk carriers' (Kemp, 1983, p. 34), had to contract with the onset of world recession. But the process of restructuring resulted in at least partially successful adjustment. Shipbuilding was a closely regulated industry in the country (see Dore, 1986, pp. 144–7; Johnson, 1982, pp. 209–11). All investments in shipyard facilities and the acceptance of orders for ships of over 2,500 tons had required a licence since the early 1950s. Shipbuilding became the subject of the first of the comprehensive rationalisation schemes in the 1970s once the international decline in the sector made its impact felt. The schemes represented a combination of capacity cuts, subsidies and various measures to assist SMEs affected as subcontractors and workers who lost their jobs. As a result of rationalisation and capacity cuts, by 1980 the industry was in a better shape in terms of international competitiveness. The 88 berths which remained were the most modern of the original 138 (Dore, 1986, p. 147; Kemp, 1983, p. 40).

The market for sea transport has always been unstable and heavily dependent on international economic conditions. The severe slump in shipping that began in 1974–5 hit first the tanker market and then the dry cargo market. Freight rates fell sharply and several major shipping firms went bust (for example, the Reksten group in Norway) or managed to survive mainly through diversification and expansion into other business (for example, the P&O in the UK) (see Strange, 1988, pp. 141–2). In sea transport and in shipbuilding, increasing international competition and the decline in the shipping tonnage registered under EC flags put considerable pressure on member states to continue and extend subsidies and various restrictive measures (see Brooks and Button, 1992). Regarding sea transport in particular, the fact that maritime shipping was not included in the provisions of the common transport policy of the Rome Treaty helps to explain the limited progress in European shipping policy until the mid-

1970s. In 1974, however, the ECJ ruled that the UN Code for Liner Conferences, which member states were about to adopt, was in violation of EC competition law. It became clear that there were problems in the evolving relations between traditional shipping policies (which included restrictive agreements between operators within liner conferences) and European competition law. It was subsequently decided to grant a block exemption for liner conferences from compliance with competition rules provided they met with certain conditions. In 1986 the Council adopted four Regulations which established the legal basis for an EC maritime policy. These provided, *inter alia*, for the application of EC competition law to shipping, with the exception of the aforementioned liner conferences. State aid in sea transport has been regulated through a series of guidelines aiming to encourage a consistent approach between member states in areas such as the reduction of manning levels, training costs, reimbursement of costs of repatriating seafarers, and operating and investment aids (Lee, 1994, pp. 225–6).

The slump of the 1970s led to the gradual adoption by Western European states of various aid schemes to declining sectors such as shipbuilding. But there were deeper causes for the crisis in the shipbuilding sector, linked to overcapacity since the late 1960s, and long-term decline continued creating acute dilemmas for policy. For example, in France, restructuring plans for shipbuilding (and similar plans for steel and coal) were at the centre of protracted political battles and marked the turn in the socialists' industrial policy after 1983, when the government plans aimed to cut shipbuilding capacity by 30 per cent over two years (Hall, 1986, p. 212).

The distinctive features of this particular industrial sector are linked, on the one hand, to the fixed nature of investments needed for its growth, and, on the other hand, to the labour-intensive nature of production, leading to significant social repercussions in the case of plant closures. The crisis of European shipyards led European governments to adopt a policy of supporting national shipyards based on the argument that closures would result in serious social and economic disturbances. The granting of national aids, however, endangered competitive conditions and did not permit reductions in surplus capacity. As a consequence, a European-wide scheme for the control of state aids to the shipbuilding industry took shape, in an effort to try to direct unavoidable subsidies towards functions that could encourage and assist adjustment in the sector.

According to competition rules on state aids, two basic options are available to the Commission when it comes to sectors in crisis. The first one concerns the introduction of appropriate measures in the context of Art. 93(1) EC. The Commission used that option in the case of the synthetic fibre industry as well as the motor vehicle industry, which will be examined below. The second option concerns the formation of a fully-fledged special legal regime which regulates the granting of aid in the particular sector. In shipbuilding the second option was followed. The special legal regime for shipbuilding was developed on the basis of Art. 92(3)d EC (Art. 92(3)f TEU). Based on that provision, the Council for the first time in 1969 decided on a Commission proposal to adopt the First Directive on aid to shipbuilding (Dir. 69/262/EEC, OJ L 206/25 1969). It was a decision taken with a qualified majority. The perceived need for a specialised regime for shipbuilding was based on three main considerations. The first was to allow operating and export aids which in principle are incompatible with the rules on state aid. Second, the development of a special sectoral regime on aid to shipbuilding aimed to promote the common commercial policy according to Art. 113 EC, to which the shipbuilding sector is also subject. Finally, it was meant to facilitate the implementation of the relevant OECD Council Resolutions on shipbuilding.

The prolonged difficulties in the sector confirmed the structural nature of the problems and contradicted the initial view that the special regime would be a temporary solution. The legal regime is changed from time to time, through the introduction of a new directive or the amendment of the directive in effect. Adjustments and modifications aim to address new developments and improve whenever necessary the functioning of pre-existing rules. Implementing the relevant rules, however, has not been an easy task for the Commission. Delays in notification of aids and cases of incompatible aids have caused tension between the Commission and the member states concerned. In general, the Commission has displayed particular rigour in ensuring the implementation of the special legal regime.

A brief examination of the directives which have been introduced demonstrates that one of their main objectives has been to secure that the aids which the special regime permits and which would normally be considered incompatible with the common market do not exceed a set ceiling. The latter was meant to be reviewed at least annually with the aim of gradually achieving a lower ceiling. Thus, operating aids (and any aid whose aim is not the restructuring of the recipient shipyard, including cases of aids to shipowners) have been under a fixed ceiling, valued as a specified percentage of the contractually fixed price. The directives refer to all shipbuilding activities, including the construction of new ships, the repair of ships as well as various ship conversion works. The only exemption concerns the construction of warships. According to Art. 223 EC, these are exempted from the prohibition of Art. 92 EC. However, the Commission has been particularly careful when distinguishing between borderline cases, having made it clear that this exemption concerns only the granting of aid for the construction of warships by the same state. In what concerns the public authority which grants the aid measure, the sectoral regime covers also aids granted by regional or local authorities. Finally, it should be noted that the regime included special provisions with respect to aids in the context of the relevant OECD Resolutions concerning export credits for ships.

The First Directive (Dir. 69/262/EEC, OJ L 206/25 1969) was launched in 1969 with the aim of introducing the harmonisation of aids in Europe in order to avoid distortion of competition in the sector against an international background which, as we have seen, was difficult for shipbuilding. The Second Directive on aid to shipbuilding (Dir. 72/273/EEC, OJ L 169/28 1972) adjusted the aid ceiling and was concerned also with the OECD agreement on export credits and actions to control overcapacity in the sector. In 1975 the Council adopted the Third Directive (Dir. 75/432/EEC, OJ L 192/27 1975) with considerable difficulty. Conditions clearly spoke in favour of a strict attitude towards the granting of aids, yet these same conditions made it difficult for Community institutions to prevail in view of widespread tendencies to re-nationalise economic policy. While the control of export credits remained in line with the OECD arrangement, special provisions were introduced regarding investment aids, which had to be notified to the Commission. The Community's reluctant approach probably contributed to the deepening of the crisis as production capacity was growing worldwide (see Schina, 1987, p. 87). In 1977 the Commission issued a Communication on the reorganisation of the shipbuilding sector in the EC (Bull. EC S7/1977), in order to promote measures that would limit the growth of overcapacity in the sector and at the same time encourage restructuring.

The Fourth Directive (Dir. 78/338/EEC, OJ L 97/19 1978) concentrated on restructuring, which became a key issue as the situation in shipbuilding did not show signs of improvement. In addition, the directive addressed the social dimension and dealt with the rules for granting rescue aid. Although the main aim (the progressive reduction in operating aids) remained the same, aids should also involve restructuring. The directive also paid particular attention to aid granted to shipowners for the purchase of ships. The focus of the Fifth Directive (Dir. 81/363/EEC, OJ L 137/39 1981) was on capacity reduction. In this respect the directive stressed the need for a rigorous policy of monitoring, particularly regarding compliance with the rules on investment aid. The directive dealt with the scope and limits of the distinction between private and state-owned shipyards, and reiterated the need for restructuring and modernisation in the sector combined with attention to the social repercussions of restructuring.

The Sixth Directive (Dir. 87/167/EEC, OJ L 69/55 1987) was adopted in 1986. Widespread subsidies led to a 1986 agreement to limit aid to a common standard percentage of cost on contracts. The Sixth Directive confirmed the importance of restructuring in all shipbuilding activities and emphasised the need for the structural adaptation of the sector. Difficulties in the sector persisted because they were not due to a 'cyclical problem of demand' but the result of 'fundamental structural crisis'. The Directive suggested the further tightening of the control of state aids, introducing an approach that distinguished between production aids and aids for restructuring. Drawing a line between the two types of aid, the Commission aimed to promote restructuring while trying to restore competitive conditions which had suffered also as a result of production aids granted by the member states. The enlargement of the Community with the accession of Spain and Portugal in 1986 had influenced the structural condition of the Community's shipbuilding industry. From this perspective also, the timing of the Sixth Directive was critical, and the Directive incorporated special provisions for Spain and Portugal.

The Seventh Directive and the OECD Agreement

Since 1990 shipbuilding aid has been governed by the provisions of the Seventh Directive on aid to shipbuilding (Council Directive 90/684/EEC, OJ L 380/27 1990). In 1994 the EU, the US, Japan, Norway and South Korea reached an agreement in the OECD context on competitive conditions in shipbuilding and ship repair, aiming to control and eliminate subsidies in the sector (*OECD Agreement Respecting Normal Competitive Conditions in the Commercial Shipbuilding and Repair Industry*, 21 December 1994). The Agreement was supposed to enter into force on 1 January 1996, following successful ratification. The latter proved difficult in the US and the previous EU regime was extended to the end of 1997. In anticipation of the new OECD Agreement entering into force, the Council initially decided that the Seventh Directive should be prolonged until 31 December 1997. But as the OECD Agreement had not entered into force by the end of 1997, owing to further delays caused by difficulties in US ratification, the Commission put forward proposals for the Council to decide on future policy. In the meantime, the regime of the Seventh Directive was extended to 31 December 1998 (see OJ L 351, 23.12.1997).

The Seventh Directive followed the differentiation approach which was introduced with the Sixth Directive. It focused on an aid control policy that would also seek to balance social considerations and the restructuring of the sector. The aim has been to reduce capacity with the assistance of tight control of operating aid and aid for restructuring. The latter, in particular, has become a major policy instrument in this as in other sectors. Restructuring aid for shipbuilding totalled 3.5 billion ECU between 1990 and 1995.

The Directive aimed also to develop the linkages between the measures for European shipbuilding and those included in the relevant OECD agreements and the DAC-list of developing countries eligible for aid. Last but not least, the Directive considered the particular conditions of the sector in member states and made some changes regarding special provisions which had been introduced with the Sixth Directive. The changes in question concerned special provisions for shipyards in Portugal, Spain, Greece and the former German Democratic Republic. Further special rules for the shipbuilding industry in these countries were subsequently introduced or re-introduced with Council Regulation 1013/97 which, as is the case with the whole regime of the Seventh Directive, possesses a transitional nature and will apply until 31 December 1998.

Applying appropriate qualitative and quantitative measures of state aid control requires an assessment of the future potential of Europe's shipbuilding industry in the international context. The European industry in the 1990s appears to possess comparative advantages in the production of high technology vessels, mainly passenger and other specialised ships, in contrast to the tankers and bulk carriers that represent the strength of most Asian yards. Accordingly, the EU state aid regime needs to find ways to accommodate relevant types of aid measures (such as innovation aid) while also ensuring the operation under strict monitoring of forms of aid measures linked to regional handicaps and environmental protection.

At the same time, in view of the continued failure of the US to ratify the OECD Shipbuilding Agreement, any assessment of the role of aid will have to take into account the view that without the OECD Agreement, the abolition of state aid in the EU 'would be the equivalent to unilateral disarmament' (witness the view quoted in House of Lords, Select Committee on European Communities, *Twenty-Third Report*, 12 May 1998). Plans to abolish all contract-related aid (aid helping European shipbuilders compete for orders) by 2001 will unavoidably become entangled in complex intra-state and interstate debates in the EU. In the UK, the House of Lords Select Committee on European Communities has already expressed its concern that, in the absence of the OECD Agreement, a radical reduction in state aid in the EU may disadvantage European shipbuilders vis-à-vis their international competitors (*Twenty-Third Report*, 12 May 1998, p. 9).

The regime and the Commission's case work

We noted that all operating aid for shipbuilding is subject to a common aid ceiling. The ceiling, which must be reviewed at least every twelve months, is fixed with reference to the prevailing difference between the cost structures of the most competitive yards in the EU and the prices charged by their main international competitors, with particular attention to market segments in which EU yards remain relatively most competitive. The common production aid ceiling is at 9 per cent for large vessels and 4.5 per cent for vessels costing less than ECU 10 million and for conversions.

State aids to shipbuilding may appear in a variety of forms. As Table 4.2. shows, shipbuilding attracts a very substantial percentage of total sectoral aid in Denmark, Belgium, Germany, Greece and Spain. It has been on the increase in 1992–4 in Belgium, Greece, Denmark and Germany. Subsidies to shipbuilding increased as a percentage of total industrial aid in Greece, Spain and Germany, reflecting the weight of substantial restructuring projects undertaken in these countries in the early 1990s (Table 4.2). A substantial part of aid in the sector concerns subsidies for the restructuring of shipyards. For example, in 1996 the Commission authorised ECU 160.5 million in aid for the restructuring of shipyards in France and ECU 128.6 million for the restructuring of shipyards in Italy. Often the issues of restructuring, problematic past practices and future changes in the nature and extent of public involvement are interlinked. The Spanish and Greek cases are interesting in this regard. In 1997 the Commission decided to clear restructuring aid

Table 4.2. State aid to the shipbuilding sector 1981–94 by member state (in percentages)

	B	DK	D	GR	E	F	IRL	I	L	NL	P	UK	Total
State aid to shipbuilding as percentage of state aid to particular sectors													
1988–90	25	84	27	60	15	16	0	27	0	64	35	35	25
1990–92	50	80	25	0	35	6	0	13	0	40	67	8	17
1992–94	67	84	60	68	28	3	0	9	0	9	2	0	18
State aid to shipbuilding as percentage of state aid to the total of state aid to industry													
1988–90	1	32	3	3	10	4	0	4	0	7	27	7	5
1990–92	1	24	2	0	12	1	0	1	0	4	37	2	2
1992–94	2	21	3	13	12	1	0	2	0	1	1	0	3

Sources: Commission (1992b), (1995), (1997b).

for Spanish and Greek shipyards (see *Competition Policy Newsletter*, 3/1, 1997, pp. 25–7). In the case of Spain, the Commission took a positive view of restructuring aid in order for public yards to return to viability, provided, first, that a capacity reduction would be enforced and, second, that the aid package[25] would have an exceptional and final character. In other words, a condition for the authorisation of the aid package was the understanding that, should any public yard fail to achieve viability by the end of 1998, no more restructuring aid would be possible.

In the case of Greece, aid to public yards (Hellenic Shipyards) was approved in 1990 as operating aid in derogation from the rules on operating aid for shipbuilding and then in 1992 as a debt write-off on the basis of an agreement on privatisation by 31 March 1993. It was only in September 1995 that the state sold 49 per cent of its shares, and then the proposed write-off had increased to approximately ECU 178.5 million instead of the approved 144 million. In making a positive recommendation to the Industry Ministers Council, the Commission considered that the conditions for the yard to become viable had been met but it also recognised the social and strategic importance of the yard for the region and the whole country. It was therefore acceptable to approve aid covering the debts as they existed when the privatisation took place. In the Spanish and Greek cases, a large part of the subsidy was meant to cover interest that the yards had to pay on loans that were agreed by them as enterprises because for budgetary or legal reasons the governments were unable to pay the aid concerned.

Even granting exemptions and derogations, complications may arise from possible links between authorised aid for a specific application and other areas of the operation of the business group in question. In 1996 the Commission decided to initiate Article 93 (2) proceedings on the spillover of restructuring aid for two former East German shipyards (MTW–Schiffswerft and Volkswerft) to other parts of the Bremer Vulkan group. There followed the initiation of proceedings on other aspects of the group's operation. It appears that not only the two East German shipyards but other areas of the group had benefited from the restructuring aid.[26] After the collapse of the group the yards were taken over by the state and a re-privatisation process was started, involving new subsidies (aiming to replace the misused funds and the expected own contributions from Bremer Vulkan) for the continuation and completion of the restructuring programmes by the end of 1998. As in the Spanish and Greek cases mentioned above, the Commission finally made a positive recom-mendation on the proposed restructuring aid. The German Government gave assurances that the capacity of the yards would remain unchanged until the end of 2000 and that capacity limitations would be extended until 2005 unless otherwise agreed with the Commission.

In assessing the total capacity aspects of the case, DGIV took into account that the group's yard in Bremen-Vegesack, one of the largest shipbuilding facilities in Germany, would be closed from late 1997. As in other cases, the Commission noted that 'comprehensive monitoring arrangements' were needed to 'supervise the use of the aid, compliance with the restructuring plans and enforcement of the capacity limitations' (*Competition Policy Newsletter*, 3/1, 1997, p. 26). In approving the aid measures, Council Regulation 1013/97 notes that 'the programme of monitoring shall include on site monitoring by the Commission assisted if necessary by independent experts'.

4.4.   A Critical Sector in Difficulty: Intervention and Overcapacity in the Motor Vehicle Industry

The motor vehicle industry is one of the largest industries in Europe, the US and the Asian industrial countries. It is, at the same time, the major customer for many other important industries, such as steel, aluminum, rubber and machine tools. And it is a major employer. In the EU in the early 1990s the automobile sector employed 1.05 million workers and, if all suppliers are added, the sector accounted for a total of 4.5 million workers, approximately 15 per cent of industrial employment in the Union (Holmes and Smith, 1995, p. 125).

The mass production of automobiles was invented in the US and became America's largest industry. It was also in the context of America's car industry that assembly-line production was perfected as a response to large and increasing demand.[27] That response, which involved the massive use of specialised machine tools, the deskilling of work and the disciplined co-ordination of many subproductions, came to symbolise both the state-of-the-art in the application of technological principles to production and the fragmentation and degradation of work associated with the unimagined productivity of industrial mass production (cf. Rueschemeyer, 1986, pp. 79–80; Sabel, 1982, pp. 29–30, 32–4). Gradually since the late 1960s, however, the US lost its export surplus in international automobile trade. By the late 1980s one third of cars sold in the US were made overseas.

It has been suggested that a crucial parameter in explaining this shift was the decision by the Detroit carmakers to concentrate on the 'family-size' car, a decision which allowed European and Japanese competitors to capture other market segments. But other, deeper problems manifested themselves gradually, such as outdated management practices and lags in technology (see Womack, 1989; Cusumano, 1990). The Japanese way proved superior on a number of counts, including the management of human resources. Continuous incremental improvements became the business of joint management–workers efforts. Because workers could not be laid off, human resources became a strategic asset and a major focus for improvement (Dertouzos, Lester and Solow, 1989, p. 19). More generally, relationships (between unions and management, technical specialists and general management, assembler and suppliers) were managed differently in American, European and Japanese production systems.

To concentrate on Europe, it is important to note the role played by national diversity and the variety of national conditions. Diversity in European conditions, before as well as after the creation of the common market, was a crucial factor and, when segmentation receded, the benefits of diversity became evident. The differences between the European and the American condition since the 1960s can be summarised by suggesting that in Europe, when trade barriers fell in the 1960s, the motor vehicle industry found itself with a wide range of products to sell in European and world markets. In the US, by contrast, a large and unified domestic market, long distances, and low gasoline prices encouraged carmakers to concentrate on a large, standard, 'family-size' car. At a later stage, while Europe's pre-eminence in smaller cars started to erode when cheaper Japanese cars began to have success in world markets, European carmakers could still utilise Europe's technologically advanced components suppliers, which pioneered developments such as electronic fuel injection and antiskid brakes (Dertouzos, Lester and Solow, 1989, pp. 178–9).

Despite the merits of European carmakers, since the 1970s a productivity gap between the Europeans and the Japanese has gradually become significant (cf. Jones, 1992). In addition, the strategic role of the car industry (as an employer, a creator of demand in the economy, a contributor to the balance of payments, and a demander of other products, including high-technology products) and its exposure to international competition encouraged national governments to intervene time and again with the aim of promoting the industry's interests. During periods of low demand (such as the mid-1970s) state aid and capital injections by governments prevented the operation of the market from squeezing out surplus capacity. During periods of intense international competition the industry has called for the negotiation of voluntary export restraints with the Japanese. State intervention (whether in the form of subsidies or through the negotiation of international trade restraints) thus marked the development of Europe's automobile industry. The American experience, despite crucial differences, suggests that anarchical intervention in the sector complicates the problem of adjustment. In the US, the move to protection for the automobile industry, which accompanied the negative shifts in America's relative standing in international competition, yielded modest results in terms of revitalisation for the sector. In fact, as William Cline has shown, the case of attempted automobile protection is a vivid example of the dominance of politics in US trade policy (Cline, 1986, pp. 227–9). When (as in 1980) petitions for protection against injury from imports were rejected by America's International Trade Commission, the administration was keen to negotiate with the Japanese voluntary export restraints under the threat of Congressionally approved US quotas.

Trade arrangements with Japan negotiated by the European Commission following protracted intra-EC debates have tended to be no less politicised. As '1992' approached, and national protective barriers were to be removed in the EC, the debate on the future of Europe's car industry focused on the common EC policy that would be replacing them. Negotiations between the Commission and Japan's Ministry of International Trade and Industry (MITI) were complicated by the circumstances of the sector in the different European states. The French and the Italians wanted to achieve substantial import restrictions, while the British, with extensive Japanese direct investment in the sector (see below), were less eager. According to the trade deal of July 1991, there would be a transition period to open trade in cars through 1999. In the meantime, trade was to be monitored by both sides in order to implement plans to share market ups and downs, the total number of Japanese imports allowed was set at a level (8 per cent) slightly below that of 1992, and certain limitations on transplants were also agreed. The ambiguities in the 1991 deal resulted in public discordance between different governments over the extent to which the agreement was specific on how import figures would be revised if Japanese transplant output in Europe exceeded forecasts and on the ways in which any fall in EU car demand would be allocated among producers. The ambiguities in the 1991 agreement between the Commission and MITI have been the combined result of the Commission's tactic to negotiate in ways that would extend its role as the industry's main interlocutor and of the existence of side deals with particular national governments (see Holmes and McGowan, 1997, pp.

163-9). French carmakers were not impressed. As with the political effects of the de Havilland decision, which we discussed in Chapter 2, the impact on the French European debate was considerable and contributed to the growth of the anti-Maastricht feelings in the country (see Ross, 1995, pp. 174–6).

Along with the crucial issue of the impact of the Single Market project, various additional trends in the 1980s reflected the concerns of the automobile industry and the new emerging conditions. On the one hand, several European carmakers felt that the EC market was close to saturation. Giant producers Volkswagen and Fiat turned increasingly towards what was then Eastern Europe, establishing various links with car producers in Czechoslovakia, Poland, eastern Germany and Yugoslavia (Harrop, 1992, p. 124).

At the same time, direct foreign investment in the sector, coming mainly from Japanese carmakers, complicated the picture. Britain is the main example in this regard. Nissan led the Japanese carmakers to the UK when it opened a factory in Sunderland in 1986. Honda followed with an engine plant in Swindon in 1989, and Toyota, Japan's biggest producer, opened an engine plant in Wales and a car factory in Derbyshire. Japanese companies also subcontract a large proportion of their production and encourage long-term relationships with a select group of efficient suppliers. Britain was thus chosen as a Japanese export base into continental Europe (*The Economist*, 28 November 1992, pp. 50–51).[28] Should cars produced by Japanese carmakers in Europe be treated as European vehicles? Does the issue of ownership play a greater role than issues such as the creation of employment or the injection of new competitive examples in domestic production systems?

The latter issue touched on a crucial aspect of the sector's problems in Europe. It concerned the sources of the problem of competitiveness. Of course, it has been the European Commission's view since the 1980s that the sector has received massive subsidies in the recent past, and that the current composition and structure of the sector reflects considerable national governmental intervention (cf. Commission, 1987). A study prepared for DG IV in 1996 suggested, rather conventionally, that surplus capacity has a structural character in Europe. According to this view, high redundancy costs and social obligations make plant closures very difficult. During the pre-1993 boom years the problem of overcapacity was less acute, because high costs could be compensated by high prices. Break-even points were kept artificially low by inflated prices which customers were able to pay (Commission, 1997a, p. 353).

Still, as it became evident in the course of the 1980s, in order to address the sources of the competitiveness problem there is need for a more comprehensive reassessment. The automobile industry was forced by intense competition to reassess its methods and forms of organisation. As the standard features of automobile mass production gave way to a production regime based on extensive product variety, just-in-time production and reformed trading methods, the European motor vehicle industry started to cope with the organisational parameters of promoting competitiveness (Coriat, 1995b; Midler, 1995). We noted above that, in contrast to the American industry, which led the world in the mass production of cars from the early decades of the century, European carmakers were placed in a position to prepare for an economy in which the competitive edge depends on variety, innovation and reactive adaptability. This, then, is a sector which has possibilities for far-reaching organisational reforms in project management systems for new products.

The Community framework for the sector

The first systematic Community involvement in the sector was the introduction in 1975 of annual reporting for the sector. Yet a Community framework for state aid to the motor vehicle industry was only introduced in 1989 (OJ C 123 1989).[29] The framework took the form of appropriate measures on the basis of Art. 93(1) EC. The new framework was not established without considerable resistance: Spain and Germany initially refused to abide by the framework and only adopted it in January and May 1990 respectively, after the Commission had decided to initiate proceedings against them.

The framework aimed to ensure transparency of aid flows and procedures in the Community and to promote competitiveness in the sector. All significant cases of aid, irrespective of their stated objective, had to comply with the prior notification requirement. The framework concerned the manufacturing and assembly of motor vehicles as well as the manufacturing of motor vehicle engines. It covered passenger cars, vans, trucks, road tractors, buses, coaches and other commercial vehicles but excluded a number of other vehicles such as motorcycles, agricultural and forestry tractors and military vehicles. The framework provides for the prior notification of state aid as well as the annual reporting of all aids granted to the sector. The framework outlined seven types of aid and provided the corresponding assessment criteria for each type.

The Commission reviewed the application of the framework in 1990 and 1993 and decided, after consulting the member states, to renew the framework's effect (see OJ C 81 1991; OJ C 36 1993). However, following an action brought by Spain, the ECJ ruled that the extension of the framework's operation should be regarded as a limited one, until a future review (Case C–135/93). The Commission proposed the re-introduction in 1996 of the framework in the form of an appropriate measure under Art. 93(1) EC with certain changes, notably, the notification threshold being fixed at ECU 17 million. In the meantime, the problems of overcapacity, which were not present at the time of the introduction of the original framework in 1989, had become significant. The Commission carried out an in-depth study of the framework assisted by independent experts and concluded that the framework was generally effective but required certain amendments. In 1996 a Council Resolution asked the Commission to improve transparency of state aid rules in this sector and ensure that authorised aid did not distort competition. The study commissioned by DG IV in 1996 included the following recommendations (see Commission, 1997a, pp. 347–8).

First, the study recommended a wider definition of the sector, so as to include parts and accessories and to make the relevant suppliers subject to Community monitoring. Second, it recommended the systematic reduction of aid intensity (by up to 3 per cent) in cases where a plan led to overcapacity in a market segment. Third, modification of the notification threshold depending on the value of the project and the amount of the proposed aid was recommended. Fourth, it recommended repayment of innovation aid where the subsidised project resulted in commercial success. Finally, the study recommended that all aid approved by the Commission should be systematically followed up and assessed *ex post*.

The new Community framework, effective from 1 January 1998, maintained the basic features of the previous one but included also certain modifications (OJ C 279/1 1997). The new framework included not only the manufacture of engines but various parts and accessories as well. In particular, it broadened the definition of the industry to include producers of modules or subsystems that constitute the primary components of a vehicle: 'first-tier' suppliers as well as cases of 'overall projects' that group together such projects. According to the guidelines all aids for the sector should be notified to the Commission *ex ante*. From the prior notification obligation are exempted cases of aids under approved schemes when their nominal amount is below ECU 50 million or the total gross aid for the project irrespective of its form and objective is below ECU 5 million. All *ad hoc* aid measures must be notified unless they comply with the thresholds and rules of the new *de minimis* notice which we examined in previous chapters.

The Community framework outlines six possible types of state aid to the motor vehicle industry. Two other types (operating aid and aid to promote modernisation and rationalisation) are not included in the framework. It has been considered that both types create lasting distortions of competition, while the nature of the objectives in question requires that they are financed from a company's own funds. If a company competing in an international market is unable to finance its own operating costs and modernisation and rationalisation, 'its ability to compete and its viability will eventually disappear' (OJ C 279/1, 15.9.1997, p. 9). Although the criteria used in assessing aid vary according to the objectives in each type of aid, the Commission uses two general tests, proportionality (that the aid granted is proportional to the gravity of the problems that will be addressed) and necessity (that the aid granted is necessary to the realisation of the project), in every instance. The six possible types of aid are as follows.

1. Rescue and restructuring aid for firms in difficulty. It is assessed under the relevant Community guidelines for rescue and restructuring schemes (OJ C 368 1994). In view of structural overcapacity in the sector, the Commission will prohibit aid which aims to increase net production capacity and may require reductions in capacity proportional to the intensity of the aid.

2. Regional aid. The Commission requires a cost-benefit analysis if the intensity of the planned aid measure is more than 10 per cent of the regional ceiling. A cost-benefit analysis aims to ascertain the costs associated with certain regional handicaps (see below).

3. Research and development (R&D) aid. It is assessed under the relevant Community framework for R&D (OJ C 45 1996). Investors must distinguish precompetitive R&D from the introduction of new technology in the form of productive investment or competitive development.

4. Investment aid for innovation. Innovation is defined as the development and industrialisation in the EU, the EEA, the countries of Central and Eastern Europe and Slovenia of genuinely or substantially new products or processes, that is, products or processes which have not yet been used or marketed by other parties operating in the industry. Innovation aid is seen as an incentive to industrial and technological risk-taking and its maximum intensity is set at 10 per cent of all eligible costs.

5. Aid for environmental protection and energy saving. It is assessed under the guidelines on aid for environmental protection (OJ C 72 1994). Assessment concerns, on the one hand, the ecological costs incurred by the investor and, on the other, the cost savings on energy, raw materials and so on which the investor has secured as a result of the environmental protection element in the subsidised project.

6. Aid to vocational training. The Commission notes that aid for training, retraining and reconversion programmes will be scrutinised to ensure that it is not used to reduce the costs a firm would normally bear.

As we suggested in previous chapters, the interlinking of the Commission's case work, the Court's case–law and political and administrative developments in the EU system and the policy environment have been crucial in bringing about policy change. Major cases of aid became significant in the years leading to the adoption of the 1989 framework. For example, in the case of Renault, which received extensive assistance in conjunction with a restructuring plan in 1984–8, the Commission applied the market economy investor principle and concluded that a market investor could not have provided the amount the French Government provided in the form of equity capital. In a 1988 Decision, the Commission requested the change of status and the completion of the restructuring plans (Hancher, Ottervanger and Slot, 1993, pp. 113–14).

The majority of cases on aid in the motor vehicle sector concern regional development aid. In general, DG IV has applied the principle of equivalence between the amount of aid granted and the level of regional handicaps. For example, in the *Volkswagen Sachsen* case (Case C 62/91), a final decision was reached by the Commission in June 1996 by concluding that aid in a sector suffering from structural overcapacity had to be confined to what was strictly necessary to offset the respective regional handicaps of the sites in question. To use the *Volkswagen Saxony* example further, the German Government proposed to subsidise (with direct grants, special depreciation allowances and refund of profits tax) *Volkswagen* in the form of regional aid for production in sites in Mosel and Chemnitz. The intensity of the proposed aid was 30.5 per cent for Mosel and 27.3 per cent for Chemnitz. With the assistance of a comparative cost-benefit analysis which aimed to ascertain if the proposed aid was in proportion to the regional problems it sought to redress, the Commission concluded that the net regional handicap amounted to 22.3 per cent for Mosel and 20.8 per cent for Chemnitz. Accordingly, the Commission approved ECU 281.7 million and prohibited the remainder of the proposed amount which was deemed incompatible with Article 92

(3)(c) of the EC Treaty in that it did not comply with the proportionality criterion (see Commission, 1997a, pp. 220–21).

In December 1996 the Commission took a positive decision on an investment aid project in favour of Ford Bridgend (South Wales, UK) (Case N 781/96). In approving this regional aid measure, concerning aid intensity which amounted to less than 2 per cent of the eligible costs of the investment, the Commission concluded that aid intensity of less than 10 per cent of the regional ceiling can be considered reasonable compensation for regional handicaps. In short, all the areas eligible for regional aid possess a certain minimum degree of structural handicaps. Accordingly, DG IV decided not to apply cost-benefit analysis in order to evaluate cases where proposed aid intensity amounts to less than 10 per cent of the regional aid ceiling (see *Competition Policy Newsletter*, 2/3, 1996, pp. 49–50).

Restructuring aid is also important in the sector. Authorisation of aid is linked to production capacity cuts and the restoration of the company's viability. To use a recent example, the Commission examined, on the basis of a restructuring plan drawn up in April 1995, aid by the Spanish authorities to *Santana Motor*. The key factors were the restoration of the company's viability and the fact that the cut in production capacity and the aid intensity (36.3 per cent) were in proportion. In 1996 the Commission authorised two loans totalling ECU 84.5 million and social aid of ECU 52.3 million to redundant workers (see Commission, 1997a, p. 221).

We noted above that, in view of the structural overcapacity which affects the motor vehicle industry in Europe, and in order to prevent surplus capacity from further distorting competition, the Commission studies a project's impact on production capacities. A 'top-up' of 3 per cent of the eligible regional investment is authorised provided that the recipient does not create extra capacity in a saturated market segment. The latter element is significant because, as the case of *MCC-France* indicates, aid may be authorised on the grounds that a new car creates a new production segment on the market while having a limited impact on existing market segments. Based on expert opinion to that effect, the Commission in this case raised no objection to the granting of aid by the French government to *Micro Compact Car-France* (*MCC-France*, a subsidiary of *MCC-AG*) for the manufacture of a new design for a micro-compact car ('Smart') (Case N 933/95).

The Commission's Report on Competition Policy for 1996 suggests that 'for the first time in the case of aid to the motor vehicle industry, the Commission has accepted that the whole of a project is innovatory in nature at European level, thus enabling it to authorise innovation aid of 10 per cent'. In the case of *MCC-France* the Commission also accepted 'that the "Smart" car occupies a distinct market segment from those currently existing and that it should therefore have a limited impact on the industry' (Commission, 1997a, p. 222).

The case of *MCC-France* is significant as an indication of the possibilities for a more comprehensive approach to the links between subsidies, competition policy and the promotion of agreed objectives. Decisions aiming to encourage innovation could encompass organisational innovation not just the creation of new market segments. For example, by authorising appropriate innovation aid measures the Community framework could encourage projects which reflect innovative managerial approaches combining more efficient outcomes and socially acceptable management of human resources. We will return to this issue in the next chapter. The Community framework could also encourage particular engineering approaches, such as the concurrent engineering principles, whereby relationships with suppliers acquire the form of co-development processes.[30]

Notes

1. According to a study prepared for the Commission in 1990. See Moussis (1992, p. 305).
2. The Community definition of SMEs was based on the following criteria: (a) a workforce not exceeding 500, (b) net fixed assets not exceeding ECU 75m, and (c) less than a third of the firm's capital held by a larger company (see, for example, Commission, 1989c, p. 3). The Commission accepted that lower thresholds might be specified in a number of sectors.
3. And either an annual turnover up to ECU 20m or a balance sheet up to ECU 10m, plus up to 25% ownership by companies not falling within this definition. Commission (1993a, p. 401).
4. Additional elements in the definition are the annual turnover of up to ECU 5m or the balance sheet of up to ECU 2m, plus the 25% ownership limit (see Commission, 1993a, pp. 401–2).
5. On the encouragement of horizontal agreements between SMEs cf. Frazer (1990, p. 620).
6. Aids to SMEs have been classified as horizontal objectives with the implication of a more relaxed policy of scrutiny. Aids granted to SMEs, research and development (COM(85) 350 final; OJ C 83 1986) as well as for environmental (SEC(74) 4264) and energy conservation purposes belong to this category of aid schemes.

7. These suggested that when the proposal refers, first, to prolongation of the aid but with no budgetary increase; second and third, to budgetary increase up to 20% of the original aid with and without prolongation; and finally, fourth, to tightening the criteria of application, the aid falls under the category of minor importance.

8. As we saw in chapters 2 and 3, the new *de minimis* rule concerns aid of no more than ECU 100,000 to all enterprises (not just SMEs), although certain sectors are excluded. The main implication is that more cases are now exempted from the prior notification obligation, enabling the Commission to concentrate on the important cases.

9. Ikenberry (1986, pp. 134–5) has shown that, depending on the particular political configuration, state institutional strength may involve a degree of withdrawal from direct involvement.

10. See, for example, EP Debates, 14 October 1981, p. 116: 'The aids which we are discussing here today lead to substantial distortions [...because] they are handed out on a first-come first-served basis and other companies have already creamed off what they can by the time the small and medium–sized undertakings have even found out that the aids are available. In my view, this is a very bad thing for the future of our Community, since it is the small and medium-sized undertakings in particular which have the flexibility necessary to produce the economic growth we need' (Mr von Wogau, Germany). Mr von Wogau had been a founder of the so-called 'Kangaroo Group', lobbying after 1979 for the abolition of trade barriers (see Colchester and Buchan, 1990, pp. 26–7).

11. Research on the expectations of small firms in the single market context indicates that small business owners are worried about large-scale programmes of assistance to industry, including EC R&D programmes, as they feel that these benefit primarily the large companies (see Jacquemin and Wright, 1993, pp. 534–5).

12. The lack of a perfect match between EC competition policy in the late 1980s and the neoliberal environment was the result of the Community's preference for an expansive use of its powers rather than a use that would be based on an economic efficiency model drawn from the Chicago approach. On the differences between the Chicago and the Community approaches see Frazer (1990, pp. 617–23).

13. Interview, DG XXIII (Enterprise Policy), Brussels, November 1992. Name and interview notes with the authors.

14. For different analyses of the corporatist potential and limitations in aspects of EC/EU policy-making cf. Andersen and Eliassen (1991); Greenwood, Grote and Ronit (1992); Obradovic (1995). On interest group activity in the EC/EU more generally cf. Butt Philip (1983; 1987), Mazey and Richardson (1993a; 1993b) and Greenwood (1997).

15. See the very interesting analysis by Ehlermann (1993b, pp. 701, 703).

16. There have been attempts by DG XXIII, disputed by DGs XVI and XXII, to utilize the 'global loan' instrument in this direction. Interviews, DG XXIII and DG XXII, Brussels, May and November 1992, February 1993. There are significant differences of opinion within the Commission on this development. For example, a senior official at DG XVI took the view that the development amounted to an attempt by DG XXIII administrators 'to increase their playground' in national small business associations, by brokering the development of intermediary agencies for administering funds by-passing state authorities. Interview with a senior administrator, DG XVI, Brussels, May 1992. The typical counterargument from DG XXIII would suggest that national administrations in several member states have a track record of considerable incompetence in absorbing and administering EC funds (cf. Lavdas, 1997).

17. By the late 1980s, Aer Lingus, Air France, Iberia, Olympic and TAP were fully public, while the rest (with the exception of BA) were under a mixed ownership regime (see Button and Swann, 1989, p. 266).

18. For a good overview of the European air transport policy before 1994 see Balfour (1994, pp. 1025–53).

19. The fact that in the air transport sector there is coexistence of different governance regimes (most of which are intergovernmental) results in limitations to the expansion of the Commission's administrative capacities. On the one hand, there are intergovernmental European as well as international organizations (Eurocontrol, International Air Transport Association, International Civil Aviation Organisation) which coordinate and regulate aviation lanes, relations between national air space areas and numerous other aspects of air transport. State authority has been strong in the international sector and such intergovernmental bodies 'only exist by permission of governments' (Strange, 1988, p. 153). On the other hand, individual member states continue to honour bilateral agreements (and, in some cases, continue to build new ones) with the US and with American and other companies and airports (e.g., between the UK and the US or, more recently, between Germany and the US). According to the chairman of the Transport Council in the first half of 1994, this coexistence of different levels and regimes creates difficulties for the Commission's efforts towards the creation of a European system of air transport infrastructure (air space control systems, airport taxes/fees, etc.). In spite of these factors, which reflect the combined weight of state intervention and bilateralism in the sector up to the early 1990s, the Commission's capacities and competencies are increasingly critical in influencing the EU carriers' responses to processes of competition and global deregulation (see Lavdas, 1997, pp. 193–4).

20. The principle is relatively new. It found its clearest formal expression first in the December 1993 conclusions of the Council regarding restructuring aids in the steel industry. The principle can also be found in the new

multilateral agreement on subsidies negotiated during the Uruguay Round (see Ehlermann, 1995).

21. Competition Commissioner Karel Van Miert has publicly underlined his interest in the competition aspects of the transport area since taking over from Sir Leon Brittan in January 1993, defending Competition's role in producing and supervising guidelines for the aviation sector. Cf. Van Miert's interviews in *The European* (17–23 February 1995); and *Financial Times* (25 October 1993; 5 December 1994). DG IV introduced the state aid guidelines for aviation in 1994, and has been involved in their application.

22. Delays in negotiations are of course a disadvantage for companies finding themselves in this position, as the debt for which the application has been made increases, with the result that additional applications may be needed later. In the months between eventual agreement between the Commission and the Greek Government and the package being actually put into operation, Olympic's debt had increased by a further Dr 48bn.

23. First, bilateral agreements on the opening of new international routes would automatically be taken to include all interested Greek private carriers; second, Olympic should accept the opening to European competition of its domestic routes, which amount to 41 per cent of its income; third, Olympic should abandon its monopoly in servicing of aircraft and other airlines (ground-handling); and finally, fourth, an independent authority should allocate arrival and landing slots to airlines at Greek airports (in accordance with a 1993 EU regulation).

24. It is reasonable to assume that if governments had not run deficits then the slump would have been deeper, since the deficits 'worked partially to offset the collapse in demand which resulted from the big increase in OPEC savings and fall in investment. Nevertheless, obsession with the size of public sector borrowing requirements began at this time' (Armstrong, Glyn and Harrison, 1991, p. 229).

25. The aid package consisted, on the one hand, of elements that were provided for in a derogation for Spain under the OECD agreement (amounting to approx. ECU 1.087 billion) and, on the other hand, various other elements that were crucial for viability: past interest payments, tax credits and a capital injection.

26. The unauthorized payment of a loan from the German privatization agency and aid for the construction of two container ships (see Cases NN 31/96, N557/96, N 108/96, OJ C 150 24.5.96, OJ C 290 3.10.96, and OJ C 168 12.6.96).

27. The assembly- line production of Ford's Model T began in 1913 in Michigan. As Sabel notes (1982, p. 29), the first car plant in Czechoslovakia to use assembly-line techniques, built by Skoda in 1925, was called America.

28. As *The Economist* put it, Britain was chosen 'not just because manufacturing wages are now among the lowest in Europe', but also because the Japanese wanted employees 'prepared to learn their lean-production methods, and a

welcoming government': they were impressed 'when Margaret Thatcher insisted in 1988 that France had to accept exports of Sunderland-built Nissan Bluebirds because they were "British"' (*The Economist*, 28 November 1992, p. 50).

29. On the issue of motor vehicle *distribution*, however, which comes under antitrust (Art. 85), the sector has been governed by successive Regulations. The most recent took effect on 1 October 1996 (Commission Regulation No. 1475/95 of 28 June 1995) and succeeded Commission Regulation No. 123/85 of 12 December 1984. The new block exemption relating to the distribution and servicing of motor vehicles has as a 'core principle' the freedom for European consumers 'to purchase a new motor vehicle, either directly or through an authorized intermediary, wherever they wish in the EU'. The Regulation aims to establish 'a balance between the supplier's interest in safeguarding its selective dealer network and the interest of European consumers in buying a car within the Community wherever they wish to do so' (Commission, 1997a, p. 33). For very interesting accounts of the debates leading to the new Regulation cf. Groves (1995) and Wijckmans and Vanderelst (1995).

30. This affects a wide range of issues. First, component price targets can be used only as a basis for the negotiation of the best technical solutions for the components themselves, not as the main criterion for deciding between different suppliers of a fixed version of a component. Second, the specifications of the contracts with suppliers can be sufficiently open to encourage co-operation in the search for solutions. Finally, suppliers can be integrated into project development teams (see Midler, 1995, p. 138).

5 The European Politics of State Intervention

What has been claimed in the preceding chapters is that European competition policy represents a new collective form of regulatory intervention and that the development of policy on state aid in particular has been a gradual and politicised process. What makes state aid policy a crucial field, we have suggested, is the fact that the European control of national subsidies increases in significance as the process of integration continues. Drawing our attention to the role of national subsidies in a changing Europe, the Competition DG of the Commission recently remarked that 'the distortive effect of aid is magnified as other government-induced distortions of competition are eliminated and markets become more open and integrated' (*Competition Policy Newsletter*, 1998/1, pp. 70–71). Subsidies constitute the most important remaining form of state intervention and concern a variety of sectoral and horizontal cases.

A superficial account of the tendencies of EU policy might lead one to hypothesise that, as integration advances and reaches new territory, the states' ability to dispense national monies and the familiar phenomena that have been associated with that ability (questionable decisions on resource allocation, particularistic practices, patronage politics and the like) become less and less significant. What is now at stake is the influence over EU-level decisions on resource allocation; new political linkages will develop accordingly. That would be a misleading view. The various forms of state aid total an amount which is now equivalent to 1.7 per cent of EU GDP. With this in mind, it is instructive to consider the difficulties involved in efforts to raise total EU budget appropriations above 1.2 per cent of EU GDP (it was 1.1 per cent at the time of the reform of the structural funds in 1988). Consider also that the bulk of EU expenditure consists of the guarantee of agricultural income, followed by the structural funds (which include the Guidance Section of the European Agricultural Guidance and Guarantee Fund–EAGGF). It is true that the overall policy picture in the EU is one of persisting national predominance in all but the regulatory policies. And it is especially true that the particular subject of this book, state aid, remains crucial. As we have seen, state aid continues to play a central role in a field which is extremely diverse and ranges from carmakers to Europe's heavily subsidised film industry. The European control of state aid is therefore a key parameter in the development of the EU's economy and its institutional edifice, which includes the emerging EU regulatory control of aspects of national distributional policies.

This book suggests that to make sense of the operation of the EU control of state aid we need an approach that combines an account of the different actor strategies and the examination of the broad line of institutional development in European competition policy. In his influential account of the political dimensions of state intervention in Britain and France, Peter Hall argued that the institutional logic which underlies policy requires an analysis of the organisation of capital, of labour, of the state and of the position of the latter within the international economy (see Hall, 1986). In the member states of today's European Union, the politics of state intervention is a new, multilevel politics in which developments come about as a result of interactions between actors situated at different levels and positions of the component parts of the emerging European political system (see Marks, Scharpf, Schmitter and Streeck, 1996). It is therefore a *European* politics of state intervention, in which the developing EU policy instruments aim to address the predominantly national causes and the collective (European) consequences of subsidisation.

5.1. EU Policy Impact on National Regimes

The examination of the EU policy impact on national regimes is the first analytical step in accounting for the emergence throughout the European Union of the politics of interconnected EU–national policy development. Exploring the impact of the EU on national competition regimes beyond the direct effects on economic actors, we can distinguish between four different levels at which this impact has been felt. First, there is influence over the parameters and the contents of the domestic policy debate. Second, European competition policy has affected the operation of public enterprises and the evolution of public–private relationships within member states. Third, the impact has been particularly significant in national legal cultures. Finally, fourth, we should be looking at the emergence of national competition authorities.

Policy debate

EC membership has been both a factor influencing domestic change and an issue that has been used in the domestic political and policy debate. We need to distinguish between European constraints and opportunities, on the one hand, and the domestic use of anticipated effects of Europeanization in attempts to bring about desired outcomes, on the other.[1] There is considerable influence over the parameters as well as the contents of policy debate, while the fusion of national and European issues and the amalgamation of the policy menu are encouraged by the growing awareness of the limitations of national policy solutions.[2]

Of course, the domestic disciplining function of Europeanization is linked to policy impact as well as the possibility that national governments use that impact as a scapegoat for a number of policy choices. More generally, however, Europeanization is giving a sense of direction as well as indications concerning the methods and the price to be paid for reaching certain goals. A different way of expressing this view is by suggesting that, like individuals, societies may need to find the ability at turning points in their evolution to gather themselves together and, utilising the interaction of diverse interests, desires and inclinations, make decisions about societal goals or commitments.

In terms of the use of EC membership in domestic politics and policy debate, the Portuguese case, with its socialist features inherited from the particular mode of regime change in 1974, presents an illuminating example. The right has pointed to the apparent incompatibility of extensive state ownership and EC membership almost continually since the late 1970s, in an attempt to expedite constitutional revision[3] and to roll back the expansion of the state (an attempt that proved moderately successful in the 1990s with the privatisation programme). The link between EC membership and domestic reform became established in the run up to the 1979 elections, when the centre-right (PSD) and the right (CDS) focused their attack on the legacy of the 1974–5 nationalisations. In short, the anticipation of EC membership became an issue in domestic politics not only directly, as a *desideratum* or a challenge, but also indirectly, regarding the forms of policy best suited to Portugal's European future.

In the context of such domestic instrumental uses of, first, the issue of anticipated EC membership and, eventually, EC membership itself, the European Commission has on some occasions felt obliged to state that the

Treaty of Rome had no bearing on the size of the public sector, provided that competition rules are observed (Tsoukalis, 1981, p. 119). Such issues acquired considerable dimensions in the 1990s in view of the new circumstances in which public enterprises found themselves and the conditions for the approval by the Commission of restructuring aid. For example, privatisation as a condition is 'obviously a delicate issue' (Ehlermann, 1995, p. 5) owing to its political dimensions and in view of the Community's principle of neutrality as regards the public or private status of companies (Art. 222 EC Treaty).

We noted that, apart from its impact on the parameters and contents of the domestic policy debate, participation in the process of integration leads to the fusion of the policy menu and the interconnected evolution of policy ideas. Delors's 1993 White Paper on *Growth, Competitiveness, Employment*, which put particular emphasis on the issue of unemployment, reflected the attempt to combine national and European perspectives in proposing a policy mix that would be at once politically sustainable and suitable to accompany and support monetary union. The policy mix included openness, employability, lifelong training and the acceptance of minimal wage increases to fund job-creating investments. The new model of European society calls for 'active solidarity' across generations and regions, and against poverty and exclusion (for a thoughtful account cf. Ross, 1995, pp. 223–6). Although the White Paper's job-creation targets (15 million new jobs by the year 2000) were largely ignored by policy development, its emphasis on a policy mix that would reflect the values of European societies signified an influential approach.

Economic and social cohesion became a Community objective with the Maastricht Treaty (Article 2 EC). In an important 1996 document on *Services of General Interest in Europe*, the Commission sought to make explicit the role of Community institutions in striking a balance between the requirements of the common market and the 'general interest objectives'. The latter were defined in relation to solidarity, social cohesion and equal treatment, values which correspond to the 'European model of society' and which foster the notion of access for all members of society to services of general benefit. The aforementioned principle of neutrality and the acceptance that member states define what are general interest services ensure that the Community's commitment to general interest objectives 'is based on respect for the diversity of the organisation of general interest services' in the different member states. To promote the 'European general interest' without becoming entangled in political debates over the scope and features of public service, the Commission proposed the 'evolutionary' and 'flexible' concept of 'universal service' to denote the need to ensure the provision of high-quality service to all at prices everyone can afford. Universal service is defined in terms of principles: equality, universality, continuity and adaptability. It is also defined in terms of 'sound practices': openness in management, price-setting and funding and scrutiny by bodies independent of those operating the services (OJ C 281, 26.09.1996).[4]

The operation of public enterprises

European competition policy has a bearing both on the operation of public enterprises and, indirectly, on the issue of public ownership. The development of the EU's competition enforcement regime has meant that states become increasingly unable to support companies in crisis. The extension of market principles to the operation of public enterprises requires greater transparency in relations between states and public firms when it comes to financing, cross-subsidies and the various strategic advantages conferred by state ownership (McGowan, 1993). As we saw in Chapter 4, the extension of market principles to the operation of the public sector has led to various transitional subsidy regimes concerning public enterprises. While in some cases the Commission's stance has resulted in rather prolonged transitional regimes, the overall picture indicates that we are witnessing a degree of convergence in 'national attitudes towards state aid' (Van Miert, 1994b, p. 54). The convergence includes the re-examination of the regime of financial guarantees provided by the state for loans taken out by public firms. The convergence in question takes place against a background of widely shared willingness to reduce government holdings in public enterprises. In short, the transitional nature of restructuring aid packages for public enterprises in crisis means that such packages are usually the prelude to partial or full privatisation.

Still, as we have seen, the notion of a public role for certain activities is explicitly accepted by EU institutions. For example, the Commission has indicated that public financing received by public television does not constitute state aid in so far as it represents compensation received in respect of particular activities which private channels are not required to perform or concerning regions to which private channels do not broadcast. Relevant activities would include coverage of the entire national territory, keeping of audio-visual archives, provision of an international channel, and broadcasting time to be made available for religious programmes (*Competition Policy Newsletter*, 2/3, 1996, pp. 48–9). The Amsterdam Treaty confirms this viewpoint in a protocol, which underlines the public roles of public broadcasting systems. Also, in 1991 the Commission had accepted that relationships between national governments and public enterprises can be approached from the prism of cross-subsidisation as it takes place within private groups, when there are long-term strategic goals involved (OJ C 257 1991).

However, it is not always easy to recognise nominally the public role of a venture without also having to face the financial issues which result from certain non-commercial burdens. The combined impact of the Treaty principles of neutrality (regarding public or private ownership) and equality (between public and private undertakings) against a political background of unwillingness to shoulder the costs associated with non-commercial duties often has the result of restructuring plans leading to full or partial privatisation. But that is a choice which depends on the political and policy environment not EU policy.

For example, in rail transport, publicly owned railway companies (which were the majority until recently) suffered from large deficits in the face of increasing competition from air, road and waterway transport. Gaps between revenues and costs were bridged by government subsidies throughout Europe. For decades, a large part of these subsidies reflected the competitive difficulties which rail transport had to face. But subsidies also reflected a recognition of the non-commercial duties imposed upon railway companies by the state: relatively low fares and the continuation of non-profitable lines in thinly populated areas. In some countries, the state imposed upon rail transport additional costs with patronage appointments and ineffective administrative practices. While the latter are burdens which result from politicisation and patronage politics, other burdens represent the genuinely non-commercial roles played by public railway companies throughout Europe.

National legal cultures

The emergent European-level regulatory system has another, more subtle impact on national policy patterns. The Italian case is particularly interesting in this regard. Along with the rest of the Southern European states, Italy lacked any effective national instruments for the control of mergers. Between 1988 and 1990 legislative activity, culminating in Law

287/1990, created Italy's first antitrust statutes. What accounts for the timing of the creation of an Italian competition policy? Two different but related factors have been at work. First, privatisation had put on the agenda the issue of the potential for collusive behaviour of previously state-owned enterprises. Against the background of a state with little if any regulatory experience, there was concern that, in the absence of an antitrust regime, the situation might get out of hand.

Second, the Italian competition debate in the late 1980s was prompted by the European debate on the adoption of an EC Merger Regulation (which was eventually adopted in December 1989). The first Italian antitrust bills were tabled in the wake of the EC measures, and Law 287/1990 was adopted by the Italian Parliament in September 1990, the month when the EC Merger Regulation came into effect. Against the background of imminent EC regulation, the Italian Government took the initiative in filling gaps in the Italian legal system with new provisions modelled on EC competition law, while at the same time inviting the European institutions to take part in a division of tasks between the Community and national levels, whereby activities that could be considered as endangering competition at the national level would be covered by the national regime (see Siragusa and Scassellati-Sforzolini, 1992).[5]

The emergence of an Italian competition policy on merger control was therefore the result of a response to two processes: privatisation and European regulatory development. That response had to address a number of problems, not least attributable to the particularities of the national legal culture. In fact, Italian company law did not fully recognise the notion of a 'group of companies' as it is known in EC competition law,[6] and the term 'undertaking' (*impresa*) was only with considerable reluctance applied to groups as economic units: even holding companies (obviously responsible for the control of a group of companies) were often not cognisable as economic units because they could not be considered as constituting a single legal entity. The notion of group is becoming part of the Italian legal system through the transposition of EC company law directives into domestic law, thereby introducing an elaborate antitrust regulatory regime while at the same time bringing about changes in Italian legal culture (see Siragusa and Scassellati-Sforzolini, 1992).

National competition authorities

To use the Italian example further, we notice that the impact on the national legal culture was a first step towards the emergence of national competition agencies. By the late 1980s, when the EC started developing a tighter antitrust regime (in application of EC Treaty Arts 85–86), only Britain, Germany and France possessed elaborate national systems of merger control (cf. Tsoukalis, 1993, p. 109).[7] Following on from the development of Italian competition policy against the background of imminent European legal regulation, a national competition agency was established in order to enforce anti-trust rules. The resulting Italian Antitrust Authority has since acquired considerable powers, and has often used them against state-controlled groups. Under former prime minister Giuliano Amato, the authority has put pressure on public companies such as Telecom Italia to adjust to EU competition law and avoid discrimination in the use of their networks. Such pressure has often been critical in the early stages in the development of new ventures, as can be seen, for example, in the case of the competition authority's indictment of Telecom Italia for abusing its dominant position and contravening EU competition law by refusing to supply lines to a small Milan-based company (see EIU, *Country Report*, 1st quarter 1995, p. 29; *Financial Times*, 20 January 1995).

European regulation provides the initial stimulus for the emergence of national competition authorities. Subsequent development presents certain interactive features, although a national authority will normally base its view of a case on the approach of EC law and on EC legal precedents concerning the concepts of business, of the relevant market, of restrictive agreement and so on. The Italian Authority has consistently subjected public enterprises to competition rules and has become 'the voice of the market and competition' in a national context that has been marked by fixed prices and market entry barriers (Amato, 1996, p. 172). In another national case which lacked any elaborate national competition policy prior to that instituted as a result of EC policy impact, the Greek Competition Committee was established with a law which was aiming to modernise the national regime following the EC merger Regulation. The Competition Committee remains, however, under the supervision of the Ministry of Commerce (Lavdas, 1997, pp. 191–2). Across Southern Europe, the emergence of new regulatory agencies along with the increasing autonomization of central banks indicate the extent to which national arrangements tend to converge into a model that combines a common policy and institutional core and a certain range of variation (see Lanza and Lavdas, 1997; Lavdas, 1997).

5.2. The Development of European Policy

European policy development has always been an essentially interactive process, in the sense that (a) the sources of crucial policy ideas (and the actual sources of policy initiative) could be found not only in the Commission but in the Council or certain national governments as well, (b) the process of policy formation involved close co-operation between EC/EU and national officials at various levels, and (c) implementation of policy relied almost exclusively on national agents. As is well known, the Commission is a relatively small bureaucracy. Within DG IV, there is a staff of 50 officials responsible for monitoring state aid and carrying out related tasks, such as the preparation of legal documents and international negotiation. From this perspective as well, successful enforcement requires close co-operation with member state administrations (Van Miert, 1994b, p. 56).

However, the relaunch of integration after the SEA led to a new mobilisation of national–EU policy linkages. Furthermore, policy development since the adoption of the Maastricht convergence criteria has become an even more closely interconnected national–European process, as the policy menu has become increasingly unified and policy convergence has involved a degree of convergence not just in policy goals and contents but in policy instruments and institutions as well.

The theoretical prism

In the account of European policy on SMEs in Chapter 4, we argued that the Commission's ability to expand its monitoring capacities in competition has been the unanticipated outcome of Council decisions, and that subsequently the Commission implicitly traded off direct involvement in small business monitoring for the consolidation of its overall monitoring position in competition. In terms of policy results, national subsidies were integrated in the policy debate as instruments of the emergent European policy-generating system. The EU cushioned SMEs from the costs associated with regulatory compliance while at the same time attempting (through enterprise policy) to channel and co-ordinate state aid to small-scale production. In the case of SMEs, state aids were explicitly recognised as European policy instruments. In terms of the theoretical prism which was discussed in the Introduction, the roles of unanticipated consequences and of the Commission's developing capacities support central tenets of the neofunctionalist framework, concerning the European institutions' expansive tasks and ability to function as supranational institutionalised mediators (Haas, 1961; George, 1991).

On the other hand, we have seen throughout the book that an intergovernmentalist perspective can be useful if applied with an interest in the explication of the political nature of the bargaining over institutional outcomes (cf. Garrett, 1992; Moravcsik, 1993). But it is a perspective which cannot account for the explanatory roles of institutions and norms and for the elements of historical inefficiency in institutional building. Furthermore, as we will see below, the development of policy through case-law suggests that the European Court's role cannot be explained from an intergovernmentalist perspective.

At the same time, however, the cases in Chapter 4 and the account of policy evolution in Chapter 2 should also lead us to question certain aspects of neofunctionalism. The Commission's capacities have been dependent on its ability to exploit windows of opportunity, and the latter did not present themselves as the result of a spill-over logic inherent in the integration process.[8] Rather than suggesting that the Commission can be regarded as a main independent variable, the present analysis stresses the explanatory weight of inter-institutional relations and organisational politics at EU level as they relate to international developments and against the background of particular domestic political contexts (cf. George, 1991, pp. 225–34) with which they interact and particular sectoral problems which they have to address.

In airlines, for example, European competition policy has tried to promote liberalisation in a symmetrical way. The Commission's mediating role (increasingly assertive control of state aid and authorisations based on competition-promoting deals) sought to ensure that a change in the response pattern to international transformations would have to take place, albeit in a negotiated manner. EU policy evolves through the politics of interconnectedness, which binds together national and European policy actors and other relevant parties. In this way, the EU is becoming an increasingly integrated policy-generating system. However, the way in which the system evolves often leads to a division of tasks which is not the result of the application of a set of effective policy principles. Rather, the division of tasks often emerges from the politics of inter-institutional bargaining and the anticipated and unanticipated consequences of different actor strategies (Lavdas and Mendrinou, 1995, p. 192). In more structural terms, this is because the new politics of state intervention is a multilevel politics in which developments depend on interactions between actors situated at different levels and positions of the component parts of the emerging European political system (see Marks, Scharpf, Schmitter and Streeck, 1996).

The international context

It is widely accepted that competition promotes increases in efficiency and productivity because, assuming that political factors do not intervene, firms which produce incompetently will exit sooner or later. Yet today's increasingly globalised economy, which manifests little collective political control, faces considerable problems of anti-competitive behaviour. The issues raised by business activity on a global scale in the area of mergers and antitrust are particularly difficult from the perspective of the EU competition authorities. A multilateral forum for competition policy is offered by the OECD and the EU co-operates closely with the parties in that forum. Still, multilateral co-operation in the OECD framework has not been able to counter the effects of globalisation. As Van Miert argues, the issue is to focus not only on government-created trade barriers but on private obstacles to trade as well (Van Miert, 1994a, p. 3). The capacity of governments to monitor the activities of international business is severely limited. Even a uniquely advanced regional organisation such as the EU may find it difficult to deal with the international operations of multinationals. Strategic decisions by major multinational firms may modify the conditions in their competitive environment overnight. Business activity may be organised in ways that bring it beyond the reach of any competition authority. At the same time, the same business activity can fall within the jurisdiction of two or more competition authorities, each applying their own national rules (see Van Miert, 1996, pp. 2–3). The EU's co-operation with its major trade partners under certain bilateral agreements is more intensive and more case-oriented. Such 'custom-made bilateral co-operation agreements' appear to work well in antitrust matters (Schaub, 1998, p. 3).

A critical part of the EU's role in the international economy is accomplished through co-operation with the US. The Union's relationship with the US is its most important bilateral relationship in both economic and political terms.[9] The economic relationship suffered a blow recently in the area of US extraterritorial legislation (D'Amato and Helms–Burton Acts, 1996). But these difficulties coexist with the development of co-operation on crucial issues of competition policy. The EU/US Agreement on the application of competition laws (1991), the result of negotiations between the Commission and the US Government, has been a significant step in that direction.[10]

The Agreement, which was approved by the Council in 1995, established a framework for bilateral co-operation in competition policy. It provides for principles as well as procedural rules whose application would enhance reciprocal co-operation in the detection of anti-competitive behaviour and the enforcement of competition policy. The Agreement establishes a commitment that each party takes into account the important interests of the other when taking enforcement measures; a procedure by virtue of which either party can invite the other to take appropriate measures regarding anti-competitive behaviour which takes place in its territory and which affects the important interests of the other party; notification of cases of common interest and exchange of information; co-operation and co-ordination of the enforcement actions of the competition authorities. Despite differences in legislation, co-operation on individual cases has demonstrated considerable similarities in the analyses of the Commission and the US authorities (Van Miert, 1996, pp. 3–5).

A schematic way to put it is that in today's international environment we witness the operations of strategic major business players but no major competition-enforcing instruments. An international competition authority would in theory be the appropriate institutional response to the globalisation of business activity. The report on international competition policy, which was prepared for DG IV by an independent group of experts,[11] argues for a multilateral framework based on a core of common principles and assisted by a developed enforcement instrument.

However, in view of the difficulties involved in such a proposal, the report also recommends the deepening of the existing bilateral EU/US co-operation in the direction of a 'second generation agreement'. The agreement would include a commitment to avoid unilateral action unless all means provided by the co-operation procedures had been exhausted, and a commitment to eliminate on a reciprocal basis the current obstacles relating to confidentiality rules applicable to exchange of information. The latter provision would be controversial as it would entail the sharing of confidential information and the use of compulsory procedures on behalf of the other party. The constraints imposed by current rules on the international protection of business confidentiality can limit both the scope and the reach of co-operation in competition policy. In cases of alleged serious and deliberate infringements, to expect a waiver from the company concerned for sharing information would not be wise. On the other hand, DG IV officials acknowledge the complications involved in sharing confidential information and the legitimate concerns of businesses (Schaub, 1998, pp. 5–6).

Any shift of competition competencies 'upwards', for example through a European Cartel Office,[12] would weaken the role of DG IV in mergers and antitrust, but the DG would remain completely responsible for state aid control. According to an influential view, an independent State Aid Control Agency would be an unrealistic solution because, as Ehlermann puts it, antitrust rules are addressed to enterprises; state aid rules are addressed to states. State aid control 'requires a wider margin of (political) discretion than decisions in antitrust matters' (Ehlermann, 1995, p. 3). Within the EU, the role played by the Union's competition system, which we examined in this book, has contributed to the creation of a more level playing field for economic activity in the integrated European market. From the perspective of the relations between the EU and its international environment, multilateral co-operation in the area of subsidies is essential in order to avoid anarchical national intervention and economic wars.

In the EU's environment, state aid rules are significant in the European Economic Area (EEA), the Europe Agreements with Central and Eastern European countries (CEECs) and the subsidy code agreed during the Uruguay Round. The Agreement on EEA, which was concluded between the EC and EFTA states and entered into force on 1 January 1994, contains provisions on state aids which essentially reproduce Art. 92 of the Treaty. According to the Agreement, the EFTA Surveillance Authority (ESA) will be responsible for the application of state aid rules in the participating EFTA countries.

Decentralised enforcement of competition policy

In previous chapters we noted the tendency towards decentralised enforcement and suggested that it involves the national courts in crucial roles in view of the direct effect of the formulation in Art. 93 (3). Based on clarifications provided by the ECJ, in 1995 the Commission published a notice with the aim of encouraging the national courts to use their powers in state aid cases and to co-operate with the Commission in the field (OJ C 312, 23.11.1995). The role of the national courts is twofold. On the one hand, when dealing with a case on which the Commission has not decided yet, the national court must ensure that no effect is given to a proposed aid measure until the Commission has reached a final decision on the measure's compatibility with the common market. On the other hand, if the Commission has taken a decision on an aid measure, the national courts must ensure the application and enforcement of that decision (see Faull, 1994, pp. 57–8).

The growing number of litigations brought by third parties using the national courts indicates the significance of decentralised enforcement. It also suggests the increasing relevance of state aid control for all parties, public and private. In this sense, the successful expansion of decentralised enforcement has been among the factors that have been responsible for the return of the issue of state aid Regulations with the increased legal certainty that these would guarantee.

The operation of national competition authorities is another key factor in this process. As we noted above, the emergence of national competition authorities in states which lacked such institutions and the increasing co-operation and policy fusion between European and national authorities in states that previously possessed them, indicate the interconnectedness of EC/EU–national processes of competition policy enforcement. Such processes to some extent presuppose and certainly reinforce the development of a common policy approach to competition. This was the view expressed in late 1991 by the then Director General for the Internal Market and Industrial Affairs, when he praised the creation of an 'effective, decentralised but inter-active, common approach' to issues of regulation across the EC (quoted in Hancher, 1996, p. 61). In its 1998 proposal for an Art. 93 Council Regulation, the Commission underlined the significance of co-operation with 'national independent supervisory bodies' on matters of monitoring and enforcement (see COM(98) 73 final).

To the extent that decentralisation involves interactive networks of implementation, it concerns the Commission co-ordinating the interactions between various national and European regulatory and other agencies. As such, this strategy invites an assessment also on grounds of its compatibility with democratic accountability, on the one hand, and the evolving balances between the Community and national strategies, on the other (cf. Hancher, 1996, pp. 64–7). We will return to the issue of democratic accountability below.

Derogations: competition policy becoming colonised

Instead of a straightforward expansion of the logic of the 'core' policy areas such as competition,[13] actual policy evolution bears the marks of a continuous interaction and interpenetration between 'core' areas (economic integration, a liberal common market, competition) and the multitude of other concerns that have accompanied integration at various stages. In this way European competition policy incorporates a number of social and political parameters. In other words, as we argued in this book, the reasons for the 'pragmatic' approach to competition policy cannot be found in the particular circumstances prevailing at a given point or the supposedly less rigorous approach endorsed by a Commissioner. 'Pragmatic' policy development, which was first suggested by von der Groeben in 1960, means taking into account the political, social and spatial context. This can be achieved through particular derogations, block exemptions or agreements over transitional measures (such as restructuring packages).

For example, the regional aid criteria incorporate the extra costs borne by investors due to their choice of location. Such regional handicaps have been addressed by competition policy, as we saw in Chapter 4, through the incorporation of mechanisms which allow state aid in forms and quantities which correspond to the alleged extra costs. Derogations can also be granted on very different grounds, such as the agreement on the need for better preparation for certain national sectoral regimes. A good example is Directive 96/19/EC, which provided for the introduction of full competition in telecommunications on 1 January 1998 and entitled five member states (Ireland, Greece, Luxembourg, Portugal and Spain) to request derogations from the deadline.

Furthermore, social parameters (such as major disruptions for a region caused by unemployment) enter the criteria of competition policy. There are of course different ways of approaching the social parameter, and these reflect in part different national styles of policy. For example, even in view of the difficulties following the global recession after 1974, differences between the British, the French and the German rationalisation plans persisted and to an extent reflected long-standing policy patterns. Thus, in Germany, both the shipbuilding and the motor vehicle industries shed thousands of workers in the 1970s without much government interference; the government chose instead to concentrate on regional aid to areas most affected by layoffs (Hall, 1986, p. 256). This is today an influential policy approach at EU level, although there is also the possibility (which is however seen as a transitional formulation) of granting aid for specific packages on the criterion that a firm is a major employer in a particular region.

As the cases in Chapter 4 illustrated, regional issues are the key factor behind various exemptions. In December 1997 the Commission decided to introduce new rules with the aim of reducing excessive amounts of regional aid to mobile capital-intensive investments. With the assistance of the new, Multisectoral Framework on regional aid for large investment projects, the Commission will not have to confine itself to investigating regional aid under sector-specific rules applying to certain 'sensitive' sectors (such as motor vehicles and steel). Instead, the largest cases of large investment regional aid in other sectors will be scrutinised for the first time even when they fall within a scheme generally approved by the Commission. The Framework will enter into force on 1 September 1998 and, after a trial period of three years, it will be decided whether to extend the new rules to the 'sensitive' sectors. According to the Commission, the Fifth Survey on State Aid, 'which showed no diminution in the overall levels of regional aid, underlined the urgency of concrete action'. The Framework aims to 'strike an appropriate balance' between the need to avoid distortions of competition and at the same time encourage regional development and job creation in the less advantaged regions of the EU. Hence the new Framework will apply only to a limited number of projects and the ability of member states to apply regional policy will be maintained 'in the vast majority of cases' (*Competition Policy Newsletter*, 1998/1, p. 71).

5.3. Policy Goals and Policy Means

A certain ambivalence has surrounded the relationships between neoliberalism, which is of course favourable to greater competition, and competition policy, which is a mode of regulatory intervention. An aspect of this lack of a perfect match between EC/EU competition policy and neoliberal economics can be gauged from the changing relationships between equivalent European and US provisions. In the past, the influence of US federal competition law was significant in the formation of the provisions of European competition policy. But there are limits to the influence exercised by relatively recent developments in American antitrust law, particularly developments moving in the direction of a minimalist policy on enforcement (cf. Fejo, 1989). The Commission's role in competition policy and its administration has been on the increase, often diverging from the economic efficiency criteria of the Chicago approach (cf. Frazer, 1990), and has been characterised by a combination of elements of greater decentralisation and more rigorous strategic involvement in the emergent enforcement system.

The lack of a perfect match between EC competition policy after the mid-1980s and the neoliberal environment was mainly due to the Commission's preference for an expansive and politically sensitive use of its powers rather than a use that would be based on a textbook economic efficiency model. As a result, European competition policy has not been associated with a strictly neoliberal perspective, despite the strong presence of Sir Leon Brittan at the helm during critical years. The institutional focus, as we suggested in the Introduction to this book, is particularly germane not only in view of the significance of organisational politics in the formation and implementation of policy, but also because the contents of policy can best be approached in terms of shifts in a market–organisational mix. From this angle, it should be noted that there exists no incompatibility in principle between European competition policy and liberal (as distinct from neoliberal–libertarian) debates about the social and institutional dimensions of economic competition and the appropriate means of enforcing different conceptions of socially acceptable policies on competition.

As we saw in the Introduction, and will have the opportunity to stress below, various strands of classical liberalism considered competition not a virtue in itself but a necessary means for the development of certain other properties. The enforcement of a level playing field and the acceptance by states of certain conditions that commit them to a tightened regime of public finance are compatible with the broader notion of competition as a multifaceted policy instrument rather than a goal in itself. Seen from this prism, the alleged gap between actual competition policy and the economist's world of pure competition criteria reflects the evolution of policy in particular contexts and the effort to combine criteria for the evaluation of particular problems.

A positive role for subsidies?

Competition policy as a form of regulatory intervention helps shape the environment of economic life also in cases where its main aim is the opening of markets. Such is the case in the Community's role in promoting liberalisation and the limiting of state intervention. For example, in December 1996 the Council adopted a directive on common rules for the internal market in electricity, which provides for a gradual opening of the electricity market within a period of six years. The directive concerns also the method of market opening and focuses on ways that would encourage the emergence of a competitive single market for electricity in the EU.

Competition policy acquires a more complex role when it comes to a perceived positive role for subsidies, that is, when there is agreement that certain state aid measures are considered desirable because they contribute to some other Community objectives. We must distinguish between the usual derogations which we discussed above, which are based on social, regional and other criteria, and the acceptance of a positive role for subsidies as such. Agreement over the latter is based on the view that the European economy faces problems of competitiveness, and that certain forms of aid are significant in promoting technological, design and organisational innovation (cf. Coriat, 1995a). Of course, active intervention at European level would amount to European industrial policy. On the other hand, the recognition of a positive role for subsidies, for example, in cases of technological as well as organisational innovation, amounts to the inclusion in the European competition framework of criteria that extend beyond the purely market-oriented view of efficiency. As we noted in the Introduction, in any event, that view was considered too narrow by a number of prominent thinkers in economic theory and political economy.

In the context of the competition–industrial policy equilibrium which we discussed in Chapter 2, Davignon's efforts in information technology concentrated on precompetitive collaborative research, which did not offend competition rules (cf. Sharp, 1989, p. 208). We noted that the accommodation thus reached was fragile. At the same time, innovation resulting from important R&D projects is both essential for economic dynamism and difficult to come by. Today, the Commission usually takes a positive view of efforts to promote R&D and protect innovation rights, accepting that new products and new production processes are pre-competitive. A new block exemption Regulation on technology transfer agreements was adopted in January 1996, introducing a less strict approach and a 'black list' of clauses or restrictions that is shorter than the previous list. The Commission still aims to ensure, however, that patent rights do not pose significant entry barriers to competitors on future markets, and that mergers or alliances between major firms with similar

R&D projects do not create dominant actors able to eliminate future competition (see Pons, 1998, p. 7).

An influential approach suggests that competition policy involves 'a form of implicit industrial policy' (Holmes and Smith, 1995, p. 138). Because of the difficulties involved in reaching a commonly accepted, well-specified industrial policy, 'competition policy is being called upon to perform tasks far removed from supporting the principles of antitrust and free trade' (Holmes and Smith, 1995, p. 139). To be sure, this approach is much more attentive to various significant nuances than the sweeping view of competition policy being based on pure competition criteria, the rest being transitional detail (cf. Dumez and Jeunemaitre, 1994; Cohen, 1996).

The issue can be approached also from a somewhat different prism. After protracted debates and periods of infighting, the current situation represents a systemic antagonistic equilibrium, by virtue of which competition policy's relative predominance, owing to the international policy environment, as a form of regulatory intervention functions as an institutional restraint which checks the impulses of an activist and *dirigiste* industrial policy. Seen from this perspective, the 'industrial policy' temptations in the domain of competition policy are by no means stronger than the 'competition policy' restraints in the domain of industrial policy. Elements of the former, which should be distinguished from the derogations (regional, social, and so on) through which other concerns and interests colonise competition policy, are evident in agreement over the positive role of subsidies in promoting technological innovation. Elements of the latter (competition restraints in industrial policy) can be found in the reluctance to engage in EU-level agreements that could be scrutinised under the dominant position rules.

Another aspect of the restraints operating in industrial policy by means of an institutionalised antagonistic relationship with competition has been the avoidance of a situation where European champions are promoted at the expense of SMEs. The analysis in Chapter 4 suggests that competition policy adopted a supporting approach to small-scale production in two ways. First, by providing an appropriate regulatory framework (custom-made provisions and minimisation of the costs associated with regulatory compliance); second, by attempting to check the most activist aspects of a European industrial policy. In addition, as we noted above, state aids to SMEs were approached by enterprise policy as European policy instruments.

The views expressed in the European Parliament's Committee on Economic and Monetary Affairs and Industrial Policy on the occasion of the consultation on the Commission's proposal for a Council Regulation on horizontal aid (COM(97) 0396) reflect the extent to which the role of aid is approached from different perspectives. It has been suggested, for example, that seeking an indiscriminate reduction in state aid may lead to confusion regarding policy goals and the role of aid as a possible policy instrument. State aids 'are also industrial policy instruments which are of direct or indirect benefit to the EU as a whole'. It was considered 'vital that the philosophy of the Union with regard to State aid as an instrument of economic and industrial policy should be clearly explained' (*Report on the proposal for a Council Regulation on the application of Articles 92 and 93 of the EC Treaty to certain categories of horizontal state aid*, A4–0100/98, 19 March 1998).

Conditions: diversity and common ground

European society has a stronger state tradition than the US and a larger place for collectivist values and state intervention (see, e.g., Keating, 1993, pp. 3–4). Hence the 'European model of society', which has been used in EC/EU debates and to which we will return, possesses a certain plausibility as a point of reference. At the same time, Europe's national political economies also manifest a series of different features and traits, the result of diverging traditions of state–economy and state–society relations (see, e.g., Müller and Wright, 1994).

Diversity in national capitalist cultures can be reflected in problems of coherence in European policy formation and asymmetries in implementation, in inter-institutional relations and in national divisions within Community institutions. At the same time, while it is undeniable that different models of capitalism[14] are at the background of several of the differences evident in the operation of national economies today, the exact implications remain somewhat elusive. While the analytical treatment of the possible links between regulatory compliance and different national capitalist features can give interesting results (Wilks, 1996),[15] there is no evidence to suggest that actual compliance deficits and significant enforcement asymmetries[16] can be associated with state characteristics rather than policy-specific or systemic parameters (see Mendrinou, 1996).

From a different perspective, it has been argued that differences in ideological positions among the member states complicate the adoption of a common depoliticised set of rules on an anti-dumping regime, in spite of the recognition of the fact that such a regime would be necessary if the Commission were to be assigned sole responsibility for anti-dumping (Holmes and Kempton, 1996). In discussing decentralised enforcement processes, we noted that these to an extent presuppose and, even more so, reinforce the development of a common approach to competition policy across the EU. Can the emergence of a common approach on competition policy affect the evolution of a model of European capitalism in the Union? Before turning to that question below, we should note that an exclusive focus on the impact of policy goals on the economy may conceal the everyday impact of policy means. Decentralised enforcement networks concern the relations between the means and ends of policy. Policy means are crucial in themselves and, as Leigh Hancher puts it, it would be irrational to gloss over the means used by European institutions by allowing ourselves to be seduced by strategies which focus on ends (Hancher, 1996, p. 64).

The evolution of competition policy is the story of the interplay of political, institutional and economic influences over policy and its enforcement in different national contexts. Often EU policy formation and its enforcement are so closely interrelated that the distinction becomes blurred (see Richardson, 1996a). As a result, concerns over the institutional and political conditions of compliance, and the inter-institutional rivalries that help shape them, become inseparable from the parameters which define the evaluation of policy *per se*. National and EU–institutional parameters are intermingled in this process, and the cleavage lines within and between institutions can be attributed to national, ideological, ideational and economic factors. As Philippe Schmitter (1996, p. 36) suggests, in the future an increasing proportion of EU conflicts will be inter-institutional conflicts which will be dealt with through novel combinations of political, administrative and judicial measures.

Development through law: judicialization

The judicialization of policy conflicts has been evident as a tendency from the early years of the Community and has gone through different phases. Scheingold had noted that institutional change in the Community had often been achieved through the ECJ, as 'the failure of the political process to provide a settlement is sufficient to transform a political dispute into a legal question' (Scheingold, 1965, p. 264). It is plain that the search for legal solutions to essentially political problems followed partly from the contrast between the highly developed legal edifice of the Community compared to its political edifice (see Weiler, 1981; 1991). The analysis of judicial politics and judicial activism has confirmed that the ECJ's approach to its role has gone through various phases (Koopmans, 1986; on judicial activism cf. Rasmussen, 1986; 1988). The development of policy through case-law was encouraged at an early point. For example, the Court had ruled (Case 7/61) that, if the interest of the Commission in pursuing a case subsists, the Commission may bring a case to the Court if compliance has occurred after the lapse of the time-limit set by the reasoned opinion.

The Commission has taken very seriously the possibility that its enforcement strategies may benefit from reinvigoration or clarification through the Court's case-law, especially with cases suited to the Commission's evolving policy agenda. By referring to the substance of the violation, the Court's judgement may be critical not only in reaffirming policies but also in overcoming Council inertia. At the same time, the jurisprudence of the Courts in Luxembourg (the ECJ and the Court of First Instance) can be seen as contributing to the shrinking of the 'originally wide margin' of Commission discretion in state aid control (Ehlermann, 1995, p. 3). This is essentially the other aspect of the same phenomenon, that is, the development and refinement of policy through law. The Court's role in policy development is especially interesting when we realise that an intergovernmentalist reading of the Court's contribution (e.g, Garrett and Weingast, 1993) is probably misleading. In other words, there emerge no general patterns suggesting that large states tend to be vindicated by the Court (see Mendrinou, 1996, pp. 13–14).

As we saw in Chapter 4, a recent (1998) Court judgement in a major state aid case vindicated private sector litigants (airlines such as British Airways) against the Commission, Air France and the French state. It was the first time the Court seriously questioned a large aid package given by a member state to an ailing state group. The case shows that private sector firms acting as litigants are able to bring judicial pressure to bear in order to counterbalance the political pressure exercised on the Commission by governments on behalf of state groups. Of course, the intergovernmental element cannot be absent: in the case in question, the governments of Denmark, Sweden and the UK, acting as intervening parties, supported the complainants against the Commission's authorisation of state aid. Overall, though, business firms emerge as key players in three respects: as interests exercising influence over policy; as major regulatory targets;[17] last but not least, as parties which promote the judicialization of policy conflicts.

Furthermore, business associations have been keen to use the relevant institutional and legal instruments. For example, in 1997 the Commission launched an investigation into claims that a major state-owned regional bank in Germany received unlawful cash injections. The investigation was triggered by a complaint from the German banking association, which represents private sector banks (*Financial Times*, 24 September 1997).

Another aspect of judicialization is involved in the role of the national courts in the context of decentralised enforcement, an aspect which was discussed above and in Chapter 2. The significance of this particular aspect is associated, on the one hand, with the roles of the national courts in the developing decentralised enforcement system and, on the other hand, with the growing propensity of private sector agents to act as litigants in order to protect their interests through EC law and in order to counterbalance the political or other pressures exercised upon the Commission.

The political criterion: democratic accountability

Issues of democracy and democratic accountability are directly relevant at three levels. First, there is the question of the extent to which the European policy-making system reduces even further the democratic controls over policy-making. It is an aspect of this more general phenomenon that European policy impact has made it difficult for governments to formulate policies acceptable to domestic interest groups (see, for example, Menon and Hayward, 1996, pp. 269–70). Even if the relative detachment of policy-making from immediate pressures at national level may have certain positive effects, the overall picture suggests that the feeble national democratic scrutiny of policy has become even weaker.

Furthermore, Europe's democratic deficit is linked to the weakness of parliamentary supervision in the EU system, despite the changes introduced with Maastricht (see Lodge, 1994; Neunreither 1994). While the EU expands in terms of policy competencies and increases its policy impact on national regimes, the parliamentary control of policy at EU level remains particularly weak. The emergence of a central European bank and the planned change to the euro after 1999 attach a certain urgency to the relevance of this dimension. In fact, as Schmitter argues (1996, p. 36), a move in the direction of increased powers for the European Parliament and the development of an overarching legislative process would ensure also a minimum of EU policy coherence.

Last but not least, issues of democratic accountability are also significant when it comes to the much-debated opaqueness of EU decision-making and policy implementation. We mentioned, for example, the reservations that have been expressed regarding implementation networks in competition policy. Such arguments are important and, as Hancher suggests (1996, pp. 66–7), need careful and urgent consideration, since they concern the shape of relations between economic power, institutional competencies and democratic control in tomorrow's Europe.

On the other hand, it is easy sometimes to exaggerate the existing problems of European democratic accountability by comparing them to a vaguely defined pre-existing democratic condition of national policy-making. In fact, European political systems were marked by tendencies such as the displacement of decision-making from the electoral partisan channel to corporate networks and the relative weakening of the role of parliaments and of the hold of parties on decision-making processes long before European integration had any significant impact on domestic political arrangements.[18] Furthermore, various policies of *national* economic decision-making bureaucracies have been opaque in the past, the result of practices to which a well-known anecdote for the press would certainly apply as well. When Wickham Steed was editor of *The Times*, and was challenged on certain editorial policies, he gave the characteristic reply that the paper's line was decided by 'a committee that never meets'. National 'committees that never met' often decided crucial issues pertaining to the concentration of economic power, public procurement or the allocation of subsidies. In comparative perspective, the extent to which national subsidies were used to preserve uncompetitive firms rather than promote development and innovation was often linked to the degree of vulnerability of the different states to pressures by interests (cf. Zysman, 1983, p. 314; Samuels, 1987, pp. 14–17).

It is now possible, for example, that the new national competition authorities and the application of competition law across Europe will lead to more transparent interactions and at least the tendency towards a less anarchical and more rational mode for the allocation of economic resources. In addition, as we noted in the Introduction, the application of competition rules and the EU control of state aid is necessary if the Community's structural policy is to make any difference.

Policy goals and policy contents

While the methods and institutional practices associated with the pursuit of alleged Community goals can be as significant as the goals themselves, the development of Europe's policy on state aid and the current juncture which leads to state aid Regulations and the re-orientation of state aid control necessitate a renewed emphasis on policy goals.

As previous chapters made clear, the evolution of competition policy was marked by interactions between institutional actors often with different perspectives. The evolution of policy has been conditioned by three main parameters: understandings on ideational frameworks for competition; institutional capacities for enforcement; and the corresponding developments at national level, where regulatory change involves the search for a redefinition of the role of the state. We have seen that Europeanization involves important shifts in the goals, contents and instruments of policy and also, to some extent, in national policy styles. There is continuous interaction between European-level developments and domestic patterns of public–private relations. The latter mediate and help shape national responses to the stimuli of globalisation and Europeanization; in turn, such stimuli redefine not only the contents but also the instruments and institutions of policy. Regulatory change is the redesigning of the rules governing public–private relations, and has been associated with a shift in the modes of state involvement from ownership to regulation. Rather than representing simply a process of state retreat, the redefinition of the state's role includes a number of diverse tendencies (cf. Moran and Prosser, 1994; Müller and Wright, 1994).

As we argued in Chapter 4, the case of airlines suggests that the strengthening of the Commission's control of state aid has a number of functions. First, it is meant to reinforce and extend processes of liberalisation and competition, mainly by breaking up relations or pockets of relative closure. This is a function which promotes marketization in the context of a European space with fewer and fewer barriers to carriers competing for business. Second, it is meant to mediate and moderate liberalisation processes, by ensuring that states and players with different levels of development and states of finances are given a chance. Rescue and restructuring packages are seen as one-off attempts to rescue state enterprises which would appear to be in a disadvantaged position even if privatisation options were immediately followed. The Commission gives the go-ahead for rescue and restructuring deals which have a number of aspects: agreed predominance of market criteria in the future management of such enterprises; opening of several of their functions to competition; avoidance of political confrontation between the states; last but not least, the states' agreement on the future impossibility of state aid. We have called this an accommodative function. Third, the Commission as an institutional mediator is supposed to take into account social parameters (for example, socially unacceptable levels of unemployment for a national or regional economy resulting from the closure of a major employer): a social function. In sum, the Commission's role in enforcing a tighter regime of competition control acts both as an amplifier and as a buffer of wider liberalisation processes. In so doing, it co-ordinates European responses to such international processes while expanding the EU institutional involvement in the policy areas concerned.

From a purely domestic perspective, the EU can be an opportunity for better policy co-ordination (at the interstate, the national–European, or the intra-state level), a source of beneficial political or financial arrangements, a source of policy constraints and possible limitations for state autonomy, or simply a convenient scapegoat for legitimising domestic policy choices. The possibility of finding co-operative solutions to policy problems has been evident even where such co-operation emerged in the context of the antagonistic policy equilibria discussed above. Such equilibria do not necessarily lead to optimal policies, however. When discussing different exemptions and derogations for subsidies, we noted that the legitimation of a special approach to certain types of aid is that it contributes to Community objectives. To the extent that some of these objectives concern cohesion, it is worth stressing that the overall picture in the state aid field is not particularly encouraging for the less developed EU economies. The four big economies (Germany, France, Italy, UK) present considerable discrepancies when it comes to subsidy patterns. In Italy aid as a percentage of value added is more than ten times as high as in the UK. But the relative importance of industrial aid is rising in the big economies in the EU compared to the four cohesion countries (Greece, Ireland, Portugal, Spain) (see Commission, 1997b, p. 9). It appears that some additional form of assessing the links between state aid control and differences in the use of aid in the member states will be necessary if cohesion is to continue playing the role of an objective.

Competition Commissioner Karel Van Miert, who took over the competition dossier from Sir Leon Brittan, signified a shift to a more comprehensive approach to competition policy. Van Miert, former chairman of the Flemish Socialist Party, has emphasised the need for competition to take into account 'what's happening in the real world', apparently alluding to the need to incorporate wider Community concerns (social, regional) into competition decisions (on Van Miert's views cf. *Financial Times*, 25 October 1993; 5 December 1994). But the shift in question, which corresponds to a period of much greater public visibility and politicisation of competition policy, should not be allowed to conceal the fact that the approach which remains attentive to issues of 'general interest' (see Van Miert, 1997; cf. OJ C 281, 26.09.1996) displays a political sensitivity that has been familiar from the Community's early years. Despite oscillations, that approach managed to maintain the conditions necessary for policy evolution. As Chapter 2 demonstrated, such conditions included striking a balance between national sensitivities and the 'Community perspective', reaching compromises between interventionism and free market philosophy and achieving member states' acceptance for the Commission's role in state aid control.

Developments in the global and the European economy, against the background of the gradual evolution of competition policy, enabled at crucial turning points the acquisition by European institutions of key policy roles. At the national level, the emergence of competition authorities having to cope with different problems but applying the same or similar rules and aiming at similar regulatory targets attached a dimension of fusion and interconnectedness to processes of convergence. This is because the structure of causation in policy-making and implementation in the increasingly integrated European polity is multi-directional. At the same time, the central European agencies are among the key institutions whose strategies can contribute in the effort to reshape the structural parameters of Europe's economic difficulties. The influential thesis on the adjustment of structure to strategy (Chandler, 1962) acquires a new dimension in the multilevel and multidirectional politics of European policy, provided that the degree of policy coherence necessary for European strategic involvement is present.

European competition policy is at a turning point on two fronts. The first concerns enforcement and is associated with the debates on the proposed Regulations. As we explained in the preceding chapters, the Commission proposals for Council Regulations (February 1998) cover all areas in which the Commission, in accordance with the jurisprudence of the European Court, has developed a practice for the application of Art. 93 (procedures regarding notification, unlawful aid, misuse of aid, existing aid schemes, monitoring and various common provisions). We have seen that the rise in the number of negative Commission decisions, the increased salience of state aid control, the growing complexity of cases and the need to codify and reinforce Commission practice in the area by means of a regulation are interlinked. Regarding notification, DG IV wishes to exempt whole categories of aid from the relevant obligation, aiming to achieve a strategic concentration of its resources on the more significant cases (cf. Commission, 1997a, p. 103).[19]

The other front concerns policy content. In particular, it concerns the specification of the positive roles of subsidies. Since the recognition of the positive role of subsidies may constitute 'a form of implicit industrial policy' (Peter Holmes), policy debate should endeavour to clarify not just the technical but the social and political criteria as well. Policy debate could also address issues linked to the organisational dimension in a dual sense. First, in terms of policy content, the dimension in question would concern the need to encompass organisational innovation not just the creation of new market segments. Using appropriate criteria and ensuring transparent application of the criteria in authorising 'innovation aid', the Community framework could encourage projects which reflect innovative managerial approaches combining more efficient outcomes and socially acceptable management of human resources.

At the same time, second, a debate concerning national subsidies as policy instruments from a European perspective cannot avoid addressing the interrelationships between competition, economic organisation, ideological perceptions and the operation of political institutions. In short, it will have to tackle substantive issues which concern the links between economic competition and the desired forms of socio-political organisation.

An interesting attempt to theorise the links between competition and socio-political development can be found in Marxian political economy. For Marx, competition, which appears historically as the dissolution of a multitude of institutional constraints within a country (the lifting of internal tariffs, of compulsory guild membership and of forms of government intervention) and on the world market (the lifting of protection and of trade barriers), is the expression of the interaction of capitals and of the relations of capitalist production. As long as capital is weak, it still relies on and interacts with a variety of institutional elements and pre-capitalist legacies. 'As soon as it feels strong, it throws away the crutches, and moves in accordance with its own laws' (Marx, 1973, p. 651). Accordingly, as Marx put it in the *Grundrisse* (1857–8), the view that free competition is 'the ultimate development of human freedom' is absurd, unless we accept 'that middle-class rule is the culmination of world history'. Rather, the Marxian scheme would anticipate that as the capitalist relations of production become barriers to technological development, the ideology of competition recedes: 'when the illusion about competition as the so-called absolute form of free individuality vanishes, this is evidence that the conditions of competition, i.e., of production founded on capital' have become barriers and are about to be changed (Marx, 1973, p. 652).[20]

Marxian teleology aside, it is probably correct to argue that the ways in which social actors in a certain temporal and cultural context define the role of economic competition are indicative of the particular mix of market and organisational principles which underlie conceptions of the socially acceptable forms of economic interaction. Attempts to define a form of economic enterprise that would correspond to the values of liberty, democracy and political equality (see, for example, Dahl, 1985), aim to address the issues raised above all by the relationships between economic competition and political institutions.

The fact is that competition within certain boundaries constitutes a central element in the modern conception of a vibrant civil society. Defining the boundaries is the main difficulty. Of course, the debate extends well beyond economics in a strict sense. Underlying the liberal notion of civil society is an approach to competition as a means for developing the rational potential of human beings. This strand is clear and possesses a strong moral dimension in Kantian liberalism. Competition is an aspect of the 'unsocial sociability' of humanity: although no virtue in itself, it encourages the development and refinement of rational properties. These allow individuals to recognise the essentially interactive construction of social order.[21] In scientific research, it is considered commonplace to suggest that ingenuity and the refinement of tools are encouraged by different combinations of co-operation (usually within centres or laboratories) and competition (usually between such institutions). And it is widely accepted in various spheres of social activity that competition results in outcomes that are more efficient and also, in a sense, more just compared to the ones that would accrue simply from inherited practice or advantages associated with an early start.[22]

As we suggested in the Introduction, the making and enforcement of competition *policy* presupposes a normative understanding about the 'proper' institutional boundaries for the play of market forces. The current normative equilibrium appears to combine notions of efficiency and fairness. In its public pronouncements, the Commission insists on this broader concept of competition. For example, in a leaflet whose aim was to inform the general public about its task and operation, the Commission

(DG IV) suggested that 'the Community has put in place a set of rules to make sure that throughout the EC firms are operating on a fair basis and that customers get the benefits to which they are entitled, for competition and price-cutting do not always come naturally to firms, whose first duty to shareholders is to maximise profits'. Noting that anti-competitive practices include cartels, artificially high prices and the blocking of market entry, the Commission went on to argue that governments may also distort competition by subsidising some firms 'so that they gain an unfair competitive advantage over their rivals' (Commission, 1992c, p. 1).

The increasing salience of competition policy demonstrates the centrality of economic competition but it also indicates that the relationships between economic competition and regulatory intervention become problematised. This is now a field of debate in which the unmistakable convergence towards a market-oriented approach does not preclude interesting differences on potentially significant issues of regulation. For example, it is becoming acceptable from a social market perspective to favour a separation of form and content in the relationship between economic competition and institutional regulation, in so far as it is agreed that competition as such should not be distorted through politicised or particularistic practices. But the role and scope of institutional regulatory mechanisms should remain open to democratic debate. For this view, preserving the European model of society requires negotiating for international institutions capable of enforcing conditions of 'fair competition' and prohibiting practices associated with social dumping (see Lafontaine and Müller, 1998, pp. 54–6, 92–4). More generally, as we noted earlier in this Chapter, the key issue today is the extent to which an international competition policy, however limited, would aim to tackle both the excessive particularism of state intervention and the harmful activities of international private actors.

We may expect the gradual crystallisation of different views on the nature and scope of European regulatory intervention and the criteria defining the positive role of subsidies after the final agreement, in May 1998, over monetary union and the founder members of the single currency, the euro. On the one hand, there can be little doubt that competition law is a 'common denominator' for all countries based on market economies (Van Miert, 1994a, p. 1). As a form of crucial regulatory intervention, competition policy is bound to remain central in future developments. On the other hand, the refinement of regulatory instruments will be influenced by the general debate on the relationships between the operation of the market economy, the central European monetary authorities and the influence of political factors. Seen from this prism, the emergence of central European monetary authorities represents a new phase in the evolution of intermediary institutions, which also include various regulatory mechanisms, situating themselves between the world of political institutions and the forces of economic competition, between politics and the market.

Notes

1. For the domestic political uses of European legislation and European rules see the very interesting, early approach in Puchala (1975).
2. For analyses of the impact of EU membership on national institutions and policies in the twelve member states (before the Northern enlargement) see the contributions in Rometsch and Wessels (1996). Rometsch and Wessels distinguish between Europeanization (increasing orientation of national institutions towards European activity and participation in EU decision-making), institutional fusion (increasing interdependence of the national and EU levels) and institutional convergence (the extent to which national institutions converge into one common model). Other analyses use a broader concept of Europeanization, encompassing policy impact as well as the European orientation of national actors (see Lavdas, 1997).
3. The 1976 Constitution (amended in 1982, 1989 and 1992) had endorsed the nationalisations and land expropriations which followed the regime change. As a result of a turbulent process of regime transition and democratization, the original constitutional document had included a number of socialist formulations, e.g., on the state's role in economic development and planning (Arts 91–94) and in ensuring that economic activities 'contribute to the development of the country and the defense of national independence and the interests of the workers' (Art. 86). The Constitution had also institutionalized (in the form of the Council of the Revolution) the influential role of the left-wing military faction MFA (Armed Forces Movement), which had been instrumental in the toppling of the Caetano regime and which was backed by the Communist Party (PCP) (cf. Dauderstädt, 1988; Chilcote, 1993).
4. The point was originally made in the context of the Commission's report on the reform of the European Treaties (*Reinforcing Political Union and Preparing for Enlargement: Commission Opinion for the Intergovernmental Conference*, COM(96) 90 final).
5. For an analysis of the political and institutional conditions which have favoured the development of a largely informal division of tasks in the enforcement of European competition policy on state aid, reinforcing, despite increasing interconnectedness, the distinctive roles of an emerging European-regulatory and a national-distributional level, see Lavdas and Mendrinou (1994; 1995).

6.   Which recognises *de facto* and indirect control as criteria for the constitution of an economic unit, 'even if in law that economic unit consists of several persons legal or natural' (ECJ, Case 170/83, quoted in Siragusa and Scassellati-Sforzolini, 1992, p. 121).

7.   In the UK competition policy (Monopolies and Mergers Act, 1965) was extended by the Fair Trading Act (1973) to cover oligopolistic markets. The Act introduced the Office of Fair Trading as an institution which is responsible for keeping under review commercial activities and restrictive agreements. The Office has powers of referral subject to the approval of the relevant Secretary of State. The Office's powers in investigating anti-competitive practices in both private and public industries were extended by the Competition Act (1980). Anti-merger legislation was introduced in the Federal Republic of Germany in 1973. For a brief account of the relations between American and German competition policy cf. Schmid (1986, p. 19). On the debate concerning the German *Bundeskartellamt* as a possible model for Europe see note 12 below.

8.   On this point see the analysis of Beukel (1994, pp. 50–51) on the case of EU educational policy.

9.   On the evolution of the EC/EU–US relationship and the prospects for future co-operation in transatlantic relations see Peterson (1996).

10. *Agreement Between the Government of the United States of America and the European Communities Regarding the Application of their Competition Laws* (OJ L 95/47, 1995). It is expected that a similar agreement negotiated with Canada will enter into force in 1998.

11. *Competition Policy in the New Trade Order: Strengthening International Cooperation and Rules* (Brussels: European Commission, 1995).

12. On the controversy surrounding the possible establishment of an independent European merger authority, built on the German model (the *Bundeskartellamt* in Berlin), cf. *The Economist*, 12 October 1991, p. 18; Ehlermann (1995, pp. 2–3); Wilks and McGowan (1995a); Lafontaine and Müller (1998, pp. 93–4).

13. As some neofunctionalists would expect. For this view, see the very interesting analysis in Pollack (1994).

14. The usual variants include the Anglo-American individualist model and the German and Northern European collectivist model, although the Northern countries are often grouped in a third, distinct social democratic variant. For an analysis based on a two-model comparison (Atlantic versus Rhine capitalism) see Hodges and Woolcock (1993).

15. For example, Wilks (1996, pp. 540–41, 550–52) makes some very interesting suggestions on the role of regulation in the evolution of European governance and on the analysis of the business firm as a key regulatory target.

16. That is, while some states tend to be generally more prominent in violations, the significant violations (concerning rules and regulations and improperly applied directives) tend to persist in all states (see Mendrinou, 1996, pp. 4–8).

17. In the US context there exist important analyses of business as regulatory targets. For a political historical analysis arguing that the forms and structures of capitalist organizations can be interpreted as being the result of their attempts to subvert state efforts to regulate them see Fligstein (1990).

18. For a balanced and authoritative overview of tendencies and counter-tendencies before the 1980s see Daalder (1983, pp. 24–7).

19. Similar developments are evident in the area of antitrust. Under the changes, the Commission will drop the requirement that companies with revenue of ECU 300 million a year must seek EU approval for deals that could restrict competition. Instead, the requirement to notify the Commission will depend on the market share held by a company or the nature of the agreement in question. This will reduce red tape for companies while allowing EU officials to focus on the significant cases (see, for example, *Wall Street Journal Europe*, 9 October 1997).

20. From a macroscopic perspective, competition is one of the conditions that led to the emergence of modernity in Europe. Consider John Hall's Weberian thesis that the rise of capitalism in Europe owes much to the competing state system in which intense economic and military competition became the key to technological and economic advances (Hall, 1985).

21. In Kant's liberalism, the realization of human potentialities can only take place in a society in which freedom and intense competition are combined with (institutional) protection of the boundaries of this freedom so that the freedom of one may exist together with the freedom of others. Competition ('antagonism'), based on competing needs, permeates all levels of human relations and is the means through which humanity's capacities come to be refined. It is through competition that individuals reach an accommodation based on the recognition that all parties have rights that accrue to them because they are ends in themselves, who cannot rightfully be used as means to one's own ends. In short, through competition individuals recognize others to be persons. Accordingly, the primary objective of the social contract in Kant is not to ensure physical well-being, but to guarantee individual and collective rights (Humphrey, 1983, pp. 12–13). The moral dimension becomes the dominant one when we consider that, unlike its Lockean counterpart, the Kantian construction of society has as its purpose not to protect pre-existing (natural) individual rights, but to encourage persons to realize that their rights and the rights of others are interlinked, and they are justly served 'when they are so limited, by virtue of their own volition, as not to abridge the rights of others' (Humphrey, 1983, p. 13). Competition is the 'natural' means through which individuals realize their rational potential and come to see this.

22. Talking about the new generation of top conductors, and responding to a point that there may be a danger that his help to a new musician could accelerate a career too quickly, Karajan remarked that competition would correct the possibly anomalous effects of an early endorsement: 'What I say to them is, don't be complacent. You are good but soon I am going to throw

into your back a whole phalanx of new ones. We all thrive on competition; without it nothing happens' (Osborne, 1991, p. 56).

References

Allen, D. (1983). Managing the Common Market: The Community's Competition Policy. In H. Wallace, W. Wallace and C. Webb, eds., *Policy-Making in the European Community*. Second edition. Chichester: Wiley.

Amato, G. (1996). The Impact of Europe on National Policies: Italian Anti-Trust Policy. In Y. Meny et al., eds., *Adjusting to Europe: The Impact of the European Union on National Institutions and Policies*. London: Routledge.

Amsden, A.H. (1985). The State and Taiwan's Economic Development. In P. Evans et al., eds., *Bringing the State Back In.* Cambridge: Cambridge University Press.

Amsden, A.H. (1989). *Asia's Next Giant: South Korea and Late Industrialization*. Oxford: Oxford University Press.

Amsden, A.H. (1990). Third World Industrialization: 'Global Fordism' or a New Model? *New Left Review*. 182.

Andersen, S. and Eliassen, K. (1991). European Community Lobbying. *European Journal of Political Research*. 20.

Andersen, S. and Eliassen, K. eds. (1993). *Making Policy in Europe: The Europeification of National Policy-Making*. London: Sage.

Andriessen, F. (1983). The Role of Anti-Trust in the Face of Economic Recession: State Aids in the EEC. *European Competition Law Review*. 4.

Armstrong, P., Glyn, A. and Harrison, J. (1991). *Capitalism Since 1945*. Oxford: Basil Blackwell.

Audretsch, H.A.H. (1986). *Supervision in European Community Law*. Second edition. New York: Elsevier.

Axelrod, R. (1984). *The Evolution of Cooperation*. New York: Basic Books.

Axelrod, R. (1986). An Evolutionary Approach to Norms. *American Political Science Review*. 80.

Balassa, B. (1973). Industrial Policy in the European Common Market. *Banca Nazionale del Lavoro Quarterly Review*. 107.

Balfour, J. (1994). Air Transport: A Community Success Story? *Common Market Law Review*. 31.

Berger, S. and Piore, M. (1980). *Dualism and Discontinuity in Industrial Societies*. Cambridge: Cambridge University Press.

Beukel, E. (1994). Restructuring Integration Theory: The Case of Educational Policy in the EC. *Cooperation and Conflict.* 29.

Binns, C. (1978). From USE to EEC: The Soviet Analysis of European Integration under Capitalism. *Soviet Studies.* 30.

Brittan, L. (1989a). 1992: Priorities in Competition Policy. *European Access.* 2.

Brittan, L. (1989b). 1992: A Bonfire of Subsidies? A Review of State Aids in the European Community. *European Access.* 3.

Brooks, M.R. and Button, K.J. (1992). Shipping within the Framework of a Single European Market. *Transport Reviews.* 12.

Brown, C., Hamilton, J. and Medoff, J. (1990). *Employers Large and Small*. Cambridge, MA: Harvard University Press.

Buigues, P., Jacquemin, A. and Sapir, A. eds. (1995). *European Policies on Competition, Trade and Industry: Conflict and Complementarities*. Aldershot: Edward Elgar.

Bull. EC 4–1960. *A European policy on competition* by H. von der Groeben.

Bull. EC 12–1965. *Debate on the activities of the EEC*. Eighth General Report.

Bull. EC 1–1969. *The Community balance sheet and prospects* by J. Rey.

Bull. EC 4–1969. *The Commission's views on the transition to the period of the full implementation of the common market.*

Bull. EC 8–1969. *The Common Market after the end of the transitional period* by G.M. Thorn.

Bull. EC 8–1969. *Current Community problems* by H. von der Groeben.

Bull. EC 12–1969. *The major European political problems* by J. Rey.

Bull. EC 3–1970. *The Community's work programme for the seventies* by J. Rey.

Bull. EC 4–1970. *Active competition policy* by E. Sassen.

Bull. EC 4–1977. *Report on competition policy: The fundamental importance of competition policy and priorities for future action* by R. Vouel.

Bull. EC 9–1979. *Proposals for the reform of the Commission.*

Bull. EC 9–1979. *On institutional reform*. Statement by R. Jenkins.

Bull. EC 9–1984. *Guidelines on public authorities' holdings in company capital.*

Bull. EC 9–1984. *Application of Articles 92 and 93 of the EEC to public authorities' holdings.*

Bull. EC 1–1989. *Control measures*.

Bull. EC 11–1991. *Declaration of the Commission on the two Intergovernmental Conferences on Political Union and on Economic and Monetary Union*. (Discussions 23, 24, 27 November).

Bull. EC Supplement 5/75. *Report on European Union*.

Bull. EC Supplement 5/75. *Letter on the Commission's Report on European Union* by F. Ortoli.

Bull. EC Supplement 1/89. *Statement on the broad lines of Commission policy* by J. Delors.

Bull. EC Supplement 2/89. *The Commission's Programme for 1989: Implementing the Single Act*.

Bull. EC Supplement 2/91. *Compliance with the judgements of the Court of Justice*.

Bull. EC Supplement 1/92. *1992: A pivotal year* by J. Delors.

Butt Philip, A. (1983). Pressure Groups and Policy-making in the European Community. In J. Lodge, ed., *Institutions and Policies of the European Community*. London: Frances Pinter.

Butt Philip, A. (1987). Pressure Group Power in the European Community. *Intereconomics*. 22.6.

Butt Philip, A. (1988). The Application of the Transport Regulations by the Administrations of the Member States. In H. Siedentopf and J. Ziller, eds., *Making European Policies Work: The Implementation of Community Legislation in the Member States*, vol. I: *Comparative Synthesis*. London: Sage.

Butt Philip, A. and Baron, C. (1988). United Kingdom. In H. Siedentopf and J. Ziller, eds., *Making European Policies Work: The Implementation of Community Legislation in the Member States*, Vol. II: *National Reports*. London: Sage.

Button, K. and Swann, D. (1989). European Community Airlines: Deregulation and its Problems. *Journal of Common Market Studies*. 27.

Cameron, D.R. (1992). The 1992 Initiative: Causes and Consequences. In A. Sbragia, ed., *Europolitics: Institutions and Policymaking in the 'New' European Community*. Washington, DC: The Brookings Institution.

Carlsnaes, W. and Smith, S. eds. (1994). *European Foreign Policy: The EC and Changing Perspectives in Europe*. London: Sage.

Case 7/61 *Commission v. Italy* [1961] ECR 317.

Cases 6 and 11/69 *Commission v France* [1969] ECR 523.

Case 47/69 *France v Commission* [1970] ECR 487.

Case 62/70 *Bock v Commission* [1971] ECR 897.

Case 70/72 *Commission v Germany* [1973] ECR 813.

Case 173/73 *Italy v Commission* [1974] ECR 709.

Case 120/73 *Gebröder Lorenz GmbH v Germany and Land Rheinland /Pfalz* [1973] ECR 1471.

Case 40/75 *Produits Bertrand v Commission* [1976] ECR 1.

Cases 15 and 16/76 *France v Commission* [1979] ECR 321.

Case 26/76 *Metro-SB-Großmärkte GmbH & Co. KG v Commission* [1977] ECR 1875.

Case 78/76 *Firma Steinike und Weilig v Germany* [1977] ECR 595.

Cases 31 and 53/77R *Commission v United Kingdom* [1977] ECR 921.

Case 91/78 *Hansen v Haupzollamt Flensburg* [1979] ECR 935.

Case 61/79 *Amministrazione delle Finanze dello Stato v Denkavit Italiano Srl* [1980] ECR 1205.

Case 73/79 *Commission v Italy* [1980] ECR 1533.

Case 730/79 *Philip Morris Holland B.V. v Commission,* [1980] ECR 2671.

Cases 142 and 143/80 *Amministrazione delle Stato v Essevi and Salengo* [1981] ECR 1413.

Cases 188-190/80 *France, Italy, and United Kingdom v Commission* [1982] ECR 2545.

Cases 213-215/81 *Norddeutsches Vieh -und Fleischkontor v BALM* [1982] ECR 3583.

Cases 296 and 318/82 *Netherlands and Leeuwarder Pappierwarenfabriek BV v Commission* [1985] CMLR 380.

Case 249/81 *Commission v Ireland* [1982] ECR 4005.

Case 84/82 *Germany v Commission* [1984] ECR 1451.

Case 191/82 *FEDIOL v Commission* [1983] ECR 2913.

Case 323/82 *N.V.Intermills v Commission* [1984] ECR 3809.

Case 324/82 *Commission v Belgium* [1984] ECR 1861.

Case 52/83 *Commission v France* [1983] ECR 3707.

Case 223/83 *RSV v Commission* [1987] ECR 4617.

Case 290/83 *Commission v France* [1985] ECR 439.

Case 52/84 *Commission v Belgium* [1986] ECR 89.

Case 169/84 *Compangie Franγaise de l' Azote (COFAZ) and Others v Commission* [1986] ECR 408.

Case 234/84 *Belgium v. Commission* [1986] ECR 2263.

Case 248/84 *Germany v Commission* [1989] CMLR 591.

Case 67, 68 and 70/85 *Kwekerij Gebroeders Van der Kooy BV v Commission* [1989] CMLR 804.

Case 310/85 *Deufil v Commission* [1988] CMLR 553.

Case 5/86 *Commission v Belgium* [1988] CMLR 258.

Case 57/86 *Greece v Commission* [1990] CMLR 65.
Cases 166 and 220/86 *Irish Cement Limited v Commission* [1988] ECR 6473 at 6501.
Case 94/87 *Commission v Germany* [1989] CMLR 425.
Case C-142/87 *Belgium v Commission* [1990] ECR I-959.
Cases C-147/87R *Belgium v Commission* [1990] ECR I-959.
Case 227/87 *Commission v Greece* OJ 1988 C199/13.
Case C–301/87 *France v Commission (Boussac)* [1990] ECR I–307.
Case C–261/89 *Italy v Commission (Comsal)* [1991] ECR.
Case C-312/90 *Spain v Commission*, OJ 1990 C288/9.
Case C-354/90 *Fédération Nationale de Commérce Extérieur des Produits Alimentaires et Syndicat National des Négotiants et Transfernateurs de Saumon v France*, Preliminary Ruling 21 November 1991.
Caspari, M. (1988). The Aid Rules of the EEC Treaty and Their Application. In J. Schwarze, ed., *Discretionary Powers of the Member States in the Field of Economic Policies and Their Limits under the EEC Treaty*. Baden-Baden: Nomos Verlagsgesellschaft.
Chandler, A.D. Jr. (1962). *Strategy and Structure*. Cambridge, MA: MIT Press.
Chilcote, R.H. (1993). Portugal: From Popular Power to Bourgeois Democracy. In J. Kurth and J. Petras, eds., *Mediterranean Paradoxes: The Politics and Social Structure of Southern Europe*. Oxford: Berg.
Cline, W.R. (1986). US Trade and Industrial Policy: The Experience of Textiles, Steel, and Automobiles. In P.R. Krugman, ed., *Strategic Trade Policy and the New International Economics*. Cambridge, MA: MIT Press.
Cohen, E. (1996). Europe between Market and Power: Industrial Policies. In Y. Meny et al., eds., *Adjusting to Europe: The Impact of the European Union on National Institutions and Policies*. London: Routledge.
Colchester, N. and Buchan, D. (1990). *Europower: The Essential Guide to Europe's Economic Transformation in 1992*. New York: Random House.
Colliard, C.A. (1969). Les aides accordées par les États. In *Droit des Communautıs Européennes*, eds. W.J.Ganshof van der Meersch et al. Bruxelles: Maison Ferdinand Larcier.
COM(77) 338 final. *Communication from the Commission to the Council. Problems posed by excise harmonisation.* 27 July 1977.
COM(78) 221 final. *Communication from the Commission to the Council. Policy on sectoral aid schemes.*

COM(81) 581 final. *Relations between the institutions of the Community.* 7 October 1981.

COM(83) 80 final. *Assessment of the function of the internal market. Report by the Commission to the Council.* 24 February 1983.

COM(84) 181 final. *First Annual Report to the EP on Commission Monitoring of the Application of Community Law – 1983.* 20 April 1984.

COM(84) 305 final. *Consolidating the internal market. Communication from the Commission to the Council.* 13 June 1984.

COM(85) 149 final. *Second Annual Report to the EP on Commission Monitoring of the Application of Community Law – 1984.* 13 May 1985.

COM(85) 310 final. *Completing the internal market. White Paper from the Commission to the European Council.* (Milan, 28–29 June 1985). Brussels 14 June 1985.

COM(85) 350 final. *On general aid schemes.*

COM(86) 35 final. *Proposal for a Council Regulation (EEC) laying down the procedures for the exercise of implementing powers conferred on the Commission.* 3 March 1986. [OJ 1986 C70/6–7].

COM(86) 204 final. *Third Annual Report to the EP on Commission Monitoring of the Application of Community Law – 1985.* 3 June 1986. [OJ 1986 C220].

COM(86) 300 final. *First Report from the Commission to the Council and the EP on the implementation of the Commission's White Paper on completing the internal market.* 26 May 1986.

COM(87) 100 final. *Making a Success of the Single Act a New Frontier for Europe.* 15 February 1987.

COM(87) 203 final. *Second Report from the Commission to the Council and the European Parliament on the implementation of the Commission's White Paper on completing the internal market.* 11 May 1987.

COM(90) 600 final. *Commission Opinion of 21 October 1990 on the proposal for the amendment of the Treaty establishing the European Economic Community with a view to Political Union.* 23 October 1990.

COM(91) 321 final. *Eighth Annual Report to the EP on Commission Monitoring of the Application of Community Law – 1990.* [OJ 1991 C338].

COM(92) 136 final. *Ninth Annual Report to the EP on Commission Monitoring of the Application of Community Law – 1991.*

COM(93) 320 final. *Tenth Annual Report to the EP on Commission Monitoring of the Application of Community Law – 1992.*

COM(94) 218 final. *Commission communication: The Way Forward for Civil Aviation in Europe.*

COM(94) 500 final. *Eleventh Annual Report to the EP on Commission Monitoring of the Application of Community Law – 1993.*

COM(96) 90 final. *Reinforcing political union and preparing for enlargement: Commission opinion for the intergovernmental conference.*

COM(97) 0396. *Proposal for a Council Regulation on the application of Articles 92 and 93 of the EC Treaty to certain categories of horizontal state aid.*

COM(98) 73 final. *Proposal for a Council Regulation laying down detailed rules for the application of Article 93 of the EC Treaty.*

Commission of the EC. (1962). *Report on the Execution of the Treaty: January 1958–January 1962*, Secretariat S/01770/62rev, Brussels, mimeo.

Commission of the EC. (1971). *Fifth General Report on the activities of the European Communities.* Luxembourg: Office for Official Publications of the European Communities.

Commission of the EC. (1972). *First Report on Competition Policy 1971.* Luxembourg: Office for Official Publications of the European Communities.

Commission of the EC. (1977). *Sixth Report on Competition Policy 1976.* Luxembourg: OOPEC.

Commission of the EC. (1981). *Tenth Report on Competition Policy 1980.* Luxembourg: OOPEC.

Commission of the EC. (1985). *Fourteenth Report on Competition Policy 1984.* Luxembourg: OOPEC.

Commission of the EC. (1986). *Fifteenth Report on Competition Policy 1985.* Luxembourg: OOPEC.

Commission of the EC. (1987). *Efficiency, Stability and Equity: A Strategy for the Evolution of the Economic System of the European Community* (T. Padoa-Schioppa Report). Luxembourg: OOPEC.

Commission of the EC. (1988). *The European Challenge 1992: The Benefits of a Single Market* (P. Cecchini Report). Luxembourg: OOPEC.

Commission of the EC. (1988b). *Seventeenth Report on Competition Policy 1987.* Luxembourg: OOPEC.

Commission of the EC. (1989a). *Eighteenth Report on Competition Policy 1988*. Luxembourg: OOPEC.

Commission of the EC. (1989b). *First Survey on State Aid in the European Community in the Manufacturing and Certain Other Sectors*. Luxembourg: OOPEC.

Commission of the EC. (1989c). *Operations of the European Community Concerning Small and Medium-Sized Enterprises: Ireland*. Luxembourg: OOPEC.

Commission of the EC. (1990a). *Nineteenth Report on Competition Policy 1989*. Luxembourg: OOPEC.

Commission of the EC. (1990b). *Second Survey on State Aid in the EC in the Manufacturing and Certain Other Sectors*. Luxembourg: OOPEC.

Commission of the EC. (1991). *Twentieth Report on Competition Policy 1990*. Luxembourg: OOPEC.

Commission of the EC. (1992a). *Twenty-First Report on Competition Policy 1991*. Luxembourg: OOPEC.

Commission of the EC. (1992b). *Third Survey on State Aid in the European Community*. Luxembourg: OOPEC.

Commission of the EC. (1992c). *Competition Policy in the European Community*. European File series. Luxembourg: OOPEC.

Commission of the EC. (1993a). *Twenty-Second Report on Competition Policy 1992*. Luxembourg: OOPEC.

Commission of the EC. (1993b). *Notice on the co-operation between national courts and the Commission in applying Articles 85 and 86 of the EC Treaty*. OJ 1993 C39.

Commission of the EC. (1995). *Fourth Survey on State Aid in the European Union*. Luxembourg: OOPEC.

Commission of the EC. (1996). *Twenty-Fifth Report on Competition Policy 1995*. Luxembourg: OOPEC.

Commission of the EC. (1997a). *Twenty-Sixth Report on Competition Policy 1996*. Luxembourg: OOPEC.

Commission of the EC. (1997b). *Fifth Survey on State Aid in the European Union*. Luxembourg: OOPEC.

Commons, J.R. (1934). *Institutional Economics*. New York: Macmillan.

Competition Policy Newsletter. Commission of the EC (1995–). Various issues.

Connolly, W.E. (1983). *The Terms of Political Discourse*. Second edition. Princeton: Princeton University Press.

Coriat, B. (1995a). Organizational Innovations: The Missing Link in European Competitiveness. In L.E. Andreasen et al., eds., *Europe's*

Next Step: Organisational Innovation, Competition and Employment. London: Frank Cass.

Coriat, B. (1995b). Organizational Routines and Competitiveness in the Auto Industry: The Case of Peugeot SA. In L.E. Andreasen et al., eds., *Europe's Next Step: Organisational Innovation, Competition and Employment.* London: Frank Cass.

Council of Ministers. *Directive 81/363/EEC on aid to shipbuilding.* OJ 1981 L137/39.

Council of Ministers. *Directive 85/2/EEC on aid to shipbuilding.* OJ 1985 L2.

Council of Ministers. *Directive 87/167/EEC on aid to shipbuilding.* OJ 1987 L69.

Council of Ministers. *Framework on general systems of regional aid.* 20 October 1971. OJ 1971 C111. Resolution.

Council of Ministers. *Regulation 17/62 for the application of competition rules to private enterprises Articles 85 and 86 of the EEC Treaty.* OJ 1962 204.

Council of Ministers. *Regulation 26/62 on the application of Articles 40–43 of the EEC Treaty for state aids in agriculture.* OJ 1962 993.

Council of Ministers. *Regulation 3094/95 on aid to shipbuilding.* OJ 1995 L 332.

Council of Ministers. *Regulation 2600/97 on aid to certain shipyards under restructuring.* OJ 1997 L 351.

Council of Ministers. *Resolution on a new approach to technical harmonization and standards.* OJ 1985 C136.

Cownie, F. (1986). State Aids in the Eighties. *European Law Review.* 2.

Cullen, P. and Yannopoulos, G. (1989). The Redistribution of Regulatory Powers between Governments and International Organizations: The Case of European Airline Deregulation. *European Journal of Political Research.* 17.

Curtin, D. (1990a). Directives: The Effectiveness of Judicial Protection of Individual Rights. *Common Market Law Review.* 27.

Curtin, D. (1990b). The Province of Government: Delimiting the Direct Effect of Directives in the Common Law Context. *European Law Review.* 15.

Curtin, D. (1992a). The Decentralised Enforcement of Community Law Rights: Judicial Snakes and Ladders. In D. Curtin and D. O'Keeffe, eds., *Constitutional Adjudication in the EC and National Law.* Dublin: Butterworth.

Curtin, D. (1992b). State Liability under Community Law: A New Remedy for Private Parties. *Industrial Law Journal.* 21.

Curtin, D. (1993). The Constitutional Structure of the Union: A Europe of Bits and Pieces. *Common Market Law Review.* 30.

Curtin, D. and O'Keeffe, D. eds. (1992). *Constitutional Adjudication in European Community and National Law.* Dublin: Butterworth.

Cusumano, M.A. (1990). *The Japanese Automobile Industry: Technology and Management at Nissan and Toyota.* Cambridge, MA: Harvard University Press.

Daalder, H. (1983). The Comparative Study of European Parties and Party Systems: An Overview. In H. Daalder and P. Mair, eds., *Western European Party Systems: Continuity and Change.* London: Sage.

Dahl, R.A. (1985). *A Preface to Economic Democracy.* Cambridge: Polity Press.

Dashwood, A. and White, R. (1989). Enforcement Actions under Articles 169 and 170 EEC. *European Law Review.* 14.

Dauderstädt, M. (1988). Schwacher Staat und schwacher Markt: Portugals Wirtschaftspolitik zwischen Abhängigkeit und Modernisierung. *Politische Vierteljahresschrift.* 29.

Decision 73/287/ECSC concerning coal and coke for the iron and steel industry in the Community. OJ 1973 L259.

Decision 3544/73/ECSC for the implementation of Decision 73/287/ECSC. OJ 1973 L361.

Decision 2320/81/ECSC on the restructuring of the steel industry. OJ 1981 L228.

Decision 3484/85/ECSC establishing Community rules for aid to the steel industry. OJ 1985 L340.

Decision 145/85/ECSC amending Decision 3544/73/ECSC. OJ 1985 L16.

Decision 3612/85/ECSC amending Decision 73/287/ECSC. OJ 1985 L344.

Decision 2064/86/ECSC establishing Community rules for state aid to the coal industry. OJ 1986 L177.

Decision 322/89/ECSC establishing Community rules for aid to the steel industry. OJ 1989 L38.

Delors, J. (1990). Bull. EC Supplement 1/90.

Deringer, A. (1963). The Distribution of Powers in the Enforcement of the Rules of Competition under the Rome Treaty. *Common Market Law Review.* 1.

Dertouzos, M.L., Lester, R. and Solow, R. eds. (1989). *Made in America: Regaining the Productive Edge.* Cambridge, MA: MIT Press.

Dinan, D. (1994). *Ever Closer Union? An Introduction to the European Community*. London: Macmillan.

Doganis, R. (1991). *Flying Off Course: The Economics of International Airlines*. London: HarperCollins.

Donner, A.M. (1963). National Law and the Case Law of the Court of Justice of the European Communities. *Common Market Law Review*. 1.

Donner, A.M. (1974). The Constitutional Powers of the Court of Justice of the European Communities. *Common Market Law Review*. 11.

Dore, R. (1986). *Flexible Rigidities: Industrial Policy and Structural Adjustment in the Japanese Economy 1970-80.* Stanford: Stanford University Press.

Dumez, H. and Jeunemaitre, A. (1994). Political Intervention versus l'Etat de droit économique: The Issue of Convergence of Competition Policies in Europe. *Essays in Regulation*. 5.

Dyson, K. (1990). *Small and Medium Size Enterprises*. London: Routledge in association with the University of Bradford and Spicers Centre for Europe Ltd.

Economist, The, various dates.

Economist Intelligence Unit, *Country Reports*.

Ehlermann, C.D. (1990). Commission Lacks Power in 1992 Process. *European Affairs*. 4.

Ehlermann, C.D. (1992). The Contribution of EC Competition Policy to the Single Market. *Common Market Law Review*. 29.

Ehlermann, C.D. (1993a). Managing Monopolies: The Role of the State in Controlling Market Dominance in the European Community. *European Competition Law Review*. 2.

Ehlermann, C.D. (1993b). Politique Actuelle de la Commission en Matiere de Concurrence. *Revue du Marche Commun et de l'Union Européenne*. 371.

Ehlermann, C.D. (1995). *State Aid Control: Failure or Success?* Text of a Speech, 18 January 1995.

Ehlermann, C.D. and Pipkorn, J. (1987). The Role of the Commission in Preliminary Proceedings under Article 177 EEC. In H.G. Schermers, C.W.A. Timmermans, A.E. Kellermann and J. Stewart Watson, eds., *Article 177 EEC: Experiences and Problems*. Amsterdam: North-Holland.

Emerson, M. et. al. (1988). *The Economics of 1992*. Oxford: Oxford University Press.

EP Debates. Various dates.

EP Doc. 1–387/81/A. *Motion for Resolution by Cattrell and Forth in accordance with Art. 47 of the Statute in respect to infringements of the ECJ and especially concerning the Italian Republic.* 8 July 1981.

EP Doc. 1–598/81/A. *Motion for Resolution on the establishment of the internal market.* von Wogau Report. OJ 1981 C287/63–5.

EP Doc. 1–608/81. *Resolution on competition policy, national aids and non-tariff barriers.* OJ 1981 C287/61–2.

EP Doc. 1–610/81. *Resolution on competition policy, national aids and non-tariff barriers.* OJ 1981 C287/63.

EP Doc. 1–1017/81/A. *Resolution on the blockage of Italian wines in France.* 18 February 1982. OJ 1982 C66/61–2.

EP Doc. 1–1046/81. *Report drawn on behalf of the Legal Affairs Committee on the maintenance of the internal market as a market of a Community ruled by law, by Mr von Wogau and others.* 18 March 1982.

EP Doc. 1–267/82. *Report drawn on behalf of the Legal Affairs Committee on the fulfilment of the obligations arising out of the EEC Treaty,* by Mr Pearce. 13 July 1982.

EP Doc. 1–1200/83/A. *Resolution on the Preliminary draft Treaty establishing the European Union.* Spinelli Report. OJ 1984 C77.

EP Doc. A 2–23/89/A. *Resolution on the decision granting discharge to the Commission in respect of the implementation of the general budget of the European Communities for the financial year 1987.* 23 March 1989.

EP Doc. A3–163/90. *Resolution on the principle of subsidiarity.* 12 July 1990. OJ 1990 C231/163–5.

EP Resolutions 1–608/81, OJ 1981 C287; 1–610/81, OJ 1981 C287.

Evans, A.C. (1979). The Enforcement Procedure of Article 169 EEC: Commission Discretion. *European Law Review.* 4.

Faull, J. (1994). More Questions and Answers About State Aid. *Competition Policy Newsletter.* 1/3.

Fejo, J. (1989). *Monopoly Law and Market.* Amsterdam: Kluwer.

Financial Times, various dates.

Fligstein, N. (1990). *The Transformation of Corporate Control.* Cambridge, MA: Harvard University Press.

Flynn, J. (1981). Force Majeure Pleas in Proceedings Before the European Court. *European Law Review.* 6.

Flynn, J. (1983). State Aid and Self-help. *European Law Review.* 8.

Flynn, J. (1987). State Aids: Recent Case Law of the European Court. *European Law Review.* 12.

Foster, J. (1991). The Institutionalist (Evolutionary) School. In D. Mair and A. Miller, eds., *A Modern Guide to Economic Thought*. Aldershot: Edward Elgar.

Frazer, T. (1990). Competition Policy After 1992: The Next Step. *Modern Law Review*. 53.

Fromont, M. (1988). State Aids: Their Field of Operation and Legal Regime. In T. Daintith, ed., *Law as an Instrument of Economic Policy: Comparative and Critical Approaches*. Berlin: Walter de Gruyter.

Garrett, G. (1992). International Cooperation and Institutional Choice: The European Community's Internal Market. *International Organization*. 46.

Garrett, G. and Weingast, B. (1993). Ideas, Interests, and Institutions: Constructing the European Community's Internal Market. In J. Goldstein and R. Keohane, eds., *Ideas and Foreign Policy: Beliefs, Institutions and Political Change*. Ithaca: Cornell University Press.

George, S. (1990). *An Awkward Partner: Britain in the European Community*. Oxford: Oxford University Press.

George, S. (1991). *Politics and Policy in the European Community*. Second edition. Oxford: Oxford University Press.

George, S. (1996). The European Union: Approaches from International Relations. In H. Kassim and A. Menon, eds., *The European Union and National Industrial Policy*. London: Routledge.

Gerschenkron, A. (1962). *Economic Backwardness in Historical Perspective*. Cambridge, MA: Harvard University Press.

Gilchrist, J. and Deacon, D. (1990). Curbing Subsidies. In P. Montagnon, ed., *European Competition Policy*. London: Pinter.

Gilmour, D.R. (1981). The Enforcement of Community Law by the Commission in the Context of State Aids: The Relationship Between Articles 93 and 169 and the Choice of Remedies. *Common Market Law Review*. 18.

Grant, W. (1993). *The Politics of Economic Policy*. London: Harvester Wheatsheaf.

Green, N., Hartley, T.C. and Usher, J.A. (1991). *The Legal Foundation of the Single European Market*. Oxford: Oxford University Press.

Greenwood, J. (1997). *Representing Interests in the European Union*. London: Macmillan.

Greenwood, J., Grote, J.R. and Ronit, K. (1992). Conclusions: Evolving Patterns of Organizing Interests in the European Community. In J. Greenwood, J. Grote and K. Ronit, eds., *Organized Interests in the European Community*. London: Sage.

von der Groeben, H. (1960). A European Policy on Competition. *Bull. EC* 4–1960.

Grote, J.R. (1992). Small Firms in the European Community: Modes of Production, Governance and Territorial Interest Representation in Italy and Germany. In J. Greenwood, J.R. Grote and K. Ronit, eds., *Organized Interests and the European Community*. London: Sage.

Groves, P.J. (1995). Whatevershebringswesing: DG IV Rebukes the Car Industry. *European Competition Law Review*. 2.

Haas, E.B. (1958). *The Uniting of Europe*. Stanford: Stanford University Press.

Haas, E.B. (1961). International Integration: The European and the Universal Process. *International Organization*. 15.

Hall, J.A. (1985). *Powers and Liberties: The Causes and Consequences of the Rise of the West*. Oxford: Basil Blackwell.

Hall, P. (1986). *Governing the Economy: The Politics of State Intervention in Britain and France*. New York: Oxford University Press.

Hall, P. (1993). Policy Paradigms, Social Learning, and the State. *Comparative Politics*. 25.

Halliday, F. (1994). *Rethinking International Relations*. London: Macmillan.

Hancher, L. (1996). The Regulatory Role of the European Union. In H. Kassim and A. Menon, eds., *The European Union and National Industrial Policy*. London: Routledge.

Hancher, L. and Moran, M. (1989). Organizing Regulatory Space. In L. Hancher and M. Moran, eds., *Capitalism, Culture and Economic Regulation*. Oxford: Clarendon Press.

Hancher, L., Ottervanger, T. and Slot, P.J. (1993). *EC State Aids*. Chichester: Chancery Law Publishing.

Hanf, K. (1982). Regulatory Structures: Enforcement as Implementation. *European Journal of Political Research*. 10.

Harrop, J. (1992). *The Political Economy of Integration in the European Community*. Second edition. Aldershot: Edward Elgar.

Hellingman, K. (1986). State Participation as State Aid under Article 92 of the EEC Treaty: The Commission's Guidelines. *Common Market Law Review*. 23.

Henig, S. (1983). The European Community's Bicephalous Political Authority. In J. Lodge, ed., *Institutions and Policies of the European Community*. London: Pinter.

Hodges, M. (1983). Industrial Policy: Hard Times or Great Expectations? In H. Wallace, W. Wallace and C. Webb, eds., *Policy-Making in the European Community*, second eition. Chichester: Wiley.

Hodges, M. and Woolcock, S. (1993). Atlantic Capitalism versus Rhine Capitalism in the European Community. *West European Politics.* 16.

Hodgson, G.M. (1988). *Economics and Institutions: A Manifesto for a New Institutional Economics.* Cambridge: Polity Press.

Holmes, P. and Kempton, J. (1996). EU Anti-dumping Policy: A Regulatory Perspective. *Journal of European Public Policy.* 3.

Holmes, P. and McGowan, F. (1997). The Changing Dynamic of EU-Industry Relations: Lessons from the Liberalization of European Car and Airline Markets. In H. Wallace and A.R. Young, eds., *Participation and Policy-Making in the European Union.* Oxford: Clarendon Press.

Holmes, P. and Smith, A. (1995). Automobile Industry. In P. Buigues, A. Jacquemin and A. Sapir, eds., *European Policies on Competition, Trade and Industry: Conflict and Complementarities.* Aldershot: Edward Elgar.

Hornsby, S.B. (1987). Competition Policy in the 80s: More Policy Less Competition? *European Law Review.* 12.

House of Lords. Select Committee on European Communities. (1998). *Twenty-Third Report.* 12 May 1998.

Humphrey, T. (1983). Introduction. In I. Kant, *Perpetual Peace and Other Essays*, translated and with an introduction by T. Humphrey. Indianapolis: Hackett.

Ikenberry, J.G. (1986). The Irony of State Strength: Comparative Responses to the Oil Shocks in the 1970s. *International Organization.* 40.

International Herald Tribune, various dates.

Ionescu, G. ed. (1979). *The European Alternatives: An Inquiry into the Policies of the European Community.* Alphen aan den Rijn: Sijthoff & Noordhoff.

Jacobsen, J.K. (1995). Much Ado about Ideas: The Cognitive Factor in Economic Policy. *World Politics.* 47.

Jacobsen, J.K. (1996). Are All Politics Domestic? Perspectives on the Integration of Comparative Politics and International Relations Theories. *Comparative Politics.* 29.

Jacquemin, A. and Wright, D. (1993). *The European Challenges Post-1992: Shaping Factors, Shaping Actors.* Aldershot: Edward Elgar.

Jenkins, R. (1989). *European Diary 1977–1981.* London: Collins.

Johnson, C. (1982). *MITI and the Japanese Miracle: The Growth of Industrial Policy, 1925–1975*. Stanford: Stanford University Press.

Joliet, P. (1981). Cartelisation, Dirigisme and Crisis in the European Community. *The World Economy.*

Jones, D.T. (1992). The Car Industry. In D. Dyker, ed., *The European Economy*. London: Longman.

de Jong, H.W. (1982). Reflections on the Economic Crisis: Markets, Competition and Welfare. In *Essays in European Law and Integration*, eds. O'Keeffe and H.G. Schermers. Deventer: Kluwer.

Jordan, J. (1975). State Aids: The Compatibility of Regional Aid Systems with the Common Market. *European Law Review*. 1.

Kassim, H. (1995). Air Transport Champions: Still Carrying the Flag. In J. Hayward, ed., *Industrial Enterprise and European Integration: From National to International Champions in Western Europe*. Oxford: Oxford University Press.

Kassim, H. and Menon, A. eds. (1996). *The European Union and National Industrial Policy*. London: Routledge.

Keating, M. (1993). *The Politics of Modern Europe: The State and Political Authority in the Major Democracies*. Aldershot: Edward Elgar.

Kemp, T. (1983). *Industrialization in the Non-Western World*. London: Longman.

Kenis, P. and Schneider, V. (1987). The EC as An International Corporate Actor: Two Case Studies in Economic Diplomacy. *European Journal of Political Research*. 15.

Keohane, R. and Hoffmann, S. (1991). Institutional Change in Europe in the 1980s. In R. Keohane and S. Hoffmann, eds., *The New European Community*. Boulder, Co: Westview Press.

Kirchner, E.J. (1992). *Decision-Making in the European Community: The Council Presidency and European Integration*. Manchester: Manchester University Press.

Koopmans, T. (1986). The Role of Law in the Next Stage of European Integration. *International and Comparative Law Quarterly*. 35.

Krislov, S., Ehlermann, C.D. and Weiler, J.H. (1986). The Political Organs and the Decision-Making Process in the United States and the European Community. In M. Cappelletti et al., eds., *Integration through Law: Methods, Tools and Institutions*. Berlin: de Gruyter.

Krugman, P.R. ed. (1986). *Strategic Trade Policy and the New International Economics*. Cambridge, MA: MIT Press.

Kuypers, P.J. and T.P.J.N. van Rijns. (1982). Procedural guarantees and investigatory methods in European law, with special reference to competition. *Yearbook of European Law*. 2

Ladrech, R. (1994). Europeanization of Domestic Politics and Institutions: The Case of France. *Journal of Common Market Studies*. 32.

Lafontaine, O. and Müller, C. (1998). *Keine Angst vor der Globalisierung: Wohlstand und Arbeit für alle*. Berlin: Dietz.

Lambert, J. (1966). The Constitutional Crisis 1965–66. *Journal of Common Market Studies*. 4.

Lanza, O. and Lavdas, K. (1997). *The Disentanglement of Interest Politics: Business Associability, the Parties and Policy in Italy and Greece*. Paper for the Workshop on 'Clientelist Politics and Interest Intermediation in Southern Europe', ECPR Joint Sessions, Bern.

Lasok, K.P.E. (1986). State Aids and Remedies Under the EEC Treaty. *European Competition Law Review*. 7.

Lasok, K.P.E. (1990). The Commission's Power Over Illegal State Aids. *European Competition Law Review*. 3.

Lavdas, K. (1992). The Impact of European Community Membership on Domestic Government-Business Relations. Mimeo, University of Manchester, UK.

Lavdas, K. (1995). Crises of Integration: Theorization and Institutional Change in European Integration. *Insight*. 8.

Lavdas, K. (1996). The Political Economy of Privatization in Southern Europe. In: D. Braddon and D. Foster, eds., *Privatization*. Aldershot: Dartmouth.

Lavdas, K. (1997). *The Europeanization of Greece: Interest Politics and the Crises of Integration*. London: Macmillan.

Lavdas, K. ed. (forthcoming). *Junctures of Stateness: Political Boundaries and Policy Change in Southern Europe*. Aldershot: Ashgate.

Lavdas, K. and Mendrinou, M. (1994). Competition Policy and Small Business in the European Community. *UWE Working Papers in Politics*. 3.

Lavdas, K. and Mendrinou, M. (1995). Competition Policy and Institutional Politics in the European Community: State Aid Control and Small Business Promotion. *European Journal of Political Research*. 28.

Lee, N. (1994). Transport Policy. In M.J. Artis and N. Lee, eds., *The Economics of the European Union*. Oxford: Oxford University Press

Lehner, S. and Meiklejohn, R. (1991). Fair Competition in the Internal Market: Community State Aid Policy. *European Economy*. 48.

Lodge, J. ed. (1989). *The European Community and the Challenge of the Future*. London: Pinter.

Lodge, J. (1994). Transparency and Democratic Legitimacy. *Journal of Common Market Studies*. 32.

Lowi, T.J. (1972). Four Systems of Policy, Politics and Choice. *Public Administration Review*. 32.

Machin, H. (1990). Introduction. In P. Hall et al. eds., *Developments in French Politics*. London: Macmillan.

Majone, G. (1989). Regulating Europe: Problems and Prospects. *Jahrbuch zur Staats- und Verwaltungswissenschaft*. 3.

Majone, G. (1990). *Deregulation or Reregulation? Regulatory Reform in Europe*. London: Pinter.

Majone, G. (1994). The Rise of the Regulatory State in Europe. *West European Politics*. 17.

Mancini, G.F. (1991). The Making of a Constitution for Europe. In R.O. Keohane and S. Hoffmann, eds., *The New European Community*. Boulder, Co: Westview Press.

March, J.G. and Olsen, J.P. (1984). The New Institutionalism: Organizational Factors in Political Life. *American Political Science Review*. 78.

March, J.G. and Olsen, J.P. (1989). *Rediscovering Institutions*. New York: Free Press.

Marks, G. (1993). Structural Policy and Multilevel Governance in the EC. In A.W. Cafruny and G.G. Rosenthal, eds., *The State of the European Community*. Vol. 2. Harlow: Longman.

Marks, G., Scharpf, F. Schmitter, P.C. and Streeck, W. (1996). *Governance in the European Union*. London: Sage.

Marx, K. (1973). *Grundrisse*, translated with a foreword by M. Nicolaus. Harmondsworth: Pelican.

Mathijsen, P.S.R.F. (1972). State Aids, State Monopolies and Public Enterprises in the Common Market. *Law and Contemporary Problems*. 37.

Mathijsen, P.S.R.F. (1990). *A Guide to European Community Law*. Fifth edition. London: Sweet and Maxwell.

Mazey, S. and Richardson, J.J. (1992). British Pressure Groups and the Challenge of Brussels. *Parliamentary Affairs*. 45.

Mazey, S. and Richardson, J.J. eds. (1993a). *Lobbying in the European Community*. Oxford: Oxford University Press.

Mazey, S. and Richardson, J.J. (1993b). Conclusion: A European Policy Style? In S. Mazey and J.J. Richardson, eds., *Lobbying in the European Community*. Oxford: Oxford University Press.

McGowan, F. (1993). Ownership and Competition in Community Markets. In C. Clarke and C. Pitelis, eds., *The Political Economy of Privatization*. London: Routledge.

McGowan, L. and Wilks, S. (1995). The First Supranational Policy in the European Union: Competition Policy. *European Journal of Political Research.* 28.

Mederer, W. (1996). The Future of State Aid Control. *Competition Policy Newsletter.* 2/3.

Mendrinou, M. (1990). *An Examination of the Relations between the European Community and Member States through the Issue of Fraud.* Master's diss., Brandeis University, USA.

Mendrinou, M. (1992). State Compliance, Monitoring and Institutional Development in European Integration. Mimeo, University of Manchester, UK.

Mendrinou, M. (1994). European Community Fraud and the Politics of Institutional Development. *European Journal of Political Research.* 26.

Mendrinou, M. (1996). Non-Compliance and the European Commission's Role in Integration. *Journal of European Public Policy.* 3.

Mendrinou, M. (forthcoming). *Integration and Enforcement: Policy Priorities and Institutional Development in European Integration.* Oxford: Oxford University Press.

Menon, A. and Hayward, J. (1996). States, Industrial Policies and the European Union. In H. Kassim and A. Menon, eds., *The European Union and National Industrial Policy*. London: Routledge.

Meny, Y. et al., eds. (1996). *Adjusting to Europe: The Impact of the European Union on National Institutions and Policies.* London: Routledge.

Midler, C. (1995). Organizational Innovation in Project Management: The Renault Twingo Case. In L.E. Andreasen et al., eds., *Europe's Next Step: Organisational Innovation, Competition and Employment.* London: Frank Cass.

Mitsos, A. (1992). A New Role for the Structural Funds? In A. Pijpers, ed., *The European Community at the Crossroads*. Dordrecht: Martinus Nijhoff.

Montagnon, P. ed. (1990). *European Competition Policy*. London: Pinter.

Moran, M. (1991). *The Politics of the Financial Services Revolution.* London: Macmillan.

Moran, M. and Prosser, T. eds. (1994). *Privatization and Regulatory Change in Europe.* Buckingham: Open University Press.

Moravcsik, A. (1993). Preferences and Power in the European Community: A Liberal Intergovernmentalist Approach. *Journal of Common Market Studies.* 31.

Mortelmans, K.J.M. (1979). Observations in Cases Governed by Article 177 of the EEC Treaty: Procedure and Practice. *Common Market Law Review.* 16.

Mortelmans, K.J.M. (1984). The Compensatory Justification Criterion in the Practice of the Commission in Decisions on State Aids. *Common Market Law Review.* 21.

Mortelmans, K.J.M. (1987a). Short and Long-term Objectives and the Choice of Instruments and Measures. In T.C. Daintith, ed., *Law as an Instrument of Economic Policy: Comparative and Critical Approaches.* Berlin: de Gruyter.

Mortelmans, K.J.M. (1987b). The Role of Government Representatives in the Proceedings: Statistical Data on the Observations of the Member States in Preliminary Proceedings. In H.G. Schermers, W.A. immermans, A.E. Kellermann and J. Stewart-Watson, eds., *Article 177 EEC: Experiences and Problems.* Amsterdam: North-Holland.

Moussis, N. (1992). *Access to Europe: Guide to Community Policies.* Second edition. Brussels: Edit-Eur.

Müller, W. and Wright, V. eds. (1994). The State in Western Europe: Retreat or Redefinition? *West European Politics.* 17, Special Issue.

Neunreither, K. (1994). The Syndrom of Democratic Deficit in the European Community. In G. Parry, ed., *Politics in an Interdependent World: Essays Presented to Ghita Ionescu.* Aldershot: Edward Elgar.

Niejahr, M. and Abbamonte, G. (1996). Liberalization Policy and State Aid in the Air Transport Sector. *Competition Policy Newsletter.* 2/2.

North, D.C. (1981). *Structure and Change in Economic History.* New York: Norton.

Obradovic, D. (1995). Prospects for Corporatist Decision-making in the European Union: The Social Policy Agreement. *Journal of European Public Policy.* 2.

OJ 1971 C 111/1. *Communication to the Council on general aid schemes.*

OJ 1975 C 153/1. *Council of Ministers. Resolution.*

OJ 1979 C 31/9. *Communication to the Member States on the application of regional aid schemes.*

OJ 1980 C 252/2. *The Notification of State Aids to the Commission pursuant to Art. 93(3) of the EEC Treaty: The Failure of Member States to respect their Obligations.*

OJ 1980 L 195/35–7. *First Directive on the transparency of financial relations between member states and their public undertakings.*

OJ 1983 C 318/3. *Communication on aids granted illegally.*

OJ 1985 C 3. *Communication on the rules applicable to cases of cumulation of aids for different purposes.*

OJ 1985 C 17. *Commission Notice concerning Regulation (EEC) No. 123/85 of 12 December 1984 on the application of Art. 85(3) of the Treaty to certain categories of motor vehicle distribution and servicing agreements.*

OJ 1985 L 229/20. *Second Directive on the transparency of financial relations between member states and their public undertakings.*

OJ 1987 C 82/2. *Commission's policy statement: On the risks of recipients of illegally granted aids.*

OJ 1988 C 212. *Communication on the method for the application of Art. 92(3)(a) and (c) to regional aid.*

OJ 1989 C 123. *Community framework on state aids to the motor vehicle industry.*

OJ 1989 C 173. *Communication on the situation in the synthetic fibres industry.*

OJ 1990 C 40. *Commission Guidelines on the notification of aid schemes of minor importance.*

OJ 1990 C 130/9–11. *Notice N340/89 on the review of 'new' state aids.*

OJ 1990 L 380. *Seventh Directive on Aid to Shipbuilding (Directive 90/684/EEC).*

OJ 1992 C 213. *Guidelines to the granting of aid to SMEs.*

OJ 1994 C 350. *Application of Articles 92 and 93 of the EC Treaty and Article 61 of the EEA agreement to State aids in the aviation sector.*

OJ 1994 L 273. *Commission Decision of 7 October 1994, Case C14/94, Olympic Airways.*

OJ 1996 C 281. *Services of general interest in Europe.*

OJ 1997 C 279/1. *Community Framework for State Aid to the Motor Vehicle Industry.*

OJ 1998 C 116. *Proposal for a Regulation (EC) laying down detailed rules for the application of Article 93 of the EC Treaty.*

Osborne, R. (1991). *Conversations with Karajan.* Oxford: Oxford University Press.

Pempel, T.J. (1982). *Policy and Politics in Japan: Creative Conservatism.* Philadelphia: Temple University Press.

Pescatore, P. (1974). *The Law of Integration.* Leiden: A.W. Sijthoff.

Peters, B.G. (1992). Bureaucratic Politics and the Institutions of the European Community. In A.M. Sbragia, ed., *Europolitics: Institutions and Policymaking in the 'New' European Community.* Washington, DC: The Brookings Institution.

Peters, B.G. (1994). Agenda-setting in the European Community. *Journal of European Public Policy.* 1.

Peterson, J. (1996). *Europe and America: The Prospects for Partnership.* Second edition. London: Routledge.

Pijnacker Hordijk, E.H. (1985). Judicial Protection of Private Interests under the EEC Competition Rules Relating to State Aids. *Legal Issues of European Integration.* 1.

Pinder, D.A. (1986). Small Firms, Regional Development and the European Investment Bank. *Journal of Common Market Studies.* 24.

Piore, M.J. and Sabel, C.F. (1984). *The Second Industrial Divide: Possibilities of Prosperity.* New York: Basic Books.

Pollack, M. (1994). Creeping Competence: The Expanding Agenda of the European Community. *Journal of Public Policy.* 14.

Pons, J.F. (1998). Innovation and Competition: A View from the European Commission. *Competition Policy Newsletter.* 1998/1.

Puchala, D. (1975). Domestic Politics and Regional Harmonization in the European Communities. *World Politics.* 27.

Rasmussen, H. (1986). *On Law and Policy in the European Court of Justice.* Dordrecht: Martinus Nijhoff.

Rasmussen, H. (1988). Between Self-Restraint and Activism: A Judicial Policy for the European Court. *European Law Review.* 13.

Richardson, J.J. ed. (1982). *Policy Styles in Western Europe.* London: Allen & Unwin.

Richardson, J.J. (1996a). Eroding EU Policies: Implementation Gaps, Cheating and Resteering. In J.J. Richardson, ed., *European Union: Power and Policy-Making.* London: Routledge.

Richardson, J.J. (1996b). Actor-based Models of National and EU Policy Making. In H. Kassim and A. Menon, eds., *The European Union and National Industrial Policy.* London: Routledge.

Richardson, J.J. and Jordan, G. (1979). *Governing Under Pressure: The Policy Process in a Post-Parliamentary Democracy.* Oxford: Martin Robertson.

Risse-Kappen, T. (1994). The Long-Term Future of European Security: Perpetual Anarchy or Community of Democracies?. In W. Carlsnaes and S. Smith, eds., *European Foreign Policy: The EC and Changing Perspectives in Europe*. London: Sage.

Rometsch, D. and Wessels, W. eds. (1996). *The European Union and Member States: Towards Institutional Fusion?* Manchester: Manchester University Press.

Ross, G. (1992). Confronting the New Europe. *New Left Review.* 191.

Ross, G. (1995). *Jacques Delors and European integration*. Cambridge: Polity Press.

Ross, M. (1986). Challenging State Aids: The Effect of Recent Developments. *Common Market Law Review.* 23.

Ross, M. (1989). A Review of Developments in State Aids 1987–88. *Common Market Law Review.* 26.

Rueschemeyer, D. (1986). *Power and the Division of Labour*. Cambridge: Polity Press.

Ryan, A. (1984). *Property and Political Theory*. Oxford: Basil Blackwell.

Sabel, C.F. (1982). *Work and Politics: The Division of Labour in Industry*. Cambridge: Cambridge University Press.

Sabel, C.F. and Zeitlin, J. (1985). Historical Alternatives to Mass Production: Politics, Markets and Technology in Nineteenth-Century Industrialization. *Past and Present.* 108.

Samuels, R.J. (1983). *The Politics of Regional Policy in Japan: Localities, Incorporated?* Princeton: Princeton University Press.

Samuels, R.J. (1987). *The Business of the Japanese State: Energy Markets in Comparative and Historical Perspective*. Ithaca: Cornell University Press.

Sandholtz, W. (1993). Institutions and Collective Action: The New Telecommunications in Western Europe. *World Politics.* 45.

Sassen, E.M.J.A. (1970). Active Competition Policy. *Bull. EC* 4–1970.

Schaub, A. (1998). International Cooperation in Antitrust Matters: Making the Point in the Wake of the Boeing/MDD Proceedings. *Competition Policy Newsletter.* 1998/1.

Scheingold, S.A. (1965). *The Rule of Law in European Integration: The Path of the Schuman Plan*. New Haven: Yale University Press.

Schina, D. (1987). *State Aids under the EEC Treaty Articles 92 to 94*. Oxford: ESC Publishing Ltd.

Schmid, K.P. (1986). Kartellrecht: Es lebe der Stärkere. Neue amerikanische Wettbewerbstheorien sorgen für Unruhe in der Bundesrepublik. *Die Zeit*, 21 February.

Schmitter, P.C. (1996). Some Alternative Futures for the European Polity and their Implications for European Public Policy. In Y. Meny et al., eds., *Adjusting to Europe*. London: Routledge.

Schneider, V. and Werle, R.. (1990). International Regime or Corporate Actor? The European Community in Telecommunications Policy. In K. Dyson and P. Humphreys, eds., *The Political Economy of Communications*. London: Routledge.

Schrans, G. (1973). National and Regional Aid to Industry under the EEC Treaty. *Common Market Law Review*. 10.

Schumann, W. (1991). EG–Forschung und Policy–Analyse: Zur Notwendigkeit, den ganzen Elefanten zu erfassen. *Politische Vierteljahresschrift*. 32.

Schumpeter, J.A. (1976). *Capitalism, Socialism and Democracy*. New York: Harper Torchbooks.

SEC(71) 363 final. *Communication to the Member States on Community framework for aids to the textile industry.*

SG (77) D/1190. *Letter to Member States.*

SG (80) D/9538. *Letter to Member States.*

SG (81) 12740. *Letter to Member States.*

SG (83) D/13342. *Letter to Member States.*

SG (85) D/2611. *Letter to Member States.*

SG (89) D/5521. *Letter to Member States.*

SG (91) D/4544. *Letter to Member States.*

SG (91) D/4577. *Letter to Member States.*

Shapiro, M. (1992). The European Court of Justice. In A.M. Sbragia, ed., *Euro-Politics: Institutions and policy making in the 'New' European Community*. Washington, DC: The Brookings Institution.

Shapiro, M. and Stone, A. eds. (1994). *The New Constitutional Politics of Europe. Comparative Political Studies*. 26.4. (Special Issue).

Sharp, M. (1989). The Community and New Technologies. In J. Lodge, ed., *The European Community and the Challenge of the Future*. London: Pinter.

Siedentopf, H. (1988). The Implementation of Directives in the Member States. In H. Siedentopf and J. Ziller, eds., *Making European Policies Work: The Implementation of Community Legislation in the Member States*. Vol. I: Comparative Synthesis. London: Sage.

Siedentopf, H. and Hauschild, C. (1988). The Implementation of Community Legislation by Member States. In H. Siedentopf and J. Ziller, eds., *Making European Policies Work: The Implementation of*

Community Legislation in the Member States. Vol. I: *Comparative Synthesis*. London: Sage.

Siedentopf, H. and Ziller, J. eds. (1988). *Making European Policies Work: The Implementation of Community Legislation in the Member States*. Vol. I: *Comparative Synthesis*. London: Sage.

Siragusa, M. and Scassellati-Sforzolini, G. (1992). Italian and EC Competition Law: A New Relationship – Reciprocal Exclusivity and Common Principles. *Common Market Law Review*. 29.

Slot, P.J. (1990). Procedural Aspects of State Aids: The Guardian of Competition versus the Subsidy Villains? *Common Market Law Review*. 27.

Slotboom, M. (1995). State Aid in Community Law: A Broad or a Narrow Definition? *European Law Review*. 20.

Snyder, F. (1989). Ideologies of Competition in European Community Law. *Modern Law Review*. 52.

Snyder, F. (1990). *New Directions in European Community Law*. London: Weidenfeld & Nicolson.

Soames, T. and Ryan, A. (1995). State Aid and Air Transport. *European Competition Law Review*. 5.

Steenbergen, J. (1987). Trade Regulation since the Tokyo Round. In E.L.M. Volker, ed., *Protectionism and the European Community*. Dewenter: Kluwer.

Stein, E. (1981). Lawyers, Judges, and the Making of a Transnational Constitution. *American Journal of International Law*. 75.

Steiner, J. (1990). Coming to Terms with EEC Directives. *Law Quarterly Review*. 106.

Steiner, J. (1993). From Direct Effects to *Francovich*: Shifting Means of Enforcement of Community Law. *European Law Review*. 18.

Steiner, J. (1995). *Enforcing EC Law*. London: Blackstone Press.

Steinmo, S. et al. eds. (1992). *Structuring Politics*. Cambridge: Cambridge University Press.

Strange, S. (1988). *States and Markets: An Introduction to International Political Economy*. London: Pinter.

Streeck, W. and Schmitter, P.C. (1991). From National Corporatism to Transnational Pluralism: Organized Interests in the Single European Market. *Politics and Society*. 19.

Sun, J.M. and Pelkmans, J. (1995). Regulatory Competition in the Single Market. *Journal of Common Market Studies*. 33.

Swann, D. (1983). *Competition and Industrial Policy*. London: Methuen.

Swann, D. (1988). *The Economics of the Common Market*. Sixth edition. Harmondsworth: Penguin Books.

Thatcher, M. (1996). High Technology. In H. Kassim and A. Menon, eds., *The European Union and National Industrial Policy*. London: Routledge.

Thomsen, S. and Woolcock, S. (1993). *Direct Investment and European Integration*. London: Pinter.

Trivers, R.L. (1971). The Evolution of Reciprocal Altruism. *Quarterly Review of Biology*. 46.

Tsoukalis, L. (1981). *The European Community and its Mediterranean Enlargement*. London: Allen & Unwin.

Tsoukalis, L. (1993). *The New European Economy: The Politics and Economics of Integration*. Second edition. Oxford: Oxford University Press.

Van Miert, K. (1994a). The Role of Competition Policy Today. *Competition Policy Newsletter*. 1/3.

Van Miert, K. (1994b). Community State Aid Policy: An Overview. *Competition Policy Newsletter*. 1/3.

Van Miert, K. (1996). Transatlantic Relations and Competition Policy. *Competition Policy Newsletter*. 2/3.

Van Miert, K. (1997). Introduction. In European Commission, *XXVIth Report on Competition Policy 1996*. Luxembourg: Office for Official Publications of the European Communities.

Van Miert, K. (1998). *Competition Policy in the Air Transport Sector*. Speech, Royal Aeronautical Society, London, 9.3.1998.

Vaughn, W.M. (1972). Transnational Policy Programme Networks in the European Community: The Example of European Competition Policy. *Journal of Common Market Studies*. 11.

Verloren van Themaat, P. (1969). Competition and Planning in the EEC and the Member States. *Common Market Law Review*. 7.

Vesterdorf, B. (1994). Complaints Concerning Infringements of Competition Law Within the Context of European Community Law. *Common Market Law Review*. 31.

Vogelaar, F.O.W. (1985). The Impact of the Economic Recession on EEC Competition Policy, Part One: State Aids. *Swiss Review of International Competition Law*. 23.

Volcansek, M.L. (1992). The European Court of Justice: Supranational Policy-making. *West European Politics*. 15. (Special issue on *Judicial Politics and Policy-making in Western Europe*).

Vouel, R. (1977). Report on Competition Policy: The Fundamental Importance of Competition Policy and Priorities for Future Action. *Bulletin of the European Communities*. 4–1977.

Wall Street Journal Europe, various dates.

Wallace, H., Wallace, W. and Webb, C. eds. (1983). *Policy-Making in the European Communities*. Second edition. Chichester: John Wiley.

Wallace, W. (1983). Less than a Federation, More than a Regime: The Community as a Political System. In H. Wallace, W. Wallace and C. Webb, eds., *Policy-Making in the European Community*. Second edition. Chichester: John Wiley.

Weatheril, S. (1990). National Remedies and Equal Access to Public Procurement. *Yearbook of European Law*. 10.

Weiler, J.H.H. (1981). The Community System: The Dual Character of Supranationalism. *Yearbook of European Law*. 1.

Weiler, J.H.H. (1988). The White Paper and the Application of Community Law. In R. Bieber, R. Dehousse, J. Pinder and J.H.H. Weiler, eds., *1992: One European Market? A Critical Analysis of the Commission's Internal Market Strategy*. Baden-Baden: Nomos Verlagsgesellschaft.

Weiler, J.H.H. (1991). The Transformation of Europe. *Yale Law Journal*. 100.

Weiler, J.H.H. (1993). Journey to An Unknown Destination: A Retrospective and Prospective of the European Court of Justice in the Arena of Political Integration. *Journal of Common Market Studies*. 31.

Weiler, J.H.H. (1994). A Quiet Revolution: The European Court of Justice and its Interlocutors. In M. Shapiro and A. Stone, eds., *The New Constitutional Politics of Europe. Comparative Political Studies*. 26.4. (Special Issue).

Weiss, L. (1988). *Creating Capitalism: The State and Small Business Since 1945*. Oxford: Basil Blackwell.

Wessels, W. (1997). An Ever Closer Fusion? A Dynamic Macropolitical View on Integration Processes. *Journal of Common Market Studies*. 35.

Wijckmans, F. and Vanderelst, A. (1995). The EC Commission's Draft Regulation on Motor Vehicle Distribution: Alea Lacta Est? *European Competition Law Review*. 4.

Wilks, S. (1996). Regulatory Compliance and Capitalist Diversity in Europe. *Journal of European Public Policy*. 3.

Wilks, S. and McGowan, L. (1995a). Disarming the Commission: The Debate over a European Cartel Office. *Journal of Common Market Studies.* 33.

Wilks, S. and McGowan, L. (1995b). Discretion in European Merger Control: The German Regime in Context. *Journal of European Public Policy.* 2.

Wilks, S. and Wright, M. eds. (1987). *Comparative Government–Industry Relations.* Oxford: Clarendon Press.

Williamson, O.E. (1975), *Markets and Hierarchies.* New York: Free Press.

Winter, J.A. (1993). Supervision of State Aid: Article 93 in the Court of Justice. *Common Market Law Review.* 30.

Wishlade, F.G. (1993). Competition Policy and the Co-ordination of Regional Aids in the European Community. *European Competition Law Review.* 4.

Womack, J.P. (1989). The US Automobile Industry in an Era of International Competition: Performance and Prospects. In MIT, *The Working Papers of the MIT Commission on Industrial Productivity.* Cambridge, MA: MIT Press.

Wulff, O. (1988). National Economic Policy: An Obstacle to the European Community? In J. Schwarze, ed., *Discretionary Powers of the Member States in the Field of Economic Policies and their Limits Under the EEC Treaty.* Baden-Baden: Nomos Verlagsgesellschaft.

Zysman, J. (1983). *Governments, Markets and Growth: Financial Systems and the Politics of Industrial Change.* Ithaca: Cornell University Press.

Index

acquis communautaire 27
ad hoc aids 42–3, 112
adjustment 32, 35, 100, 110, 148
    process of 14, 21
    structural 5, 28
Aer Lingus 91, 94, 119
Air France 91, 93, 94, 95, 119, 143
air transport 89–97, 119, 120, 127
Alcatel 22, 24
Amato, G. 127
Amsterdam Treaty 125
Andriessen, F. 14, 19, 24, 32, 33, 38
antagonistic equilibrium 140
antitrust 18, 21, 46, 120, 127, 128,
    132, 133, 137, 140, 154
Association of European Airlines 94
automobile industry 108, 110, 111,
    112
    see also motor vehicle industry

Bangemann, M. 24
Belgium 22, 82
Bertelsmann group 25
block exemptions 43, 78, 139
    see also competition policy; ex-
    emptions; state aid policy
Boeing 24
British Airways 90, 97, 143
Brittan, L. 24, 37, 39, 48, 120, 138,
    147
business firm 7, 49, 127, 153, 154
business interests 5, 13, 143, 145
    see also lobbying; public–private
    relation; state

capitalism 5, 142, 149, 153, 154

carmakers *see* car manufacturers;
    motor vehicle industry
car manufacturers 108, 119
case-law 31, 32, 36, 38, 40, 41, 50,
    51, 52, 61, 69, 73, 74, 75, 143
Central and Eastern European
    Countries (CEECs) 134
Chicago school 46, 138
civil society 150, 153
cohesion 1, 4, 125, 147
    see also economic and social
    cohesion
Colonna Report 80
Committee of the Regions 89
Common Market 3, 49, 53, 55, 59,
    60, 70, 74, 101, 108, 125, 135,
    136
comparative politics 10–11
compensatory justification criterion 53
competition 1, 2, 3, 5, 7, 8, 103,
    109, 132, 138, 153
    economic 24, 138, 149, 150,
    151, 152
    excess competition 6
    ideologies of 5, 150
    perfect competition 6
    see also competition policy;
    mergers; Schumpeter; state aid
competition law 16, 17, 30, 31, 42,
    46, 49–70, 127, 128, 129, 143,
    150
competition policy 1, 2, 3, 16–22,
    27, 44, 127, 128, 136, 137,
    140, 148, 151
competitiveness 112, 117, 119,
    138, 139

compliance 12, 13, 41, 61, 62, 63, 64, 67, 107, 130, 141, 143, 153
  see also enforcement; European Commission; monitoring
concentration 17, 18
conciliatory phase 68
corporatism 87, 119
corruption 5
cost-benefit analysis 116
Council of Ministers 29, 37, 86, 130, 133, 139, 143, 148
  relations with the European Commission 45
Court of First Instance 42, 143

Davignon, E. 18, 139
De Havilland 24, 110
de minimis aid category 56, 73, 85, 117
Delors, J. 20, 24, 125
Delors Report 38
democratic accountability 135, 145
democratic deficit 145
Denmark 22, 105, 143
DG III 18, 20, 24
DG IV 18, 20, 22, 25, 28, 29, 33, 37, 39, 40, 45, 47, 55, 82, 84, 91, 97, 107, 110, 114, 115, 130, 133, 151
DG VII 24, 92, 97
DG XIII 19, 81
DG XVI 40, 55
DG XXIII 88, 118
discretion *see* European Commission
domestic politics 9, 10, 87, 130, 147
dominant position 18, 24, 81
dumping 151

Eastern Europe 110, 114
Economic and Monetary Union (EMU) 122, 151
economic nationalism 5, 18, 24, 29, 30, 101, 109
economic policy 5–7, 101
economic and social cohesion 125, 148

economies of scale 19, 20, 35
Ehlermann, C.-D. 20, 21, 36 40, 135
energy crisis 31, 99, 120
enforcement 40, 41, 46, 60, 61, 63, 73, 74, 86, 134, 135
  decentralised enforcement 134–5
  see also compliance; European Commission; monitoring
enterprise policy 80, 81, 82, 88, 132
equality principle 127
European Agricultural Guidance and Guarantee Fund (EAGGF) 74, 122
European Cartel Office 134
European Coal and Steel Community (ECSC) 50, 58
European Commission 3, 4, 8, 14, 22, 26–36, 37, 54, 55, 85, 86, 92, 93, 96, 101, 131, 143, 146, 152
  discretion in monitoring and enforcement 42, 64, 65–7, 69, 74, 75
European Community Treaty 2, 4, 16, 17, 27, 29, 30, 31, 49, 50, 54, 57, 59, 60, 63, 65, 66, 67, 91, 95, 115, 124
European Court of Justice (ECJ) 8, 27, 30, 31, 32, 33, 36, 38, 41, 42, 43, 45, 46, 47, 50, 51, 52, 61, 62, 63, 64, 70, 73, 74, 75, 91, 93, 114, 131, 143, 148
European Economic Area (EEA) 114, 134
European Free Trade Association (EFTA) 134
European general interest 125, 126
European integration 1, 8, 10, 11, 12, 145
  see also Europeanization; interconnectedness
European Investment Bank 80

European model of society 125, 141, 151
European monetary authorities 151
European Parliament 33, 40, 80, 85, 86, 87, 117, 141, 145
European Surveillance Authority (ESA) 134
European politics of state intervention 122, 123, 131
EU budget 122
EU policy impact 1, 3, 8, 10, 11, 12, 14, 122, 145
EU/US competition policy agreement, 133
Europeanization 8, 124, 152
  see also interconnectedness; policy convergence; regulatory change
exemptions 51, 52, 53, 56, 81, 107, 136, 137, 138, 146

family-size car 108, 109
Fiat 22, 110
flexible specialisation 7
Ford 115, 120
France 17, 18, 24, 82, 93, 110, 114, 116, 120, 122, 143

George, S. 11
German competition policy 153
Germany 22, 25, 81, 103, 105, 107, 112, 114, 119, 136, 153
globalization 132, 133, 146
Greece 22, 82, 95, 97, 103, 105, 107, 129
Greek competition policy 129

Hall, J. 153
Hall, P. 123
Hancher, L. 135, 142, 145
Holmes, P. 142, 145
Honda 110
horizontal aid 45, 77

Iberia 91, 93, 96, 98

industrial culture 12, 88
industrial morality 87
industrial policy 3, 4, 16–22, 34, 81, 140, 149
  see also mergers; positive role of subsidies
industrial structure 79
information technologies 19, 139
innovation 116, 139
innovation aid 103, 114, 120, 149
institutionalism 7, 9
interconnectedness 8, 10, 11, 12, 131
  see also Europeanization; policy convergence
interest groups 88, 118, 144, 145
intergovernmentalism 10, 130, 131
international economy 109, 132, 133, 135
international relations 11, 14
investment aid 102
Ireland 22
Italian competition policy 126, 127, 129
Italy 22, 24, 82, 127, 128, 129, 147, 152

Japan 20, 99, 109, 120
Japanese carmakers 109
Jenkins, R. 18, 46
judicial activism 141
judicial politics 10, 13, 27, 42, 143
judicialization 42, 43, 93, 141, 143
justice 8, 9, 151
Johnson, C. 6

Kantian liberalism 150, 153
KLM 97

laissez-faire 1, 17
legal culture 13, 127
liberalism 7, 138, 153
  see also competition; democracy; Kantian liberalism; neoliberalism

liberalisation 44, 90, 91, 96, 98, 131, 138, 148
lobbying 2
Lockean liberalism 153
Luxembourg 22, 25, 82
Luxembourg Compromise 30

Maastricht Treaty, 50, 51, 52, 85, 125, 130, 144
Mancini, F. 41, 46
market economy investor principle 16, 45, 114
market failure 6
Marxian political economy 149
merger Regulation 22, 128
mergers 17, 34, 153
    see also competition policy; international context
Mill, J.–S. 8
Millan, B. 24
modernity 150, 153
monitoring 107, 112
motor vehicle distribution 121
motor vehicle industry 108–16, 121, 137,
    market fragmentation 109
multinational firms 132

national competition authorities 129, 135, 146
national courts 43, 44, 48, 69, 70, 135
national diversity 109, 142
national interest 22, 25, 31
neofunctionalism 10, 11, 131, 153
neoliberalism 11, 87, 118, 119, 137
Netherlands 22, 82
neutrality principle 91, 125, 127
new aids 55
new institutionalism 11
    in EC politics 9, 14
    in political analysis 9
Nissan 110, 121
non-compliance *see* compliance
Norway 99

OECD Shipbuilding Agreement 103
Olympic Airways 91, 96, 97, 98, 120
Organisation for Economic Co-operation and Development (OECD) 132
OPEC 120
Oreja, M. 98
organised interests 12, 13
Ortoli Facility 81
overcapacity 95, 111, 112

Pareto efficiency 6
patronage politics 122, 127, 145
Patronat Française 17
policy analysis 11, 12, 13
policy areas, 2
    core 2
    institutional 2
    issue-driven 2
policy content 89, 146
policy convergence 1, 10, 126, 130, 148, 151
policy debate 124, 125, 151
policy evolution 10, 12, 18, 22, 26, 58, 78, 81, 88, 136, 137, 142, 149
policy goals 22, 137, 141, 146
policy ideas 12, 13, 14, 17, 22, 86, 141
policy impact 8
policy implementation 138, 141, 142
policy instruments 12, 20, 30, 32, 33, 37, 38, 39, 42, 65, 85, 86, 88, 89, 122, 138, 141, 145
policy-making process 9, 145
policy mix 1, 17–22, 122, 138
policy networks 13
political science 3, 9
politicisation 2, 5, 22–6, 55, 137
Portugal 82, 96, 102, 103, 124
positive role of subsidies 138–41
pragmatic approach 28, 29

pre-competitive research 19, 139
prior notification requirement 45, 63, 64, 74, 85, 118
privatisation 89, 91, 125, 126
protectionism 5, 110, 111
public broadcasting systems 127
public enterprises 126
public–private relations 126, 127, 141, 146
  see also interest politics; liberalism; regulatory change; state

rail transport 127
realism 11
reciprocity 13, 14
regional aid schemes 53, 72, 73, 114, 137
regulation 2, 6, 8, 12, 20, 122, 139, 140
regulatory change 90, 128, 145, 147
  see also competition policy; policy convergence; privatisation; regulatory policy; state
regulatory competition 14
regulatory compliance 141
regulatory intervention 122, 139, 149, 151
regulatory policy 2
remedies 68–70
Renault 115
rescue aid 91, 92
research and development (R&D) 114
restructuring aid 90, 92, 101, 102, 103, 114
Richardson, J. 13, 142
Rome Treaty 27, 49, 58, 124
Ross, G. 24, 125
Ryan, A. 8

Sabena 91, 94
Samuels, R. 13
Santana Motors 115
SAS 97
Schmitter, P.C. 142, 144

Schumpeter, J. 7
sea transport 99, 100
second generation agreements 133
sectoral aid regimes 4, 77, 100
shipbuilding 98–107, 136
shipbuilding Directives 101–104
Single European Act (SEA) 81
Single Market project 20, 21, 33, 110
Skoda 121
small business 4, 7, 20, 78–89, 130
  see also enterprise policy; industrial policy; mergers
small and medium-size enterprises (SMEs) 118, 131
Smart car 116
social contract 154
social market perspective 151
Southern Europe 14, 129
Spain 82, 95, 102, 103, 105, 107, 111, 119
state 141, 145, 146, 147
  see also Europeanization; public–private relations; regulatory change
state aid 1, 21, 22, 42, 113, 138
  forms of 31, 50, 105
  see also competition policy; regulatory change
state aid control of 2, 34, 39, 59, 61, 77, 84, 92, 146
state aid policy 16, 21, 26–33, 37, 49, 58, 84, 85, 89, 94, 97, 99, 111, 112, 122, 123, 137, 138, 140
state aid regimes 2, 4, 57, 78
  see also competition policy; horizontal aid; sectoral aid; state aid
state aid Regulations 30, 31, 36–8, 43–5, 71, 148
state intervention 5, 6, 16, 17, 19, 21, 27, 32, 38, 42, 59, 70, 99, 121, 123
structural policy 3, 4, 89, 146

subsidiarity 88
subsidies *see* state aid
Sweden 143

TAP 91, 92, 96
Telecom Italia 129
telecommunications 19, 136
third parties 61
Thorn, G. 19
Toyota 110
Treaty on European Union (TEU) 44, 73, 79
Treaty of Rome *see* Rome Treaty

UK competition policy 153
unemployment 124, 147
Union des Confederations de l'Industrie et des Employeurs d' Europe (UNICE) 17
United Kingdom (UK) 12, 22, 24, 25, 90, 99, 104, 110, 115, 120, 123, 143, 147, 153

United States of America (USA) 12, 20, 32, 46, 47, 89, 90, 99, 102, 108, 133, 153, 153
universal service 126
    see also European general interest; neutrality principle
Uruguay Round 119, 134
US competition law 46, 47, 137
    see also European integration; international context; regulatory change

Van Miert, K. 24, 98, 119, 132, 147, 151
Volkswagen 110, 114
von der Groeben, H. 27, 28, 136
Vouel, R. 19, 32, 46

warships, 101
White Paper 33, 124